FIGHTERS FROM THE EAST END

FIGHTERS FROM
THE EAST END

Aldgate, Stepney & Whitechapel

Bob Lonkhurst

Published by

B L Associates

Published by

B L Associates 2018

A catalogue record for this book is available from the British library

ISBN 978-0-9540271-7-9

Printed and bound by 4Bind Ltd, Stevenage, Herts. UK

DEDICATED TO THE MEMORY OF THE LATE

RON OLVER

A GREAT FRIEND AND WRITER WHOSE LITERARY
CONTRIBUTION TO BOXING WAS ADMIRED OVER
MANY YEARS

Also by Bob Lonkhurst

MAN OF COURAGE:	*The Life and Career of Tommy Farr*
GENTLEMAN OF THE RING:	*The Life and Career of Jack Petersen*
EAST END IDOL:	*The Amazing Story of Terry Spinks MBE*
FEN TIGER:	*The Success of Dave 'Boy' Green*
LIFE IS JUST A SCHEME:	*Autobiography of Danny Clark (in aid of charity)*
TERRY SPINKS MBE:	*Life Was A Rollercoaster*
CHATTERIS THUNDERBOLT:	*The Eric Boon Story*
BIG FIGHT BANNED:	*Bombardier Billy Wells & The Jack Johnson Affair*

CONTENTS

Foreword   ix
Acknowledgements   xi
Introduction   xiii
1. Judean Club   1
2. Wonderland   5
3. Premierland   15
4. Jack 'Kid' Berg   23
5. Harry Brooks   29
6. Johnny Brown   32
7. Young Johnny Brown   38
8. Sid Burns   46
9. Benny Caplan   53
10. Young Jack Cohen   58
11. Dutch Sam   62
12. Al. Foreman   65
13. Danny Frush   76
14. Jack Greenstock   86
15. Jack Hyams   91
16. Freddie Jacks   97
17. Young Joseph   106
18. Sam Kellar   114
19. Tom King   121
20. Lew Lazar   124
21. Mark Lesnick   129
22. Ted 'Kid' Lewis   137
23. Sammy McCarthy   148
24. Charlie Magri   158
25. Alf Mansfield   169
26. Harry Mansfield   178
27. Harry Mason   188
28. Daniel Mendoza   201
29. Harry Mizler   204

30. Sid Nathan   214
31. Al Phillips   217
32. Johnny Quill   224
33. Harry Reeve   229
34. Jewey Smith   236
35. George Walker   245
36. Joe Wilson   250
37. Jack Goodwin (Trainer)   258
38. Nat Sellar (Trainer)   264
39. Johnny Sharp (Trainer)   267
40. Harry Jacobs (Promoter)   270
41. Honourable Mentions   275
42. Reflections   292
    Bibliography

FOREWORD

A book such as this is long overdue because as far as I am aware there hasn't been one written which is devoted entirely to East End boxers. That is a shame because there have been so many over the years especially in the early part of the 1900's.

I was born and brought up in Stepney, a very hard working-class area of the East End. When I was a boy there seemed to be a boxing club on almost every street corner and in many cases young lads trained alongside hardened professionals. Like many others I got involved after my brother persuaded me to join a club and learn to look after myself.

Of the many great fighters who came from the East End, a large number where Jewish. The most famous were Ted 'Kid' Lewis and Jack 'Kid' Berg, both of whom became world champions. I was fortunate enough to get to know them both long after they had retired and found them extremely nice men.

Being a professional boxer myself I got to know many others, a lot who were Jewish. I have great respect for Jewish folk of whom there were many in the East End before and during my career. I found them hard working, very family orientated and easy to make friends with. When I was a youngster I used to help my father, who pushed a barrow around the streets of Stepney selling veg. Many of his regular customers were Jewish folk well known for preparing hearty meals for their families.

Boxers generally were well respected and in many cases an inspiration to youngsters. Back in the early 1900's it was not uncommon for the lads to have well over 100 fights. Many started out when they were only fourteen or fifteen because they could often earn more money fighting than holding down a regular job. There were lots of shows in those days particularly on Sundays, but now it is a very different story.

The author and I have been friends for many years. He has a good understanding of boxing and has chosen his subjects well for this book. Men like Jack Hyams, who used to box as Young Froggy, Benny Caplan, Al Phillips, the Mizler brothers, the Lazars, trainers Nat Sellar and Johnny Sharpe both of whom I knew very well, all had interesting lives which are well worth recalling. I am delighted to have been asked to provide this foreword.

Sammy McCarthy
Wanstead - 2018

ACKNOWLEDGEMENTS

The foreword is an extremely important opening to any book especially those about well-known personalities. I am therefore extremely privileged that former British featherweight champion Sammy McCarthy agreed to provide such for this publication.

I have known Sammy for many years and he was very helpful to me when I wrote Terry Spinks' biography *East End Idol* back in 2002. Born and brought up in Stepney, he has maintained a close interest in the fight game throughout his life. Now aged almost eighty-seven he remains one of the most popular men in the sport. Although he is featured in a chapter, I can think of no better person to open this book.

I am particularly indebted to my close and very dear friend Sandie Ball whose skill and patience ensured we reached publication by the intended date. She has brought new ideas to the project particularly regarding design for which I am extremely grateful.

I have received considerable help from Essex EBA secretary Ray Lee regarding boxers from bygone years. His daughter Tracy provided great help in the early stages of design.

As with most of my previous publications my good friend Larry Braysher provided most of the photographs from his extensive private collection for which I thank him.

Another long-standing friend who I thank is Nigel Wood, managing director of 4Bind limited at Stevenage, for the printing and binding of the book whilst his daughter Emma undertook the laborious task of the proof-reading.

My sincere thanks also go to Kevin Moore for the cover design and production of photographs.

The staff at the National Newspaper library in Colindale, who provided great support over a number of years during my research.

Finally, I acknowledge the works of the late Ron Olver, Fred Snelling and Gilbert Odd, three fine boxing writers. Their respective articles provided essential background information during my research.

Ron was a particularly good friend who was always on hand to provide guidance in the early days of my writing. A highly respected man throughout boxing, particularly with the EBA's, I therefore dedicate this book to his memory.

INTRODUCTION

Whenever boxing addicts gather and swap stories about the sport, there is no better place to start than in the East End of London which, certainly decades ago, was frequently referred to as the home of boxing. East End folk were essentially boxing-minded and the sport virtually a way of life. For many it provided meals on the table during times of extreme hardship.

From their midst emerged some of the finest fighters to ply their trade in British rings. Some rose to great heights, their names going down in boxing history whilst countless others who failed to make the grade vanished into obscurity. The Noble Art, as it was referred to in the early days, was practised at a host of venues in the area long before the sport was licenced or regulated. Most were hostelries and during the late 1800's Whitechapel had its fair share. The Horse & Groom at Church Lane, Queen Adelaide at King Edward Street and Garrick Tavern were particularly popular. Jack Baldock's East London Gym at Dean Street, Shadwell and Aldgate Baths were other busy venues.

As long ago as 16 August 1878, the Assembly Rooms at Bull Lane, Stepney, was the venue for what was claimed to be the longest recorded fight to have taken place in Europe. Tommy Hawkins from Mile End drew with Joe Fowler (Bristol) in what was billed as 'the English 7st 12lbs championship'. They wore two-ounce gloves and fought for £25 – a – side and the original Joe Hoiles championship belt which was originally won in 1854. The contest came to a conclusion when it became too dark to see.

Tainted with notoriety, the East End has always been one of the roughest and toughest parts of Britain. A densely-populated area stretching along the capital's huge

Docklands, it has for centuries been a breeding ground for fighters of all levels. Blitzed by enemy bombs during two world wars, devastation was heaped upon a region already deprived of any form of luxury. Exceptionally high levels of unemployment, countless run-down properties and a large immigrant population were just a few of the factors which contributed to make the region a haven for fighting.

The 1920's and 1930's were particularly hazardous times in the East End. From Aldgate, a deprived area adjacent to the City of London, to Canning Town and beyond, fighting was the only thing that threw many youngsters a lifeline. It ensured they put food on the table for their families and gave them dignity.

During the early decades of the 20th Century, hundreds, maybe even thousands of East End youngsters took to the ring, yet the thought of fighting for a championship was the furthest thing from the minds of the majority. Many virtually stepped out of the gutter to become professional fighters using false names (especially 'Young', 'Kid' and 'Boy') so that their parents wouldn't know what they were doing. The few pounds or even shillings that they were there for was all that mattered. Starting as young teenagers, they were prepared to take on anyone put in front of them. A hiding in the ring was often par for the course, but worth it from their view providing they got paid.

Most promoters had their house fighters, those who could draw the fans. Provided they kept winning or putting on exciting performances, they got regular work. Consequently, many names cropped up with regularity on promotions at arenas and small halls throughout the East End. It was not unusual for the popular and more successful to build records approaching or exceeding 100 contests within a relatively short period of time.

Despite the need for boxing and the advantages it presented, there can be no denying that in those early days it was crude and often barbaric. The British Boxing Board of Control was not formed until 1929 and even then, it was far less stringent than at present. There was no equivalent to modern day Health and Safety Regulations and consequently crowds far exceeding reasonable levels frequently crammed into venues of all sizes especially for an attractive billing. Ignoring the possible consequences, promoters often took the view that the more admitted, the greater the box office takings.

Conditions generally were an age away from modern times and with ringside betting rife, disorder was commonplace at the East End halls. These were not places of luxury, the air being thick with smoke while the stench of jellied eels, a favourite East End delicacy, was an added discomfort.

With the benefit of hindsight, the medical aspect was the most lax. Whilst a doctor was usually present at shows, there was no comparison to provisions now in force where at least one team of paramedics, an anaesthetist and a minimum of two general practitioners are a strict requirement at every promotion. Restrictions were rarely placed on a boxer who was knocked out or stopped with a serious injury. Nothing was in place to prevent an individual fighting again within a few days if he declared himself fit.

Sadly, many boxers, whilst being raw tough individuals who thought nothing of injury, pain and suffering, were not the most responsible of people and could therefore be manipulated into a fight long before they were ready. There were many cases where desperate people did desperate things, a classic example of which related to Aldgate flyweight, Alf Mansfield, back in 1919. Having been knocked out in round 13 of a demanding contest with world class Welshman, Jimmy Wilde, he allowed himself to be pushed into a British championship eliminator just 16 days later by the promoters of the National Sporting Club. It was nothing less than irresponsibility by all parties especially as Alf was blind in one eye and the other was failing.

Many others also paid the price in later life for recklessness during their ring careers, albeit brought on by desperation in most cases. They included Young Joseph who tottered around the street on crutches some years after his retirement; Jewey Smith, a pre first world war favourite was reduced to living off charity and only just able to afford his lodgings at an East End Rowton House; Andrew Jeptha, blind and penniless was once turned away from a hospital when it was discovered that he had been a professional boxer, former Stepney welterweight, Fred Archer, who ran a barber's shop on the Commercial Road, had hands which shook so badly that customers risked serious injury by simply asking for a shave. There were many others who suffered permanently from the effects of punishment received in the ring; punch-drunkenness and cauliflower ears being commonplace.

Boxers generally, however, have always been well respected individuals and long before glove – fighting and the introduction of Queensberry rules, bare-knuckle combat was very much an organised sport. Yet despite being illegal throughout its existence, it nevertheless gained in popularity. Organised contests received considerable publicity and often attracted wealthy patrons, sometimes even members of the Royalty.

Since the early days of recorded prize-fights, men from the East End always figured amongst the best. Daniel Mendoza was recognised as heavyweight champion of England during the late 1700's, while Dutch Sam was considered by many followers to be the finest of the bare-knuckle lightweights during the early 1800's. Jem Ward (1825-27) and Tom King (1862) both reigned as heavyweight champions and were rarely beaten.

In the days of men such as Medoza, Sam, Ward and King contests generally took place in open air spaces outside London in order to avoid the authorities. The introduction of glove fighting and the Queensberry Rules during the mid-1860's, however, brought about change with many fights taking place at pubs, private clubs, gymnasiums and other suitable establishments in the heart of the Capital.

During the early days of gloves, weight divisions bore no resemblance to those of modern times. In fact, until 1909 when the National Sporting Club decided to introduce the standard eight divisions (flyweight to heavy) there were championship bouts at every two pounds up to and including 138 pounds. Despite the respective changes, the East End continued to produce an abundance of good quality fighters at all weights, many of whom laid claim to the original form of English championships in the lower divisions.

Over the years, small halls, local baths and the like have been used by promoters to stage boxing shows throughout the East End. Crowds flocked to the Whitechapel Arena, Poplar Hippodrome, Hoxton Baths, Mile End Arena and the Devonshire Club to name just a few. There were of course the larger and more famous arenas which represent a huge part of the East End boxing history. The Judean Club situated just off Cable Street, Wonderland in the Whitechapel Road and Premierland at Back Church Lane off Commercial Road were arenas of intense atmosphere. Always intimidating, smokey and packed to capacity, they were the nurseries for thousands of fighters. Consequently, some of the finest boxers in the country emerged from the East End.

Fighters and boxing in the East End generally, have fascinated me since I took up writing as a hobby more than 20 years ago. The urge to research and pen stories of the many characters and venues which helped shape the sport in the area has been immense. Yet soon after embarking on the project I realised how vast it would be. Serious consideration needed to be given to the size and intensity of the region and the vast numbers of men and boys living there who had embarked on ring careers amid times of sheer hardship.

Boundaries therefore needed to be set in order to do justice to those men by highlighting their courage, commitment and achievement whilst battling adversity. It soon became apparent that a thoroughly researched book about East End boxing could reach encyclopaedia proportions, so I had to come up with something more practical. Having floated and rejected several possibilities, I was eventually convinced that the only satisfactory conclusion would be to divide the East End into three sections and over a period of time, health permitting, produce three books. With that in mind it made sense geographically to start at one end of the region and accordingly I have, for the purposes of this book, concentrated on Aldgate, Stepney and Whitechapel, producing potted biographies of fighters from those areas. Those from surrounding districts will be considered in further publications in due course.

In attempting to present a balanced picture of the East End boxing scene, the opening three chapters of this book are devoted to the Judean Club, Wonderland and Premierland which featured in the careers of most of my chosen subjects. Elsewhere I have not concentrated solely on men who have reached the top as in a number of cases their successes have been well documented, some in the form of biographies. I have therefore included chapters of some of the lesser known and less successful whose hunger and commitment contributed to and represented a huge part of the sport in the region.

During the early 1900's it was the impoverished Jewish boys who struggled so desperately. Coming from large families many had to hustle for themselves as mere children and fighting often came naturally to them. Battling in the ring for a few shillings meant the difference between a wholesome meal and starvation.

With the passing of time, however, the quality of life improved in the East End and venues such as the Judean Club and Premierland ceased to exist. By the 1950's fewer Jewish lads took to boxing and Lew Lazar was one of the few to keep the Star of David on his shorts in London rings.

Throughout the book, I have focused not only on the achievements of my subjects but also the obstacles they faced. Many travelled to America to ply their trade and by doing so received better purse money and gained an abundance of valuable experience. Australia and South Africa were other faraway places where they sought work. The majority were active during the early 1900's and have been selected because, due entirely to period hardships, they were generally of greater ability than those of more recent times.

In conclusion, the reader should be aware that during those years men invariably had far more fights than reported by the media. Consequently, some records quoted may not be complete and should therefore be used merely as a guide.

Bob Lonkhurst
Potters Bar 2018

JUDEAN CLUB

The Judean Social and Athletic Club was the most legendary of all Jewish clubs and one of London's earliest and best fight venues. It was founded in 1902 by brothers Dave and Barney Stitcher to encourage members of the Jewish fraternity, particularly youngsters, to participate in all branches of sport. Situated above a stable at 54 Princes Square just off Cable Street, it was the only club open on the Christian Sabbath. Entry was up a steep ladder and through a door into what was, in reality, a workshop high above the stable. All-comers were welcome, and it had gentiles on its committee. By 1909 the club claimed to have over 1,000 members who paid an entry fee of sixpence (2.5p) while non-members were charged one shilling (5p).

Boxing promotions took place every Sunday afternoon and drew huge crowds that packed the small venue almost to suffocation. With only a few seats the majority were forced to stand shoulder to shoulder occupying every inch of space. Many had come not only to watch the fights but to place a few bets. With large sums often at stake, their riotous antics were more often directed at the referee in an attempt, to influence the decision.

A rough and ready run-down establishment, the Judean typified this part of the East End in the early 1900's. In an area of extreme poverty and high unemployment, the reputation of the club spread far beyond its locality. Kids in ragged clothes frequently fought vicious six round contests before baying crowds for meagre rewards of between sixpence and two shillings and a cup of tea. Some had been caught by coppers scrapping in the streets and after a hefty clip around the ear, told to get along to the club where they could get paid for fighting. Despite being brash and aggressive, many were terrified once amid the hostile surroundings. Needs, however, conquered their fear and helped them overcome it with the result being that they often went back for more.

It was no secret that Jewish lads were given every encouragement to succeed whilst those from the south side of Blackfriars Bridge usually went into the ring as underdogs and were expected to lose. That, however, made little difference. Their needs were as great as the local boys.

Operations at the club were, for many years, generally run by Sam Kite who acted as secretary, often refereed and also shared the promotional work with Dave Stitcher. They were assisted by another tireless member, Morrie Isaacs. One Christmas Day, Kite staged a seven-fight programme to a packed house.

Despite their efforts there was always an element of danger about the activities. Critics often claimed that too many young boys were pitched into the ring without proper precautions being in place. Frequently, the ropes were too slack and there were rarely doctors present to treat injuries. Basic crudeness existed openly because there was no regulatory body like a Board of Control in existence to impose and enforce safety regulations.

Despite its faults, the Judean Club was undoubtedly an establishment built on experience of no little excellence. It produced championship-class fighters right up until it was reduced to rubble by Zeppelin bombs during the First World War. Men like Young Joseph, Harry Reeve, Mike Honeyman, Joe Fox, Sid Burns, Alf Mansfield and a host of others all learned their trade in its ring. There were so many talented lads performing there regularly that it became a recruitment hall for promoters from other venues in and around the East End working to feature them on their bills.

The star pupil at the club was undoubtedly Ted 'Kid' Lewis who made his debut there on 29 August 1909 at the age of sixteen. Although he lost his first two contests there, he went on to have 73 fights within the space of three years, losing only three. He never regretted that grounding, although, probably with tongue in cheek, he often described it as 'Little more than a room above a cowshed'.

Despite the intense and continuous activity at the club, there came a time in about 1910 when proceedings became somewhat disorganised and it required fresh faces with new ideas. With that in mind the Stitcher brothers approached Moss Deyong, later to become one of the top referees in the country. He had been successfully running small boxing shows elsewhere in the East End and was willing to become involved.

Moss quickly recognised that the club was badly in need of refurbishment and was not happy with the meagre money being paid to novice boxers in view of the risks they were taking. Matters which concerned him most, however, was the conduct of several boxers which in his view, was causing attendances to fall away. Jack Swift, who had been refereeing at the club for some time confirmed that some of the lads were endeavouring to terminate proceedings according to their own private arrangements by either faking a hand or arm injury or going to the floor from a soft blow and being counted out.

Jack originally became involved at the club when 'kidded' into taking charge of a fight one Sunday afternoon between local lads Young Cohen and Joe Shears. It was an extremely close affair, but he awarded the decision to Cohen. Afterwards he explained that despite his considerable experience, refereeing at the Judean was like nowhere else. 'The members were definitely connoisseurs of all thing pugilistic', he remarked.

Moss Deyong also knew his way about and agreed to referee one night. He quickly found that Swift's concerns were justified when contestants in two contests sought an early exit. After being put firmly in their places and told of the possible consequences, those attempting to quit agreed to carry on. Moss extinguished the problems quickly and everything got back to normal. That was the start of 20 years unpaid service for Deyong at the Judean Club, four of which were as chairman. He learned his trade as a referee there and encouraged good Jewish boxers such as Young Joseph and Sam Keller to officiate occasionally on Sundays. Their presence alone was an incentive to many youngsters.

By early 1911 there was a huge improvement in general facilities at the club with a new enclosure being constructed, more seating and the seconds to wear spotless white uniforms.

Throughout the existence of the club, many of the contests were between lads unknown to the ordinary boxing enthusiast and it was largely for that reason that the Sunday shows were so well attended. The contestants had to be 'triers' and give their best from start to finish. Even a lad with a good record would be shown the door if he failed to put on a good show. The continued existence of the club was of huge importance to social life in the East End as well as boxing as a sport. The general set-up there was accurately portrayed by *Boxing* during September 1913 when it stated:

> The Judean club, resplendent in new paint and new ring trappings was packed to suffocation yesterday afternoon on its reopening. The one drawback to the afternoon enjoyment was caused by the white wash on the ring floor. The clouds of dust that sprang therefrom in response to the beating of the boxer's feet were dense enough to choke one. The volume at times reached an opaqueness that seriously threatened the vision of the referee. But the whole heartedness of the boxing compensated for these trifling defects. It cannot be described more appropriately than that trite phrasing, 'it was real Judean slamming'

WONDERLAND

Boxing as a sport had much to thank the National Sporting Club for, the old club in Covent Garden having opened at a time when the game had no regular home. There came a time, however, when it was insufficient for the needs of the many people who wanted to watch it. The problem was that it was a club and a very select one at that, to which admission was only gained through membership.

The general public, especially those living in the East End, clamoured for a venue where they could watch boxing at a popular price, which is what led to Wonderland being created. Once established it did as much for the sport as the National Sporting Club in that it encouraged novice boxers and catered for patrons with a limited purse.

Situated at 100 Whitechapel Road, next to St Mary's station, it was originally the Effingham Theatre which was forced to close due to competition from the Whitechapel Pavilion on the opposite side of the road. When the building reopened during the early part of 1899 it was a bizarre institution furbished in shabby Victorian music hall style. At first it became the home for all types of shows of the fairground variety. For admission fees of two shillings and sixpence (12.5p) and one shilling (5p) for standing, the public came to see 'lion-faced' ladies, 'living skeletons' and a host of similar attractions.

It was not long, however, before the building was converted to enable it to concentrate mainly on boxing promotions. Research reveals that fights had taken place at Wonderland some years earlier, albeit on a much smaller scale than what was now being proposed. One contestant was Lambeth lightweight Jim Kendrick, who boxed there on five occasions between 1883 and '84, all in three round affairs.

The first man to stage boxing at the venue under the new plans was 'Professor' Joe Smith. Other promoters followed, particularly Harry Lee and Harry Wright, who was manager of the establishment for several years. Finally came Jack Woolf who owned the site on which Wonderland stood and kept the tavern next door. He also promoted at the nearby Paragon Theatre.

Apart from his theatrical, vaudeville and licenced victualler's businesses, Woolf took control of boxing and turned the venue into one of the most famous arenas with a tradition all of its own. Rules were frequently made to fit the occasion just as championships were fought between men who were no more entitled to the honour than the novices. If a particular pairing looked attractive enough, the matchmaker or one of the promoters would bill it as being for a championship.

One such occasion was during the early 1900's when Charlie Knock, (Stratford), a Wonderland regular, was matched with Tom Woodley. Both were welters but agreed to fight for a so-called British lightweight title. Neither went to the scales and the fight, which was never officially recognised (Due to Jabaz White being the champion) at that weight, nevertheless went ahead under the house rules.

Championship belts were always a great bait for the boxers. One belonging to some former champion was often rescued from a pawn broker or junk shop and put up as the main prize for a competition or 'special' contest. It happened regularly at Wonderland and never failed to attract a good entry or draw a full house.

Wonderland became a hard school and one of the roughest arenas in the country for a young boxer to learn his trade. Fights outside the ring were often as fierce as any inside it. The audience were never out of action for long on fight nights often crowding around the referee who, in those days, sat or stood outside the ring. Most were gamblers who tried everything possible to influence his decision upon which hundreds of bets depended. Whilst he was seldom interfered with physically during a fight, he was frequently irritated by those whose business it was to 'talk home' one or other of the boxers. Their tactics were simple; Two or more would stand on either side of him shouting how 'so & so' was winning the fight hands down. If their tactics worked, all well and good, but if the decision went against their man, the official was told in the strongest language possible how utterly incompetent he was. Other unruly individuals frequently resorted to jeering, cat-calling and even singing at the desperate men slugging it out in the ring.

Aside from the unruliness, boxing was exploited wholeheartedly at Wonderland. Whilst plenty of genuine championship fights were contested, programmes were often comprised entirely of six round bouts with as many as a dozen in an evening. The most important were over three-minute rounds and the remainder over two minutes. The star boxer usually received three pounds ten shillings, win, lose or draw but there was nothing for any man disqualified.

Any ambitious youngster could get started with a six, two-minute round fight and earn himself a pound if he won, less half a crown which he had to pay his seconds. Many a novice went into the ring hungry but rarely complained if a close decision went against him. He had the consolation of knowing he would at least be able to eat that night.

A huge building, Wonderland had a seating capacity of 2,000 albeit in a minimum of comfort and frequently with no regard for health and safety. Almost twice that number were often packed in on occasions of important championship contests. As many as another thousand crowded around in the streets outside waiting to hear the result, especially when a local fighter featured.

Jack Woolf was a showman in every sense of the word and ran Wonderland with ardent efficiency, never balking at officiating in all manner of roles. He had countless admirers and did more in the boxing world, especially in the East End, than any other. He gave an immense amount of time, money and help to needy boxers as well as raising funds for local hospitals. On fight bills he was described as 'The Man with a Name!'.

Woolf was probably best remembered for his fiery business partnership with Harry Jacobs who became his matchmaker. They occasionally ran in harness, but a more ill-assorted couple were rarely associated in business. Both were very domineering and masterful in their ways and as such sought to rule the roost. The inevitable result was that there was often chaos and bad feeling. Bitter arguments broke out and it was not uncommon to find them engaged in a slanging match in the main hall or box office. Every so often they would dissolve their partnership and then either one or the other would make a dramatic announcement that the venue would be under the sole control of whoever considered himself to be the top man of the moment.

People generally associated the boxing with Jacobs who despite his aggression was an excellent matchmaker and certainly the man who turned the venue into a great centre for boxing. Once he had thoroughly entrenched himself he assumed a very dictatorial attitude to everyone having business dealings with him. 'Those are my terms, take them or leave them,' was his recognised way of addressing boxers and their managers. He was rarely open to negotiation so usually, badly in need of money, they accepted his offer.

One man who did not bow to the aggressive attitude of Jacobs was world heavyweight champion, Tommy Burns, who was in London having defended his title against Gunner Moir at the National Sporting Club in December 1907. Burns liked the capital, particularly the West End, but in the hope of earning more easy money, took a taxi to the less salubrious East End and visited Wonderland. There he met Woolf and Jacobs and asked if they would like to stage a world heavyweight title fight. They rubbed hands at the prospect of a full house paying inflated prices just for the purpose of being there. Burns, however, soon put a dampener on their excitement by stating his terms. 'Don't worry about the size of the purse,' he assured them. 'I'll be on fifty percent by the gate'.

'Who will you fight?' asked Jacobs, who was in charge of all the matchmaking.

'Jack Palmer of Newcastle' replied the champion. 'He was champion before Moir'.

'He won't stand a chance' said Jacobs. 'That's just the point' snapped Burns.

Tommy was in the game to make money and although he had an associate who attended to minor matters relating to his fights, he kept a firm grip on the financial side himself. Although terms were eventually agreed for the Palmer fight to take place on 10 February 1908, Burns' first job was to secure an estimate of the total holding capacity of Wonderland. He turned a deaf ear to Jacobs sharp assurance of 'You can leave all that to me old man!'.

Woolf, and Jacobs in particular, had an even bigger shock on the night of the fight when the champion arrived at the arena armed with padlocks to fasten all the entrances and exits with the exception of the main door. Once the task was completed he sat in the main box office and made sure that every customer paid for their ticket. Only when he was satisfied that no more could be expected did he lock the door, count all the takings and put his share in a leather bag which he took to the dressing room with him.

The fight itself was a farce, with Palmer looking beaten within the first minute. To his credit, Burns allowed him to survive until the fourth round by which time he considered that the fans had received their money's worth. He then proceeded to knock out the challenger with a few crisp accurate punches.

Despite his domineering attitude, Jacobs had a real gift for making attractive contests, putting together some of the finest ever seen at East End arenas. Having several star performers, he would carefully select opponents capable of bringing the best out of them without too much risk of damaging their future. One such man was Charlie Knock from Stratford, a championship-class welterweight with a terrific punch who had a following sufficient to pack Wonderland.

Knock, Ernie Veitch of St Georges and Curley Watson from Chatham laid the foundation for Harry's success as a promoter. He kept them apart for a year or two, but then matched Knock and Watson in a fight billed for the 10st 4lbs championship of England. A terrific contest ensued and there was very little between them by the end of the 17th round. During the interval, however, Watson's second gave him smelling salts, but as he did so the boxer jerked his head forward causing some of the pungent substance to splash into his eyes, temporarily blinding him and rendering him incapable of continuing. Seven months later the shrewd Jacobs staged a return which Watson won on points. The result was of no concern to Harry because he made a considerable sum from two packed houses. On a tragic note, he lost a good fighter in Curley who later died as a result of injuries sustained in a subsequent contest with West Indian boxer, Frank English.

There was an abundance of characters associated with Wonderland, the majority of whom were Jewish. Boxing had been a favourite sport of that fraternity since the days of Daniel Mendoza and on Saturday nights they flocked to Wonderland where they could get a full evening's entertainment for as little as one shilling and sixpence, (7.5p). Few people objected to the fact that it was a dirty smelly place, thick with cigarette and cigar smoke and crowded with ringside bookmakers constantly yelling the odds. Although large notices were displayed throughout the building declaring that gambling was forbidden, punters used to wager on even the small fights. Those there to keep order and prevent it were invariably the worst offenders.

Such activity and presence of characters was all part of the entertainment. Constantly on public view was Ben Harris, the Master of Ceremonies, who seemed to be a fixture in the place. A rare personality, he used an abundance of hair oil and was known as one of the world's greatest tale pinchers. In between his spells as M.C at

Wonderland he ran small boxing shows at the Oak Club off Leman Street.

Refreshment in the form of soft drinks and fruit was always available but Monty the jellied eel man, a true East End character, provided his own brand of fun. Smartly dressed in a white jacket and apron he would perambulate the building carrying a huge tray containing some 30 small ivory and blue coloured basins filled with the favourite local delicacy. When empty, these were thrown at police whenever they had the unsporting habit of intervening to protect a referee from rowdies who disapproved of a particular decision.

More than a few referees deemed themselves to be fortunate enough to escape from the arena unscathed after giving a decision which did not meet with the approval of those supporting the losing fighter. Officiating at the venue was strenuous, both physically and mentally, but the referees still did the whole card for Jack Woolf's payment of £1.

There were countless stories relating to the goings-on at Wonderland, not least because it was unique and had an atmosphere all of its own. They ranged from violence to sheer humour. It was once claimed that a famous amateur boxer walked backwards through Jack Woolf's private door pointing a revolver at his pursuer. On another occasion a boxer was allegedly stabbed in the leg after defeating a local favourite. There were also many occasions when boxers and their seconds had to be rescued from dissatisfied backers of local losers, particularly if they had been disqualified.

A situation which involved both violence and humour arose one night when the Lord Mayor was due to attend the arena on behalf of a well-known charity. Boxing commenced prior to his arrival and one important contest was between two aspiring East End featherweights, George Moore and Cockney Cohen. Being bitter rivals, both were viciously intent on emerging victorious and during the course of battle broke almost every rule in the book. After a few rounds during which both received a number of warnings, the referee left the ringside as they were fighting on the floor. When the bell sounded, they returned to their corners believing it was the end of the round. On being told that the referee had ruled it a no contest, which would probably have meant no purse, each contestant picked up their stool and the battle started afresh.

Meanwhile, Jack Woolf had arrived at ringside in evening dress and was nervously awaiting the Lord Mayor's arrival. When the alarm was raised that Moore and Cohen were having a free-for-all and bleeding profusely, Harry Jacobs sprinted to the ring and threw them both out. Sawdust was quickly thrown over the blood-stained canvas and the ringside area tidied up before the Mayor and his party were escorted to their seats on the stage. Once they were comfortably seated, cornermen smartly dressed in clean white jumpers made their way to the ring followed by two boxers clad in full length black tights. After the first bell, they moved skilfully around boxing in a very gentlemanly manner for a few rounds. At the end of the contest Jack Woolf climbed into the ring and introduced the Lord Mayor to the audience. After his charity appeal and saying how much he enjoyed the boxing, the collection boxes were taken round. The guests then departed to more salubrious surroundings.

One of the bloodiest and most ferocious fights ever witnessed in a London ring took place at Wonderland in 1910. American middleweight, Bob Scanlon and Blink McCarthy, so named because he only had one eye, engaged in sheer cold-blooded fury with no regard for the rules. Bitter rivalry existed between the two over matters unconnected with boxing. When Harry Jacobs heard about it he went to great lengths to get them into the ring.

Among the many noted boxers who appeared at the venue were Johnny Summers, Pat O'Keefe, Pedlar Palmer, Matt Wells, Ben Jordan, Jimmy Britt, Young Joseph as well as a host of others. In 1910, Bombardier Billy Wells made his first public appearance in the Wonderland ring before a full house for which Jacobs paid him £8

By September 1909 boxing had been staged there for over 10 years, during which time it was estimated that no fewer than 11,000 fights had been staged by various promoters. Yet it was Woolf and Jacobs who, despite their constant differences lasted longest and turned the venue into an extremely successful enterprise. Their association came to a predictable ending in 1910, by which time it was common knowledge that they were arch enemies. Jacobs was forced out prompting a comment in a *Boxing* editorial: 'He had done his best to damage boxing and his enforced retirement has been followed by a boom that augers well for everyone'.

Jacobs though, was far from finished and soon began operating at the nearby Paragon Music Hall where he advertised mammoth promotions in direct competition to Wonderland. The bitterness raged on as he and rival promoters engaged in poster battles by plastering each other's fight bills with adverts for tonic pills and other merchandise. Such behaviour degraded the reputation of boxing as a sport and in another editorial, the trade paper was quick to take issue with the perpetrators by saying: 'Just at present there is, in the London camp of promoters, an amount of friction that is a serious indictment against the honour and manlihood of some of them'.

The antics only ceased when Jacobs was eventually forced out of the Paragon by the London County Council following a series of complaints from local residents. Yet, as time would show, he was quick to set about planning his future.

Boxing came to an abrupt halt at Wonderland in 1911 when the building was totally destroyed by a fire on Sunday 13 August. It broke out shortly before 4pm and within a few minutes was a blazing furnace. The flames spread so rapidly that a number of nearby premises were in danger and had to be evacuated. The adjoining East London Palace was particularly vulnerable and only the skill of the firemen saved a great part of it from destruction.

Although there were reports of an explosion, the cause of the blaze or what caused it to spread so rapidly was never established. There were a number of theories but officially it remained a mystery. Despite nothing being stated on record, it was strongly suspected that the disaster arose as a direct result of the bitterness which existed between Woolf and Jacobs. That theory did the rounds again four months later when Jacobs opened Premierland just a short distance away at Back Church Lane.

Jack Woolf suffered a huge financial loss following the fire at Wonderland and ceased to be involved in boxing. Despite his bitter disputes with his former business partner he was remembered for his commitment to good causes. He organised collections at most Saturday night shows in aid of the London Hospital of which he was a life governor. On another occasion in 1911 following the great mining disaster at Bolton, he collected over one hundredweight of money for a fund opened by the Lord Mayor of London for the widows and orphans.

As much as it could be an intimidating place, Wonderland played a massive part in East End boxing. It had character and attracted crowds of people from all walks of life. Pick pockets were in their element. Boxing-minded youngsters teemed around outside the main entrance fascinated yet respectful of the men who were there to fight. Champions were developed, titles contested and many a dispute resolved. Former British middleweight champion, Tom Thomas had his last fight there and coincidentally passed away the day the great arena was destroyed by fire. Eugene Corri, the top referee of the time once remarked, 'There was no better place than Wonderland for a young boxer to embark on a professional career'.

── 3 ──

PREMIERLAND

Never before had Back Church Lane known such a din, nor had it been so brightly lit as on the evening of 11 December 1911 when Harry Jacobs opened Premierland for its first promotion. Everyone in the East End was aware of the event because of the massive advertising campaign in which multi-coloured bill posters were plastered on virtually every available wall space around the area. Announcing himself as 'England's Greatest Promoter', the flamboyant Jacobs did things in style and would continue the activity long after he was established.

Four months earlier when Wonderland was mysteriously destroyed by fire, the East End was left without a suitable boxing arena. Anxious to retain control of the sport in the region, Jacobs, having failed to establish the Paragon Music Hall as a venue to compete with Wonderland, rented an empty warehouse at Back Church Lane just off Commercial Road.

The drab building which dominated the thoroughfare that wound down to Cable Street and the London Docks was owned by Fairclough's, a meat contractor. A massive barn of a place with huge steel girders lining its glass roof made it more reminiscent of a railway station. Despite its appearance, the shrewd Jacobs knew that once developed it could accommodate massive crowds.

Thousands flocked to the opening show made up of a nine-fight bill headed by Aldgate middleweight, Harry Mansfield against Bill Curzon. There was plenty of other local interest with Sid Burns, Nat Brookes and Harry Reeve on the undercard. In a further contest a young Ted 'Kid' Lewis outpointed Billy Taylor (Bethnal Green) over eight rounds. It was the first of his 48 at the venue, 35 of which would take place between January and December the following year.

Throughout the evening, Jacobs, smartly attired in evening dress, sat centre stage with a few acquaintances. Another full house the following Saturday saw a bill of 13 contests. The main event was over 10 rounds with eight contests of six rounds and the remainder of four.

The routine was set and the new East End venue quickly followed along similar lines to Wonderland with an atmosphere all of its own. Half the patrons were Jewish, the remainder mainly cockney Christians. The air was thick with smoke and throughout the arena, boys selling fruit did a roaring trade as did the purveyors of jellied eels.

By 1912 there were very few fight fans who would dispute Jacobs claim to be considered as the leading promoter in England. The huge attendances at Premierland were testimony to his business and matchmaking skills. The arena, like The Ring at Blackfriars, almost adjacent to the River Thames, was a place where embryo champions learned their trade before the most critical of audiences. Both staged Sunday afternoon shows at which variety stars would often be seen in the best seats at ringside. Elsewhere, ordinary working men could watch top class boxing for as little as one shilling, (5p).

Jacobs only ran Premierland until July 1913, but despite being an instant hit with the fans he reaped very little financial reward for the enterprise. The following year he was declared bankrupt having gambled away a small fortune. Although he built the venue from scratch it was never the personal success that Wonderland had been, most probably because it lacked the input of Jack Woolf.

Following the departure of Jacobs, Harry Morris took over in partnership with promoter Jack Callaghan until Autumn 1914 when the doors were closed to boxing. During the war years, it operated as a cinema but following the declaration of peace Callaghan re-introduced boxing promotions. His tenure, however, only lasted until the early 1920's and the lease was passed to boxing manager Joe Morris, backed by Ted 'Kid' Lewis. Joe, who had a large stable of fighters, eventually stepped down following a lack of financial success and continued complaints from other managers. Lewis was left to run Premierland alone but still being an active top-level fighter, was not ready for the rat race of promoting. Within a short time, he therefore signed the lease over to his brother-in-law, Manny Lyttlestone, who for some while had worked in the arena box office.

Manny joined forces with Victor Berliner, a local sportsman with fresh ideas and they re-opened in style in 1922. Joe Morris, who had built an impressive stable of boxers mostly from the East End, including Harry Corbett, Teddy Baldock, Alf Simmons, Archie Sexton and Johnny Curley (Lambeth), took on the role of matchmaker until 1925 when he severed ties with Berliner.

Three shows a week were staged, the first being on a Thursday evening with a programme usually consisting of five or six contests of 10, 12 or 15 rounds. Admission prices ranged from sixpence (2.5p) to three shillings and sixpence(17.5p). There were two shows on Sundays, a matinee at 3pm and an evening event at 8pm. The afternoon programmes were the most popular because the fighting was torrid and the atmosphere exuberant. Admission prices were hiked up to between one shilling and sixpence (7.5p) and five shillings and sixpence (27.5p) because four 15 round contests were usually staged and often featured some of the leading fighters in the country. Admission prices for the Sunday evening promotions were the same as on Thursdays.

From the day Berliner took over fans flocked to Premierland in their thousands. No matter who was fighting there was rarely a seat to be had and more often than not hundreds were turned away. The only place for unrestricted movement was in the ring. The new man paid crowd favourites reasonably well and gave them regular work. He even signed Jack 'Kid' Berg on a 10-year contract.

Quality boxers from around the country who topped Berliner's bills included Nel Tarleton, Dom Volante, Len Harvey, Jack Hood, and Harry Mason. Whilst the hardest

East End patrons were prepared for anything, even they did not anticipate what occurred one Sunday afternoon during the late 1920's.

To the surprise of everyone, regular Master of Ceremonies, the talented, charismatic Buster Cohen, whose voice carried far and beyond the confines of the stadium, the catcalls and whistles of the crowd, climbed into the ring and announced there would be an extra bout. It was not on the programme and arose following a series of disputes between drivers from two taxi ranks at Aldgate and Whitechapel. They had agreed to settle their differences over territory poaching by each nominating a champion who would enter the ring to decide the matter. Sam Russell, a former professional from Limehouse had agreed to referee.

The whole affair, whilst being completely devoid of skill and an observance of Queensberry rules, had the crowd yelling. Within a very short space of time a blatant foul by one man left his opponent writhing on the canvas prompting a near riot as opposing groups of supporters stampeded towards the ring. There was pandemonium and order was only restored when two van loads of police arrived.

In another amazing incident during 1929, a grudge fight took place between Kid Herman of Aldgate and Cockeye Davis from Spitalfields. A bitter dispute between the two originated over a bet at the dogs and, although only preliminary fighters, they went away and trained with all the fanfare of champions. On the day of the fight Premierland was packed and the main event dwarfed into insignificance. Both men went to the ring accompanied by a dozen seconds and handlers with all the ceremony of a world championship contest.

Although proceedings were quite orthodox during the opening round neither man could land a telling blow in the second, so they resorted to all the unpleasantries of a street fight. The finish came in round three when both lost their heads and kicking became the general mode of attack. After warnings to fight in the correct fashion the referee finally lost patience and called it 'No Contest' because as he explained afterwards, he was unable to judge a contest that featured more kicks than punches.

Premierland was far from being luxurious which was to be expected in an area as rough as Commercial Road amid a district adjacent to the London Docks during a period of high unemployment. As with Wonderland before it dense smoke filled the air on fight nights and hung in thick clouds beneath the skylights. This was no fantasy land, this was Dockland in the heart of London's East End.

The place also had its seedy side as pickpockets took advantage of the dense crowds in a confined space. Another attraction for the many of the punters was the ringside betting just as it had been at Wonderland. Small groups of bookmakers would stand around the pillars at the corners of the ring adorned with posters which read 'Betting Strictly Prohibited'. Nobody took any notice and huge sums of money changed hands every night often prompting violent arguments. Frequently, a free-for-all would kick off when a local boxer lost a close decision. Fist fights and bottle throwing considerably damaged the image which management wanted to present to outsiders.

Not surprisingly, the continuous unruly behaviour eventually attracted the attention of both Stepney Borough Council and the Metropolitan Police based at nearby Leman Street headquarters. By the late 1920's both authorities were closely monitoring events at the arena. When officers made an unannounced visit, they recorded that all aisles and exits were blocked. In a subsequent written report to the council it was concluded that Premierland was a disaster waiting to happen and that official action was necessary. The events at the arena gave rise to two particular cases of concern, the first of which related to crowd safety. In a report in November 1928 the Stepney Borough Surveyor brought his concerns to the attention of the council. Aware that the building was a former cinema with a seating capacity for 1,500, he estimated that on the day of his visit there were up to 3,000 people crammed in. It was his opinion that such conditions could lead to a serious injury or loss of life in the event of a fire or panic among spectators. He concluded that although neither Stepney Borough Council or London County Council had any power over the situation, some form of control should be in place.

Earlier in 1925 there had been an incident at Premierland concerning the safety and welfare of contestants in boxing. Following a sixth-round stoppage defeat, 21-year-old boxer Teddy Shepphard died in the ring. The referee, Sam Russell, had called a halt when he noticed that the boxer was unduly hanging onto his opponent. Having shaken hands with the opponent, Sheppard slowly collapsed to the floor as he made his way to his corner.

This occurred during a period when there were continuing debates as to the legality of boxing following several deaths in the ring. Following a lengthy investigation into matters concerning Teddy Sheppard, the Director of Public Prosecutions ruled that on the evidence available there would be no criminal proceedings.

The eventual outcome regarding concerns at Premierland was that, at a subsequent meeting of the London County Council, it was ruled that from 1 January 1931 all premises used for the purpose of boxing would require a licence, the stipulations of which would vary from hall to hall.

From the day that Premierland first opened under Harry Jacobs, thousands of fighters earned their bread and butter in its ring. Every preliminary boy was a budding champion and virtually every top-line contest carried a needle element. The fighters always gave their best and urged on by the crowd generally endeavoured to give even more.

Despite changes in management, the comings and goings at the venue basically remained the same. The bills were as varied as the paying customers with barrow boys, dockers and street traders from nearby Petticoat Lane rubbing shoulders with vaudeville stars. Princes of harmony at the time, Layton and Johnstone along with xylophonist Teddy Brown were always to be found there when they were playing at the London Palladium or Holborn Empire. This American trio were often accompanied by other stage stars. Teddy's 20 stone plus frame was almost as broad as it was long, so two ringside seats were knocked into one to accommodate him.

The set up at Premierland bore no resemblance to modern day boxing. There were no weigh-ins except on occasions where there was a 'money-match' and even then, nobody could ever vouch for the accuracy of the scales. Until the formation of the British Boxing Board of Control in 1929 there were rarely doctors at ringside to treat injuries and no officials to supervise proceedings or enforce rules. Yet it survived until 1930 by which time Manny Lyttlestone was the sole manager, Victor Berliner having moved a short distance to become manager of The Ring at Blackfriars.

Although huge crowds gathered at each show, Lyttlestone owed money to the owners who planned to repossess the building and return it to its original purpose of a storage depot. In many respects this was a blessing in disguise because it had become run down and was a danger. The steel girders were rusty, the roof leaked badly and the floor and brickwork were badly in need of repair. The heating apparatus had also completely gone, the boilers having burst and been thrown out into the open.

Sadly, the grand old arena had reached the end of the road and on Thursday 30 October that year it closed its doors for the final time. The last show consisted of just four contests with Bert Taylor (Birmingham) outpointing Lew Pinkus (Mile End) over 15 rounds in the main event. Charlie McDonald (Sunderland) beat Jack Hyams (Stepney) who was disqualified in round ten for persistent holding; Billy Jones (Hampstead) beat Kid Rich (St Georges) on points over 10 and Charlie Wye (Hoxton) took a similar decision over Len Fisher (Millwall).

Predictably, a huge crowd assembled for the final show, but although boxing continued to thrive in the East End, the Back Church Lane arena was the last of its kind. It was a nursery for champions and men such as Lewis, Berg, Mason, the Corbetts, the Browns, Baldock, Pattenden, Reeve and others built their early careers there.

There was an abundance of memories and the presence of great characters. No Master of Ceremonies could match

Buster Cohen. Former boxer, Jack Hart born Moses Solomon, the house referee during the 1920's, who worked from a seat at ringside, took no nonsense from boxers or their handlers. Born in 1900, he boxed at middleweight before becoming one of the top referees in the country.

There was respect too as demonstrated one night in February 1929 when the whole audience stood for a minute silence as respect following the death of Harry Jacobs. Memories of Premierland were so imprinted in the minds of those who attended its shows regularly that it would never be forgotten.

4

JACK 'KID' BERG

(Whitechapel)

World Junior Welterweight champion (NBA Version) 1930-1931

British Lightweight Champion 1934-1936

Only an extraordinary man could have won the world light-welterweight title at the age of twenty-one, lost only a handful of almost 200 fights as well as been able to become the first man to get the better of legendary Cuban star, Kid Chocolate in a professional ring. Yet, that is exactly what Jack 'Kid' Berg did. In doing so he became one of the most celebrated names in British boxing history. Few others have done more to uphold the prestige of this country in the American ring.

Born Judah Bergman, of immigrant Russian-Jewish parents at Whitechapel on 28 June 1909, he grew up in the East End and went to school with such latter-day fighters as Jack Hyams, Phil Lolosky and dozens of other Jewish kids. As a young teenager he gained a fearful reputation for scrapping in the streets of the region and when he was fourteen used to look after cars parked outside Premierland on fight nights for which the owners gave him tips.

Jack was very enthusiastic about his responsibilities and one night in early June 1924 when an older youth decided to sit on the bonnet of one of the cars, he flew into a rage and set about him with both fists. The ruckus attracted the attention of venue promoter Victor Berliner, who on discovering what it was all about took hold of Berg saying; 'Why fight for nothing?'. He took the youngster inside, handed him over to the matchmaker, Joe Goodwin, and a few days later, just three weeks short of his fifteenth birthday he had his first professional fight.

Premierland became Jack's ring home ground and he would engage in 51 contests there in less than four years. Within five months he was fighting 15-rounders against seasoned professionals and after just 12 months faced future British feather-weight champion, Johnny Cuthbert, who outpointed him over that distance and again three months later. Berg was a mere sixteen years and four months old when he outpointed British feather-weight champion Johnny Curley over 15 rounds in a non-title contest.

The '*Whitechapel Windmill*' or '*Yiddle*' as he had become affectionately known was recognised as one of the outstanding lightweights in Britain. His record during 1926 included two victories over good French champion Andre Routis, who in 1928 would become World featherweight champion. He also won, drew and lost against Harry Corbett, who in 1928 would take the British featherweight title from Johnny Cuthbert. Yet, despite his considerable talent and success Jack found his path to a shot at the British title blocked.

Anxious to keep his career moving forward he went to America in 1928 where he won his first five contests inside two months. He was then matched with Billy Petrolle, a great favourite of the American fight fans. Known as '*The Fargo Express*' he had over 100 contests behind him. He was a tremendous obstacle for Berg, but after getting a draw he became an instant hit with both the fans and the media.

It was such an exciting fight that they were matched again four weeks later but Berg injured an ankle in training. Stubbornly refusing to pull out of the fight was utter stupidity against a man of Petrolle's quality and when the ankle gave way again in round two it proved to be the beginning of the end. Unable to avoid the American's big punches he was smashed to the canvas 16 times before finally submitting in the fifth. Despite having to be helped from the ring he received a huge ovation from the admiring crowd.

Jack returned briefly to England at the end of 1928, but after taking two fights at The Royal Albert Hall, one of which was a points defeat of Alf Mancini, he returned to the States by popular demand early the following year. Between May and December, he had an unbeaten run of 15 contests, three victories coming against Bruce Flowers, rated as one of the most dangerous lightweights in the world and another against Mushy Callahan, all on points over 10 rounds.

After beating former world featherweight champion Tony Canzoneri on points over 10 rounds in New York in January 1930, Berg returned to London where four weeks later, he won the world junior welterweight title by knocking out Callahan in 10 rounds at The Royal Albert Hall. When the decision was announced, Lord Lonsdale rose from his ringside seat and waving his walking stick, angrily protested that there was no such title.

Berg's stay in London was a short one and by the beginning of April he was back in America determined to cash in on his crown. During the next 12 months, he was undefeated in a dozen contests, nine of which some records claimed were in defence of his title. His victims included the great Cuban, Kid Chocolate and old foe Billy Petrolle.

After three more victories in as many months at the beginning of 1931, Jack faced Canzoneri at Chicago in a challenge for the world welterweight championship. Three days before that he was presented with a National Boxing Association belt in recognition of him being the light-welterweight (or junior welterweight) champion.

Almost 13,000 fans crammed into the Chicago Stadium, Illinois, expecting a tense battle. Back in the East End the area was alive with excitement and in the street where Berg's parents lived, few went to bed anxiously awaiting the outcome. Alas, it was a disappointing result as their man was knocked out in the third round.

The winner claimed both titles which Berg disputed and after six more victories he was matched with Canzoneri again at the same arena five months later. Although Jack fought much better, the American took a close, hard earned victory. Despite Berg being floored twice in the opening round the British press were adamant that he was robbed. Their American counterparts, however, did not share that view.

After a single contest in London at the end of 1931, Berg returned to the States where, based in New York, he won four of five contests including a 15 rounds points decision over Kid Chocolate. During the next two years, he fought both there and in Britain but deeply regretted never having been a champion of his own country. That, however, was eventually rectified in October 1934 when he took the lightweight title from fellow East Ender, Harry Mizler, who was forced to retire in the 10th round of their contest at the Royal Albert Hall.

Yet it proved to be a false dawn; Jack's form nose-dived following that success. He lost two of three contests with Gustave Humary of France, was beaten on points by Laurie Stevens in South Africa for the vacant Empire title and in April 1936 lost his British title to Jimmy Walsh.

Due to a series of injuries mostly to an ankle, that contest had to be postponed on four occasions before eventually going ahead at Liverpool Stadium. Berg, who had also experienced weight difficulties, was floored twice and when he could barely stand due to the pain in his damaged ankle, the bout was stopped.

After a six-month break he moved up to welterweight and had reasonable success throughout 1937 when he was undefeated albeit against a mediocre opposition. He returned to America the following year where he had a long and successful stay winning 18 of the 24 contests, mostly at small arenas in Brooklyn. Yet the days of the 20,000 crowds were gone as, had the big pay days. Back home he fell out with the Board of Control, was suspended for a period and also commenced divorce proceedings with his wife.

Returning to the ring in England, Jack still beat fighters of average ability at small halls including the Devonshire Club where he fought on three occasions during 1940. Success, however, was spasmodic and although he beat Harry Mizler on points and Eric Boon on a controversial disqualification, he lost to Arthur Danahar, Ernie Roderick and George Odwell. Serving in the Royal Air Force during the Second World War restricted his ring activities. He boxed only twice in 1942, and once in 1943, but after a short comeback in 1945, during which he won all three contests, his second wife Moyra ordered him to quit.

Although he was recognised in America as the world junior welterweight champion during 1930 and 1931 Berg never became a fully-fledged world title holder. He was, however, one of the outstanding light-welterweights of his time and may well have become champion of that division had he been able to get a contest with the title holder at the right time. When Sammy Mandell was champion between 1926 and 1930, Jack was never able to secure a fight with him. When Al Singer took the title from him in 1930 a match with Berg was an obvious one but never materialised. At the time, it was believed that the reason was because the British boxer had previously refused to meet Singer who was a close friend.

Life treated Berg well after he retired from the ring. During the early 1950's he was the proprietor of a popular restaurant at Denman Street, Soho, for a short while. Then after getting an equity card, he became involved in the film industry spending many years performing as a stuntman. Talented author, Louis Golding wrote a novel entitled 'Magnolia Street' said to be based on Berg's life and there followed a film called 'Money Talks' in which Jack played the leading role himself. He also appeared in a theatre comedy 'Is Zat So?'

Although he moved home on several occasions from St Johns Wood to Sussex, then back to London before finally settling in Essex, Berg kept in touch with the fight game until his dying day. On 6 March 1991, he sat ringside at Wembley for the Lennox Lewis v Gary Mason British heavyweight championship contest. Even chronic arthritis failed to stop him eventually climbing into the ring to a wonderful ovation. A few weeks later he was taken ill and admitted to hospital at Southend but even then, insisted on being taken to London in order that he could attend the annual Boxing Writers dinner on 11 April. It was an evening of emotion and handshaking for the great East End fighter and a fitting end to his life. He passed away 10 days later aged eighty-two.

Traceable Record;
192 Contests
157 Won
26 Lost
9 Drew.

5

HARRY BROOKS

(Aldgate)

There could never be any doubt that Harry Brooks had been a fighter for many years. The scars etched about his craggy face along with the misshaped broken nose were all mementos of a long professional ring career between 1926 and 1945. It was claimed that he had over 500 contests during that period although it is unclear how accurate that claim was. Yet from his records there is no doubting that he was an extremely tough gritty character generally capable of holding his own with the best men around.

Born in Aldgate of Lithuanian parents in the early 1900's Harry soon discovered that by living in one of the poorest quarters of London, he had to be ready to defend himself against bullies of all ages and sizes. Being a diminutive figure, they enjoyed battering him with their hard-hitting fists, particularly at school. Despite all the bruises and bloody noses, he quickly learned the art of playground and street fighting. Soon after leaving school he decided to fight as a professional to augment his meagre wage of ten shillings a week.

By the age of fifteen, Harry was having three or four fights a week generally at East End venues and considered himself rich when paid seventeen shillings and sixpence for a six-round contest. After winning about 90 six-rounder's, Harry took two ten round contests in one day and won both. He was then matched with undefeated George Rose from Bristol and won by a third-round knockout. The success elevated him into championship class resulting in him facing men such as Johnny Curley in 1929, to whom he lost on points over 15 rounds. Ernie Izzard and Fred Webster both similarly outpointed him as did Nel Tarleton over 12 rounds in 1934. His record is littered with top class fighters and among those he beat were Bugler Harry Lake, Fred Green, Phil Richards, Norman Snow and Bep Van Klaveren.

Willing to face anybody, Brooks agreed to meet world featherweight champion, Freddy Miller, at The Ring, Blackfriars in March 1935, but was knocked out in the seventh round. The American was a class act and floored Harry for two long counts in the fourth. He hung on gamely until a vicious body shot, which appeared extremely low, brought matters to an end.

The defeat did nothing to deter Harry and two weeks later he travelled to Edinburgh and faced Scottish lightweight champion, Tommy Spiers in an eliminator for the British title. In a see-saw 15-rounder he was floored in rounds 10 and 13 but came very close to victory in the final round when he knocked Spiers virtually out of the ring. The Scot held on gamely to take the decision.

Back in London two weeks later Brooks faced rising star, Pedro Montanez at Mile End Arena. The undefeated, hard-hitting Puerto Rican was on a European tour during which he had scored 13 consecutive knockout victories including two in London. The tough Brooks, however, took everything thrown at him but was beaten on points.

In the latter years of his career he won only four of his last 20 contests. One was against an up and coming Eric Boon at the Devonshire Club in 1937. When his opponent failed to arrive at the venue, Eric agreed to face Brooks despite giving away over a stone in weight and about 20 years in experience. Harry was too big for the youngster who retired after four rounds with eye problems.

Although he was regarded as a lightweight contender in 1927 and again in 1934, Brooks never got a championship shot which he richly deserved. Trained by Nat Seller during the mid-1930's, he eventually managed his own affairs. When he officially retired in 1945 it was estimated that he had engaged in about 500 contests. He was very proud of the fact that he was never disqualified. Harry also had two brothers, Joe and Nat who also boxed professionally during the mid 1930's and were usually billed as from St George's.

Harry served with the British Army during the Second World War and on being discharged wanted to continue boxing. The Board of Control, however, refused him a license on grounds of his age. In retirement, he worked for many years for Western Union Cables and spent an active life until he passed away in May 1991.

Traceable Record:
156 Contests
78 Won
61 Lost
16 Drew
1 NC

JOHNNY BROWN

(Stepney)

British Bantamweight Champion 1923-1928

British Empire Bantamweight Champion 1923-1928

European Bantamweight Champion 1923-1924

Born on 18 July 1902 in the St Georges district of Stepney of Lithuanian–Jewish parents, his real name was Phil Hickman, but he changed it to Johnny Brown when he started boxing as a young amateur because he did not want his widowed mother to know what he was doing. He developed into a promising young fighter prompting East End manager, Joe Morris, to suggest that he turned professional. 'You can earn enough money to prevent your mother having to go out to work' he told the youngster. 'You can save her all those hours she puts in as a cook'.

The idea appealed to Johnny, but loving his mother dearly, he insisted that it was done honestly, and she would have to give her consent. It took a lot of coaxing from her son and the manager before she finally gave her blessing.

Johnny was three months short of his seventeenth birthday when he had his first professional contest at The Ring, Blackfriars, which he won. After almost 30 contests within two years he lost only four. Even though he won a dozen inside the distance there was little to indicate he could progress to becoming a champion. In 1921 he entered a bantamweight competition at The Ring for which the proprietors put up a belt and guaranteed the winner 20% of the takings plus an additional three contests at the venue. The losing finalist would get two further contests. Brown fought his way into the final but was outpointed over 10 rounds by Kid Davis.

Although he was knocked out in the first of his guaranteed fights, he won the second after which he was offered a series of contests in the United States and Canada. Joe Morris advised him to go because he was convinced that the experience he would gain would be far greater than if he stayed at home. Johnny was away for nine months during which time he had 14 contests at venues as far apart as New York, Montreal and Philadelphia losing only two on points.

Returning home in the Spring of 1922, he was convinced that he was a much better fighter and after drawing with another rising East End star, Al Foreman over 15 rounds at Premierland, Morris was anxious to move his man towards a shot at the British bantamweight title. Bugler Harry Lake was a top contender at the time and in order to assess his man's potential, Morris agreed to a fight in the champion's home town of Plymouth. The ex-marine, however, was too smart and easily outpointed the East End youngster.

Clearly not ready for a title fight, Brown returned to the United States in March 1923 where he had a further six contests losing just one, the remainder being of no decision. During this trip, however, he developed considerably more power in his punches which became evident when he returned home and scored two quick victories.

He then faced the vastly more experienced Johnny Curley, a professional since 1912 and who, in 1925, would become British featherweight champion. Although he lost on points over 20 rounds Brown put up a credible performance and in doing so convinced the National Sporting Club that he was worthy of a championship shot against Bugler Lake. They met at the club on 26 November over 20 rounds with the British, European and British

Empire titles at stake. The East End boy won clearly on points thus gaining revenge for the defeat he suffered to Lake 15 months earlier.

Anxious to become a fighting champion, Johnny had nine contests during 1924, winning six inside the distance. His only defeat was to Harry Corbett (Bethnal Green) who had been one of his sparring partners as he prepared for the Lake fight. To protect his title, the contest at Hoxton Baths was made at two pounds above the bantamweight limit, which was fortunate for Brown because he was outpointed after a terrific battle. A return with the title at stake was a natural, but Joe Morris was dubious about his man's chances because since returning from America he had become lax in training and developed a chain smoking habit. More than once when he was supposed to be in the gym, Joe found him walking about in the street with a fag in his mouth.

Desperate for his man to be in top shape, Joe sent him to Jack Goodwin, one of the best trainers in the business and a strong disciplinarian. He immediately clamped down on Brown's smoking habit, but within a few days was faced with pleas from the boxer to 'let me have a fag'. Eventually, after careful negotiation, Jack relented slightly allowing the boy to have half a cigarette in the morning and the other half at night. The trainer was convinced he had broken Johnny's habit, but after their last day together was horrified to find a full box of butt ends under his bed.

Rumours were circulating that Brown was proving difficult to handle and would have trouble making the weight yet come fight day it was his opponent who looked the more drained of the two. Goodwin told Joe Morris very little about the smoking issues but did remark that training Brown had put years on him.

Johnny looked a picture of health and despite having been beaten by Corbett two months earlier, he oozed confidence. He looked bigger and stronger and as the fight developed he slowly but surely reduced the challenger's stamina and fighting spirit. Harry had trained so hard for his big fight that he had left most of his strength in the gym. He was floored twice in round 15, only the bell saving him from a knockout. Vicious body shots in round 16 left Corbett in a heap on the floor and although he rose gamely he collapsed again under the champion's next big attack whereupon the towel was thrown in.

Johnny kept busy and among his successes were disqualification victories over good Frenchman, Andre Routis and old foe Johnny Cuthbert. In the meantime, however, he relinquished his claim to the European title as he was not generally recognised as champion on the continent.

The next defence of his British and Empire titles was against Mick Hill from Tooting, a real box office attraction who had battled his way through a series of eliminators. The National Sporting Club was packed when they faced each other on 19 October 1925. Despite earlier concerns, Brown just made the championship weight of 8st 6lbs, but Hill was six ounces over and it took him an hour of strenuous exercising to remove it. Mick made all the running and was well ahead by halfway but faced two disadvantages. Apart from the effect the weight reducing was likely to have, he was without his chief second who was ordered from the ringside for urging encouragement to his fighter by clapping his hands during the fourth round. Coaching of any kind was strictly against National Sporting Club rules.

In what was a thrilling contest from the start, Hill continued to give the champion problems until the 11th round when Johnny set up a big two-fisted attack. Although a big right to the jaw changed the course of the fight, he was sent to the floor briefly as the challenger made his last desperate stand. Both men went for the finish in the 12th, but Brown was by far the harder puncher, flooring his opponent three times to keep his titles by way of a knockout. Victory also ensured that he made the Lonsdale Belt his own property in less than two years.

Anxious to secure a world title shot, Johnny returned to America in early 1926, but returned home disappointed having lost all six contests there, three inside the distance. After being outpointed by good South African, Willie

Smith, in Johannesburg in a catchweight contest, he was out of action for six months.

When he returned to action in July he was undefeated in four contests, one of which was a 15 round points victory over young Liverpool prospect, Nel Tarleton at Premierland. After that, however, there were signs that Johnny was past his best. Defeats to Alf Pattenden (St Georges), Kid Socks (Mile End) and Sammy Shack (USA), who stopped him in 14 rounds at Mile End, were a clear indication that his best days were behind him.

Johnny's ring career ended in August 1928 when he was stopped in two rounds by former world bantamweight champion, Teddy Baldock. Although the contest was billed as being for the British and Empire titles, this was in dispute because the Board of Control had withdrawn recognition from him some months earlier. Alf Pattenden was recognised as champion having beaten Kid Nicholson at the National Sporting Club in June.

Although the defeat by Baldock brought about his retirement from the ring.

Johnny was determined to stay in boxing. On being granted a referee's licence by the newly formed British Boxing Board of Control he handled bouts for several years in various parts of the country, particularly London. His judgement was always considered to be beyond question. One incident of particular interest occurred, however, when he was refereeing a 10-round contest at Mile End Arena on 17 June 1934 between Bermondsey boxers, Johnny English and Billy Palmer. In round three, much to the amazement of virtually everyone present, Johnny called a halt and declared it 'no contest'. People were even more bewildered when in announcing the result, the Master of Ceremonies gave no reason for the ending. The press seized on the situation and subsequent reports bitterly criticized Brown for his action.

The backlash irritated Johnny to the extent that he took the unusual course of giving a press interview explaining his reasons. He claimed that as early as the first round he realised something strange was afoot and warned both men for hugging and holding. During the second round, he refereed from inside the ring and had to stop them from talking to one another. When English went to the canvas from a mere flick of his opponent's glove, Brown cautioned them both again. In the third round after more holding and muttering, he claimed that Palmer said, 'give me one on the chin and I'll go down'. At that point Johnny left the ring and declared it 'no contest'. He explained that he had enough experience in the ring to know what was going on and was determined to stop it.

Brown continued refereeing for several more years before eventually emigrating to South Africa where he remained until his death in 1975.

Traceable Record
99 Contests
54 Won
5 Drew
25 Lost
15 ND

7

YOUNG JOHNNY BROWN

(Stepney)

Almost five years younger than his brother, Young Johnny Brown started his ring career at flyweight and developed into one of the brightest of many Jewish boxers in the East End. After a good education at King Edward Street School his widowed mother got him an apprenticeship in the tailoring business. Boxing, however, soon became the lad's ambition and he took part in amateur contests whenever he could.

Much to his mother's disappointment he soon broke the apprenticeship and turned professional. This was due in no small part to the fact that his older brother had adopted that course in 1919 (when) three months short of his seventeenth birthday. It was an inevitable course of events for Young Johnny as with money extremely hard to come by, his brother and many other lads of his age were earning far more from fights than most businesses were prepared to pay them.

His first paid contest was at Manor Hall, Hackney, where he gave a severe beating to another Stepney lad, Young Dyer. It was a perfect start for the youngster who followed along the same lines as his brother. In August 1922, the pair travelled to Plymouth where at the famous Cosmopolitan Club, they faced Bugler Harry Lake and his brother Percy. Both were beaten but Young Johnny sustained serious hand damage and had to have long term treatment from Dr Matthews, a renowned bone specialist whose picture hung in the National Sporting Club.

The injury eventually healed but the boxer bore evidence of it for the rest of his life. There was disfigurement due largely to the fact that Young Johnny did not have the patience to wait until it had fully recovered. When he fought Johnny Hayden at Premierland in February 1924, he suffered acute pain with every blow he landed and was forced to retire after 10 rounds.

On examination, Dr Matthews found that it had fractured again, this time in three places. The boxer was unperturbed as he walked about the East End with his arm in a sling often joking: 'I am back to my second childhood nursing a doll again'. His happy go lucky attitude did not last for long and he soon became very despondent because he had begun to see a bright future ahead of him. Not wanting to lose one of his most promising youngsters, Manny Littlejohn, the manager of Premierland where Young Johnny had become a popular competitor in recent months, gave him a ray of hope. He took him to see Jack Goodwin, one of the most capable and experienced trainers in the sport. When the young boxer explained his predicament about not being able to support his mother, Jack insisted he would get him fit enough to fight again within a month.

Showing incredible sympathy, he visited Brown at his house twice a day, applied manipulation to the damaged hand until it was fully healed. He didn't charge him a penny but said he wanted to get him a fight to see the result of his work. It was a testimony of Goodwin's skill that the young boxer returned to the Premierland ring just two months after sustaining his injuries and beat Johnny Jones in 11 rounds. His weight was 7st 11lbs.

Brown then travelled to South Africa where three fights had been arranged for him in Johannesburg at monthly intervals between June and August 1924. In the first he beat national bantamweight champion, Scotty Fraser on points over 20 rounds. At the same venue four weeks later, he was adjudged to have been outpointed by Norman Mulligan over 20 two-minute rounds, but the decision was so hotly disputed that police had to be called to restore order among the irate spectators. In a return bout four weeks later, Mulligan again got the decision, this time over 15 rounds without dispute. He was an experienced fighter who had held the bantamweight title until beaten by Scotty Fraser in November 1923.

On his return to London, Johnny was quickly back in action, taking three fights in as many weeks at Premierland, winning all inside the distance. Early in the New Year his brother, Johnny the Elder, who by this time was British, British Empire and European bantamweight champion, was due to fight Kid Nicholson of Leeds at Premierland in a non-title fight over 15 rounds at 8st 8lbs. When he was taken ill Young Johnny went to the promoter and offered to take his place. Despite only boxing at flyweight he outboxed and outfought the much heavier Nicholson and took a good decision.

Brown had progressed well beating some of the best flyweights in the country. His victory over talented and experienced Frankie Ash of Plymouth, who he stopped in nine rounds at Premierland in February 1925, was particularly impressive. In May the previous year, Ash put up a tremendous display at Brooklyn only to lose a close 15-round points decision to world flyweight champion, Pancho Villa. He was without doubt Johnny's most experienced opponent since turning professional, yet he handled him well.

That success brought Brown his first big chance and his next contest was a challenge for the European flyweight title against Glaswegian, Elky Clark, at The Royal Albert Hall on 30 April. Young Johnny was trained for the fight by Jack Goodwin who also prepared his brother Johnny the Elder and Ernie Izzard for contests on the same bill.

Young Johnny gave it everything against Clark but was heavily knocked out in the final round and remembered nothing until he came round in his dressing room. Once he had recovered, Elky went to see him and shook his hand. He told him that he had never been in such a hard fight and added; 'If you look after yourself, you are sure to become a world champion. I am a lot older than you'.

After a six-month break Brown returned to South Africa where he had three more fights in as many months. As with the previous trip, the opponents were all of high quality. After beating Joe Michael in 11 rounds he faced Ernie Eustice who, four months later would become South African flyweight champion. He proved too strong for Young Johnny who was forced to retire after nine rounds.

Four weeks later he met hot prospect, Willie Smith, who three months earlier had beaten bantamweight champion, Scotty Fraser but the South African Board of Control refused to sanction the contest as a title fight. Brown gave Willie a great fight only to be outpointed over 20 rounds but drew satisfaction from the fact that his opponent went on to win the South African featherweight title in November 1929 and held it until he retired in 1936.

Young Johnny had become extremely popular in South Africa and would be invited back on three occasions in the future. In September 1927, he knocked out Johnny Sullivan in seven rounds in Johannesburg. The trips enhanced his bank balance considerably.

On returning to Britain in early 1926, he scored eight successive victories, mostly at Premierland, only one of which lasted the distance. Recognised as being of championship class, he then proceeded to take on a string of top quality opponents over the next two years, albeit with limited success. Jack Hyams, Johnny Curley, Johnny Cuthbert (twice) and Alf 'Kid' Pattenden all outpointed him over 15 rounds while Teddy Baldock knocked him out in three. He outpointed Cuthbert over 10 rounds between losses to him and also stopped Phil Lolosky in 12. With the exception of Hyams and Lolosky all were or would have become champions. Curley was British featherweight champion when he faced Brown, Baldock was just three months away from becoming world bantamweight title holder, Cuthbert was British featherweight champion having taken it from Curley two months earlier and Pattenden would win the British bantamweight title four months after beating Young Johnny. It was a testimony of Brown's skill and toughness that, with the exception of Baldock, he handled himself with such credit.

Pattenden, a fellow East Ender from Mile End, became British champion by knocking out Kid Nicholson at the National Sporting Club in June 1928. His first defence of the title was against Brown at the same venue on 26 November. Before a packed house Young Johnny made a spirited effort to bring the title back to his family but the champion was too strong and forced his retirement in round 12. The end came when Pattenden landed three straight lefts to the face followed by two hard rights. Brown crashed to the floor whereupon his seconds jumped into the ring and went to his aid before he was counted out.

From a career point of view, worse was to follow for Johnny and when he returned to the ring at Crystal Palace in February the following year, he was knocked out in the opening round by Dom Volante. It was a worrying situation and on advice he took a year out from boxing.

He resumed in February 1930 winning three straight fights in four weeks at Premierland, two coming inside the distance. Refreshed, Young Johnny then made his fourth trip to South Africa. On returning home, he faced British Empire bantamweight champion, Dick Corbett from Bethnal Green in a non-title bout at Premierland. Dick had won the title in May by outpointing former Brown opponent Willie Smith at Olympia and was expected to be too good for Young Johnny. Nevertheless, the arena was packed to the rafters for what was expected to be a Sunday East End classic. Unfortunately, the fight did not live up to expectations due largely to Browns tactics. He did everything but box during the opening four rounds, being guilty of holding, palming and general rough tactics for which referee, Jack Hart, issued only the mildest of cautions.

Corbett had entered the ring with a strip of plaster covering his left eyebrow to protect a recent cut, but Johnny palmed it off before the end of the opening session. As the fight progressed, however, the Bethnal Green man took control due mainly to the accuracy of his left jab. By the end of the 15 rounds he was considered by many onlookers to be at least ten rounds ahead but to everyone's amazement, the referee called it a draw. There was uproar and even the usually jovial Master of Ceremonies, Buster Cohen, pulled a face before announcing the official decision. Punters left Premierland in bewilderment and press reports described the result as amazing. In what was his last fight before going on a tour of the United States, Young Johnny Brown got extremely lucky.

After taking just one fight in America, Young Johnny returned home for Christmas, but still found time to top a Sunday afternoon promotion before a packed audience at Shoreditch Olympia. Although billed to engage in a 15-round contest, he proved too strong for late substitute, Fred Cook from Birmingham whose corner threw in the towel during the fourth round.

Returning to the United States, Young Johnny fought at arenas in Philadelphia and New York including one at Madison Square Garden. He engaged in seven contests during the four-month stay of which he lost only two. In his last fight, however, he suffered a heavy defeat being stopped in three rounds and when he returned to the ring in London he looked to be well past his best.

Young Johnny won only one of his six contests after returning from America and there were signs that he was nearing the end of his career. This was never more apparent than when he was forced to retire during the eighth round of a fight with Sandy McEwan from Birmingham at The Ring, Blackfriars. During the early stages of the contest the exchanges had the packed Sunday afternoon house roaring with delight, especially as McEwan, the smaller of the two, bundled into Brown with great vigour. By the fifth the Londoner appeared to be in control as McEwan tired but in the eighth the unexpected happened. A hard-right swing to the jaw put Johnny down for a short count and on rising a similar shot floored him again. This time he looked badly hurt and the towel was thrown in from his corner during the count. It was a particularly bad defeat for Brown when considering that his opponent had recorded only two previous victories from over 40 contests.

With no apparent prospect of future success in the ring it was generally believed that he had retired following the defeat by McEwan. With that in mind a long-awaited testimonial was organised for Young Johnny at the Whitechapel Pavilion during the afternoon of Sunday 13 December that year. The venue was packed to the doors with many ring notables including Jack 'Kid' Berg being present. East End boxers on the bill included Moe Moss, Alf Pattenden, Kid Farlo and Albert Danahar. Larry Gains boxed a three-round exhibition whilst Moss Deyong in his usual glib manner, extracted £65 from ringsiders for the cause.

Still not able to quit with dignity, Brown, billed as from Wealdstone, unwisely faced Herbie Hill at a small hall venue in Wembley the following month, but was widely outpointed. After two further contests (a draw and a victory) his career finally came to an end in August 1932, when he suffered a heavy defeat at the hands of Dick Corbett who stopped him in two rounds at Southend Football Ground on Bank Holiday Monday. Having stated publicly that he was extremely fit and had the desire to work his way back to the top, more was expected from him.

Due to wet conditions the boxers were kept waiting for over an hour before the fight could get underway and there were signs of impatience among the huge crowd, many of whom had travelled from the East End. Although Brown started aggressively when the fight got underway, Corbett soon took control landing big punches to the head and body. By the end of the opening session he was well on top and resumed where he left off in the second. Hooking accurately, he quickly sent Young Johnny to the canvas for a count of 'nine'. Very unsteady on his feet when he rose, more hooks sent him down for 'eight '. Again, he rose bravely but when Corbett continued the vicious assault, the seconds threw the towel in as a token of surrender sensing that their man was badly hurt and about to be knocked out.

Realising the extent of the defeat Johnny sensibly called time on his career. He was a brave, gutsy little fighter with plenty of natural talent. He was afraid of nobody and pursued a demanding ring career to help support his mother in times of dire hardship. Although he did not reach the heights achieved by his brother, Johnny the Elder, he was an exciting and extremely popular ring man particularly in the East End. He outlived his brother by five years and died in 1983 aged seventy-eight.

Traceable Record
92 Contests
64 Won
5 Drew
23 Lost

8

SID BURNS

(Aldgate)

Born in Aldgate on 26 May 1890, Soloman Bernstein had every incentive to make a career from boxing as he lived just a short distance from the celebrated Judean Club. There, from an early age, youngsters could pick up the rudiments of the sport. Also nearby was the famous Wonderland Arena; an ambitious youngster was spoilt for choice.

Towards the end of the summer of 1909, Soloman decided to go to the Judean Club because he wanted to fight. When he gave his name to the matchmaker he was told: 'We can't have that, people will think you are a Jew boy and we already have four on the bill. I'll put you down as Sid Burns'. The name stuck throughout his subsequent career.

Sid's first fight was on 2 September that year against Bill Myers, a local lad who he outpointed over six rounds. When the Master of Ceremonies announced the winner, however, it didn't register with Sid because he had already forgotten his change of name.

Burns had several contests at the club winning the majority by knockout. A particularly impressive performance came a few weeks later when he floored a Bermondsey lad named Cleary four times in the opening round including the count.

Moving to Wonderland a few months later, he scored a knockout on his debut at the venue against Bill Jordan. Five more victories followed in quick succession and then a member of the National Sporting Club committee witnessed him dispose of well-known Wally Pickard in two rounds and recommended him to the club matchmaker.

Sid was matched with Andre Bayard of France and before a packed audience on 7 March 1910 he disposed of his first continental opponent in the opening round. The importance of fighting at the headquarters of the sport held no fears for the youngster and the victory ensured plenty of work in London rings.

The Aldgate lad's winning run since turning professional reached 24 before he was held to a draw by Young Nipper (real name Chamberlain) over 10 rounds at Wonderland. Two weeks later he travelled to Newcastle for his first contest outside London. It was also to be his first over 20 rounds but he stopped his opponent, Bob Docherty in the 15th. It was a hectic period for Sid and within three weeks he faced Young Nipper again and won on points over 10 rounds at The Ring, Blackfriars.

Burns engaged in 26 contests during 1910 losing only one, that being on points to Jack Goldswain, a veteran of over 70 fights. He had held the British lightweight title from 1906 to 1908 and challenged Young Joseph for the welterweight crown in March 1910 only to lose on points. It was a massive step-up in class for Sid and resulted in a points defeat over 20 rounds, his first set back in two years as a professional. Although he took a beating, a report in *Boxing* vividly summarised the intensity of the fight and the effort each man out in:

> The fiercest, toughest, hardest contest seen in London these many years. The gathering that packed The Ring to the rafters saw a glove battle that will live in their memories for many years to come. They witnessed a struggle between two men for mastery that simply beggars belief.

Despite his herculean effort, Sid was back in the ring within three weeks to continue where he left off, scoring a number of victories. He did drop a six-round points decision to Dick Lee (Kentish Town) at the Holborn

Empire on 9 January 1911, a Monday, in a fierce contest, but appeared to lack urgency. This was believed to be due partly to the fact that he had knocked out Lee in two rounds in a previous contest. The decision, however, was a popular one with the audience although press opinion was that a draw would have been a more accurate reflection on what had occurred.

Meanwhile, flamboyant promoter, James White, had arrived on the London scene and booked the huge Olympia Arena at Earls Court for his first show on Wednesday 11 January just two days after Burns fought Lee. His top liner featured popular heavyweight, Bombardier Billy Wells against former champion Gunner Moir.

In the chief supporting contest Burns was paired with Jack Meekins of Battersea over 10 rounds. In what was his second contest in 48 hours, Sid was grim and determined in scoring a convincing points victory which induced the promoter to use him again two months later at the same venue against experienced American, Ray Bronson, from Iowa, a veteran of some 70 contests. He was a typical smart American who had fought three men who would go on to win world titles – Jack Dillon, Freddie Welsh and Jack Britton, and was visiting London following an unbeaten tour of Australia.

By the halfway stage of the contest, Bronson was well ahead and, increasing the pressure, shook Burns several times and floored him for a count of 'eight' in round 14. The Londoner, however, absorbed everything and hit back bravely. Becoming frustrated, the man from Iowa became wild in his attacks and leaving himself open, was floored for 'nine' in round 18. He was desperate to finish Burns who still appeared strong but in the next round forced his fist up hard under Sids chin and slammed a right hook well below the belt-line. Burns sank to the floor and without hesitation the referee sitting at ringside indicated that Bronson had been disqualified. It was a popular decision and Sid's game effort impressed the promoter to the extent that he promised him further work on his next big show.

In the meantime, Burns faced old foe Young Nipper at The Ring two months later. After another absorbing contest in which Sid floored his man in the 15th and final round, the referee called it a draw despite the Aldgate man appearing to have won. Afterwards, Billy Papke, in London to fight Jim Sullivan for the World middleweight championship, told the press; 'That was the best fight I have seen in a long while.'

After three more successes Burns faced young French welterweight champion, Georges Carpentier at Olympia on 2 October. It was top of James White's big promotion, replacing a planned contest between Bombardier Billy Wells challenging Jack Johnson for the world heavyweight title. Sid had joined Johnson at his training camp at the Black Bull, Whetstone but had barely settled when the heavyweight fight was cancelled on the instructions of the Home Secretary backed by a court ruling.

Carpentier quickly revealed his outstanding skill and punch, flooring Burns in round four. Sid recovered and fought back well but was down again in the sixth. Courage and determination kept him going until round nine when he was down again, but still not out and still there at the end of the 15th and final round. Although he lost widely on points, he would remain the only British boxer to have lasted the full distance with the talented Frenchman who, in his next contest, knocked out Young Joseph to take the European title. Carpentier went on to become World light-heavyweight champion in 1920 and challenged Jack Dempsey for the heavyweight title the following year.

Defeat to the great Frenchman did not deter Burns and after a break of six months he was busy again. A points victory at Hoxton Baths was followed by a 10-round success over Sam Lucas on the opening night promotion at the new East End arena, Premierland. He followed this by outpointing experienced British welterweight champion,

Johnny Summers over 20 rounds at Liverpool Stadium in January 1912. It was an unexpected victory which ultimately led to him facing Summers again eleven months later for the championship.

In the meantime, he kept active taking eight further contests during the course of the year, losing two, one of which was to American prospect, Mike Gibbons, who forced him to retire after five rounds at Madison Square Garden, New York.

Sid's title fight with Summers took place at the National Sporting Club on 9 December 1912 and this time the champion got the decision. Shortly afterwards he took the championship trophy with him on a tour of Australia and after being there for a few months and winning three contests, he wrote to Sid saying: 'Come out here, fight me for my title and make some real money'. Without hesitation, the Aldgate man set sail and shortly after arriving in Sydney was matched with Summers in a contest advertised as being for the British and vacant British Empire titles.

Burns did not have a good start to his trip; he had to pull out of a warm up fight after injuring a hand in training. Once he was fully recovered the fight with Summers was re-scheduled and took place at Sydney Stadium on 11 June 1913 with the champion taking a very close decision.

Burns was in no hurry to go home because he loved the new surroundings and the Aussie fans appreciated his aggressive style and fighting spirit. He stayed for another six months taking on five more contests. Showing no ill effects from the Summers fight he took a 20-round points decision from fellow Londoner, Young Nipper at Sydney but two days later was knocked out in 10 rounds by Arthur Evenden in the same ring. In a return two months later he forced Arthur to retire after 13 rounds at Melbourne, but after decisioning, Sid Stagg at the same venue in December, decided it was time to return home.

With war looming it was not long before Sid was called into the army, whereupon his ring appearances were few and far between. During the next three and a half years he had just six contests, all in London of which he won only two. Despite his lack of success, Burns was still highly regarded especially by top trainer Jack Goodwin. They had met in Australia where Jack was looking after Harry Mansfield and when London promoter, Jack Callaghan, was looking for an opponent for British welterweight champion, Johnny Basham, Goodwin told him Burns was ideal.

At the time, Sid was engaged on special work in the army transport department at Osterley and immediately agreed to the fight despite knowing he would not be allowed enough leave for special training. This badly affected his performance and he was knocked out in nine rounds. Seven months later, however, he caused a major upset by knocking out reigning middleweight title holder Bandsman Jack Blake in six rounds at Liverpool.

With the war over, the lack of ring activity during the years of unrest appeared to have affected Sid's performance and motivation as between 1919 and 1921 he won just three of 11 contests, being stopped on four occasions. One of these was in Paris where he faced French middleweight champion, Ercole Balzac. It was a vicious toe-to-toe punch-up throughout six rounds and became so torrid that during one mix up on the ropes, both men fell out of the ring with Burns landing on his head. The timekeeper immediately began his count and on reaching 'seven' Balzac scrambled back into the ring. Burns, however, was too dazed to make it and was counted out. The crowd booed the decision but cheered the Aldgate man all the way back to his dressing room.

Despite being game to the end of every fight, Sid failed to win any of his last six and following a first round knockout in Glasgow in March 1921, he reluctantly hung up his gloves. He never considered a comeback.

Sid Burns mixed with the best and was far better than his record indicates. To have been the only British boxer to stay the distance with the great Georges Carpentier is a testimony in itself. His ring surname lived on as his son Sam Burns became a leading figure on the British fight scene. For many years, he was a knowledgeable and respected member of the sport. He became an associate of top promoter, Jack Solomons in the 1950's and 1960's and manager of many top boxers including Terry Downes who became world middleweight champion. Sid died on 26 October 1948.

Traceable Record
86 Contests
57 Won (25 inside the distance)
5 Drew
24 Lost

9

BENNY CAPLAN

(Stepney St Georges)

SOUTHERN AREA FEATHERWEIGHT CHAMPION

Another extremely competent and popular fighter of Hebrew heritage, Benny was recognised as having one of the best left hands in the business. Although throughout his career he boxed out of the St Georges area of Stepney, he was in fact born at Richard Street, Poplar, on 26 March 1911. He took to boxing at a very young age and was a product of St. Georges Boys Club as was his elder brother, a hard-bitten battler who fought professionally as Phil Richards.

In 1925, at the age of fourteen, Benny won a national senior schoolboy championship. After joining the Polytechnic Club, he was beaten in a preliminary round of the 1929 ABA senior championships, but took the featherweight title in 1931, beating J Jones of the Royal Welsh Fusiliers in the final. In an earlier round he beat Harry Mizler in one of the best amateur contests ever seen at The Royal Albert Hall.

Turning professional later the same year, Caplan won his first ten contests mainly on points over eight rounds. His debut took place on the grand opening show of the Whitechapel Pavilion during the afternoon of Sunday 11

October. The place was packed to the doors with hundreds of other fans unable to gain admission. The scenes confirmed that East End fans had eagerly awaited the revival of boxing in the area following the closure of Premierland, which along with Wonderland before it, had for so long been the main venues.

The show was staged by a syndicate of promoters under the direction of former British welterweight champion, Young Joseph. The top-liner featured Caplan's brother, Phil Richards in a 15-rounder against Harry Brooks, also of St Georges, who won the local derby clearly on points. Despite appearing nervous and over anxious, Benny restored family pride, albeit by the narrowest of margins, over eight rounds against Young Heasman from Brighton.

After suffering his first professional defeat in the final of a featherweight competition at Crystal Palace in May 1932, Caplan's only reverse in his next 20 contests between then and February 1935 was by way of disqualification. At that time, he was looked after by Harry Stokes, a top corner man who had worked with greats such as Ted 'Kid' Lewis, Johnny Summers and Young Aschel Josephs. Hard working and conscientious he was described by Lewis as being 'as honest as the day is long'.

The quality of Benny's opponents improved rapidly during that period in which he beat Johnny McGrory on points and drew with him seven months later. There were victories over Cuthbert Taylor, (twice) and Dave Finn but his finest hour was on 20 January 1935 when he held world champion, Freddie Miller, of America to a draw at The Ring, Blackfriars.

A veteran of over 150 fights dating back to 1927, Miller gained revenge with a 10-round points victory at The Ring four weeks later after a terrific contest. Although Benny took five long counts, the world champion could not keep him on the floor.

Caplan was back in action within three weeks and remained undefeated in his next nine contests, included a 12-round victory and draw over 15 rounds with Southern Area champion, Dave Crowley. They were two of the most intriguing contests of skill witnessed during 1935. The first was at The Royal Albert Hall on 13 April and after a great battle which swung one way and then the other, Benny got the decision.

There followed a return six weeks later in the open air at Clapton Greyhound Stadium on the 28 May with Crowley's Southern Area featherweight title at stake. Again, it went the distance and was a see-saw battle packed with skill throughout. Although he was floored for a count of 'nine' in the third round, Caplan recovered well and fought back with courage and skill. There was always a 'needle' element present during the tense exchanges and at the end referee, Moss Deyong, couldn't separate them. His decision prompted tremendous controversy with each side believing they had won. It was that close!

It was another 12 months before Benny lost again, this time on points over 15 rounds to Dick Corbett (Bethnal Green) in a challenge for the Southern Area title. After losing to Jimmy Walsh (RSC.3) and Alby Day (Old Ford) on points, however, he went on another winning streak of ten, one of which was a stoppage over Nipper Fred Morris in an eliminator for the Southern Area title. In August 1937 after five more winning fights, he took the title from Dick Corbett before a crowd of over 12,000 after a great fight on what was the first ever promotion staged at Hackney Wick Stadium. He retained it two months later by outpointing Joe Brahams (Mile End) in a disappointing contest at Earls Court.

Established as an area champion, Benny commenced 1938 by beating Frank McCudden in an eliminator for the British featherweight title and in March won the final eliminator by outpointing Johnny Cusick at Leeds. In between those contests, however, he was outpointed by

Dick Corbett who proved to be a master tactician in a wonderful battle of wits. Caplan's long-awaited chance to contest the British title was eventually set for August when he was matched with champion Johnny McGrory, who also held the British Empire title. To everyone's amazement and Benny's utter disappointment the champion was over the stipulated weight when he went to the scales on the afternoon of the contest and therefore forfeited both titles. The fight went ahead as a non-title affair at the end of which it was declared a draw.

As a legitimate challenger, Caplan was matched with Jim 'Spider' Kelly for the vacant titles in Belfast three months later and before a crowd of 8,000 the Irishman took a clear-cut decision ending the East Ender's chance of winning a major title he so richly deserved. In February 1939, American Boxing Magazine *'The Ring'* ranked Benny as the number nine featherweight in the world albeit at a time when such ratings usually referred to a boxer's form three months before publication.

At the beginning of 1939 there were signs that Caplan was past his best as he suffered more defeats than he gained victories. Leading up to the outbreak of war there were points defeats to Billy Charlton and Jim Kelly, whilst he was knocked out in two rounds by Ronnie James and forced to retire in six against Len Benyon. Although he outpointed Len Wickwar in an eliminator for the Southern Area title it was to no avail because war was declared and he had only six more contests before quitting the ring in 1942.

Benny signed up for military service and became a Sergeant Instructor in the Welsh Guards. Back in civilian life in peacetime he worked as an inspector on the London buses. Still retaining his love of boxing, he was appointed as a British Boxing Board of Control referee, a position he held for 30 years. At the end of the last contest at which he officiated fans threw £50 in 'nobbins' into the ring in appreciation of his service. Afterwards he remarked: 'I was delighted to go out on a high note and obviously I shall remember this contest for the rest of my life'.

Living in Hackney at the time he applied for and was granted trainer and manager licenses by the Board of Control. Although he never made headlines in those capacities, he did train Billy Walker (West Ham) for his fight with Eduardo Corletti at San Remo in August 1965. Billy had previously been beaten by Brian London and Caplan was engaged to improve his skills. 'With Benny Caplan training him I feel sure that he can fight his way to the British title', his brother George told the press. It didn't work out, however, with Billy fortunate to get a draw at the Italian arena.

During the later years of his life, Benny did incredible work for charity, in particular, by organising sponsored greyhound meetings. His first in 1978 raised £1,000 for his chosen cause and despite the big money, he always refused to take anything by way of payment for expenses.

Benny died at Homerton hospital, in the East End in late July 1987 aged seventy-eight following a heart attack.

Traceable Record:
82 Contests
58 Won
7 Drew
17 Lost

—.10.—

YOUNG JACK COHEN

(Aldgate)

Of the many young Jewish boxers to have grown up in the East End and embarked on a ring career, Aldgate born Young Jack Cohen showed as much promise as most. Starting as a flyweight in September 1909 he had a dozen contests in just four months, the majority of which were at the Judean Club. Within less than two years as a professional he had engaged in almost 60 without being stopped or knocked out. During that period, he moved up to bantamweight and graduated to Wonderland where he had been discovered by Harry Wright fighting in a novice's competition.

A tall lad with great skills, particularly his left jab, Jack was being tipped by experts as a future champion. Despite being matched with better quality opposition he was rarely beaten. His victims included experienced campaigners Young Joey Smith, a win and two draws, Bill Kyne, Johnny Russell and Jim Kenrick, all of whom had, at some stage, claimed English championships at the lower weights. The fights with Russell and Kenrick were both staged at Wonderland over 20 (3 minute) rounds under the control of *Sporting Life* who appointed referees and supplied the gloves. The contest with Russell was made at 8st-6lbs for a purse of £130 plus side stakes and against Kenrick at 8st-4lbs with side stakes and a purse of £150.

Cohen was a real star at Wonderland where he had a huge following. Yet when he knocked out Harry Williams in three rounds on 12 August 1911, little did he know that the following afternoon the great arena would be burnt to the ground.

After an unbeaten run of over 20 fights, Jack went to America in September 1911 just two years after turning professional. He was full of confidence and during a nine month stay faced some of the best men at his weight having been convinced that it was the best way to get noticed. Following three wins and a draw in two months he faced world featherweight champion, Abe Attell. At the weigh-in Cohen was two pounds inside the stipulated limit but Attell refused to go to the scales. Despite him having an estimated advantage of about five pounds, Jack still gave him one of his hardest fights in a long time.

Some reports from America were very unreliable, an example being one relating to his next contest against Biz Makey who was disqualified in round 13 for persistent holding. It was claimed that Jack suffered such serious injuries that it was feared he would never box again. It transpired, however, that the foul tactics of the American were considerably exaggerated because 10 days later Jack was back in the ring to upset the aspirations of Johnny Dundee. Despite taking three counts in the opening round, he gained a popular newspaper decision.

According to the majority of reports Cohen was rarely in a bad fight during his stay in the United States. On New Year's Day 1912 one of the largest crowds ever to attend a boxing show at Utica saw him score an easy victory over Kid Julian. A few days later at Bridgeport he out-boxed Fred Bosse in a no decision contest after which one paper reported; 'No cleverer boy with his hands and footwork had ever been seen there'.

In two losing fights to promising Joe Shugrue, Jack was warmly applauded for his gameness and his final contest in the States against substitute, Jimmy Coffey, was described as being 'As good a scrap as any seen in New York this season'.

Cohen retuned to London in August 1912 and wrote an extremely informative two-page article about his experiences in America which was published in the 10 August edition of *Boxing*. News of his return aroused interest from promoters, particularly those at Premierland who wasted no time in staging his first fight back on home soil. The arena was packed to capacity for the contest against Seaman Arthur Haynes (Hoxton) who, six years earlier, had claimed the English 126-pound title. The ovation Jack received as he climbed into the ring was incredible but although he won on points, reports indicated that he appeared jaded after his exploits in the States. The victory, however, set up a mouth-watering encounter with another East End favourite, Fred Halsband.

Predictably, Premierland was again full to overflowing and after an intense battle, Cohen got the 15-round decision. Yet there were indications that he may have seen better days. Although he scraped a draw with Billy Marchant three weeks later, consecutive defeats to Young Joe Brooks was the start of a period of decline in which Jack only won eight out of almost 30 contests.

In 1915 he returned to America but failed to win any of the seven contests there over the next two years. As he faded from the scene his only two fights were in Germany and France before he finally retired in 1921.

Jack was an extremely talented youngster who promised so much, yet like many others of his era, failed to progress to the top. He took part in almost 100 contests, 88 of which were in his first five years as a professional. Many were long gruelling affairs due, in no small part, to his ability to absorb tremendous punishment. He was stopped only twice and never knocked out. His style of fighting undoubtedly took its toll and prevented him challenging for a championship.

Traceable Record
97 Contests
58 Won
10 Drew
28 Lost
1 N.C

11

DUTCH SAM

(Whitechapel)

Another great Jewish fighter from the East End was Dutch Sam. Born in Petticoat Lane of Dutch immigrant parents on the 4 April 1775, his real name was Samuel Elias. Although only a lightweight by modern day standards, he often defeated men more than 30 pounds heavier than himself.

Strong and muscular Sam was a scientific boxer and possessed devastating punching power that earned him the nickname of 'the man with the iron fist'. He was also known as 'the terrible Jew'.

Fighting regularly between 1801 and 1814, his major fights were against Tom Belcher who he beat three times in 1806 and 1807, even though there was a serious dispute about the second result with some reports claiming it was a no contest. In all three, Sam was seconded by Daniel Mendoza.

An excessive drinker, Sam often boasted that he could train on gin. His final contest which took place in 1814 actually arose as a result of a dispute when he was drunk. His opponent, Bill Nosworthy, was much fitter and won in nine rounds, but not before there were the most incredible scenes.

Particular areas of the East End, Aldgate and Whitechapel in particular, were heavily populated by

Jewish folk who gave incredible support to fighters of their heritage. They accepted Dutch Sam as the natural successor to Mendoza because he had dominated the lighter weights throughout the first decade of the 19th century. Consequently, his following was immense and there had been tremendous betting on the fight with Nosworthy.

During round nine it was apparent that Sam was on the verge of defeat which prompted a mob of his backers to storm the ring armed with weapons of every description. Their intention was to end the fight and give their man the chance of getting it deemed no contest.

When order was eventually restored Sam proudly and honourably insisted that they proceeded to an honest conclusion. Despite his sportsmanship, it turned out to be poor judgement because after 50 minutes he was beaten for the only time in his career. It was estimated at least £100,000 was lost in bets by his East End supporters.

Excessive drinking brought Sam's life to a premature end just two years later at the age of forty-one. He had suffered considerably and passed away at the London Hospital, Whitechapel Road, on 3 July 1816. He was a pauper, being buried 'without boards', the following day at the Jews' burying ground, Whitechapel. Yet his ring skills were never forgotten and in 1997 he was inducted into the Boxers Hall of Fame.

The memory of Dutch Sam was more than adequately preserved by his son, also Samuel Elias. Born at Stepney in 1808, he had his first fight at the age of seventeen and proved to be a real chip off the old block. Like his father, he was an extremely confident and skilful ring man, although not such a powerful puncher. This made little difference, prompting one writer of the time to comment 'Young Sam cannot punch anything like his late papa, nor hit as hard but he has a knack of hitting twice on a place which amounts to nearly the same thing'.

Known as 'The Phenomenon', Young Dutch Sam had a massive following within the Jewish community and was never beaten between 1825 and 1834. He then ran pubs in the Leicester Square and Covent Garden areas but was often at odds with the law. Living life to the full, he also abused his health to such an extent that he passed away at the young age of thirty-six.

12

AL FOREMAN

(St Georges)

BRITISH LIGHTWEIGHT CHAMPION 1930-1932
(Undefeated)

BRITISH EMPIRE LIGHTWEIGHT CHAMPION 1930-1933

BRITISH EMPIRE LIGHTWEIGHT CHAMPION 1933-1934
(Undefeated)

When Al Foreman stepped off an Atlantic liner at Southampton in the spring of 1930, he was about to cause mayhem in the lightweight division of British boxing. After six successful years battling in the rings of Canada and the United States of America, he had acquired a reputation of being a ferocious puncher. On returning home his intention was to win the British title and stake a claim for World honours.

Born of Jewish parents in the St Georges district on 3 November 1904, he was no stranger to the London boxing rings. He started fighting at the age of sixteen when hungry and out of work. Most of his early battles took place at venues such as Manor Hall, Hackney, Premierland and at Hoxton, Bow, Stratford and Canning Town.

Fighting as Bert 'Kid' Harris of Bow, he was undefeated for more than 20 contests and in less than two years was only beaten twice in over 40 bouts, many of which were over 10 rounds. Before reaching the age of eighteen, he was elevated to 15-round contests and in July 1922 boxed a draw over that distance with fellow East Ender, Johnny Brown at Premierland. An indication of the youngster's potential could be derived from the fact that Brown would become British and European bantamweight Champion the following year.

Fighting regularly against good class opposition, Foreman progressed well. A testimony of his ability comes from the fact that just a month after his eighteenth birthday he boxed a draw with tough and experienced Dutchman, Battling Van Dyk, in his first contest over 20 rounds. He also beat a number of other good fighters including Johnny Murton, Billy Palmer and Harry Pullen and drew twice with the extremely talented Ernie Izzard who would progress to become British lightweight champion within a couple of years.

In 1923, however, things began to go wrong for Foreman. After scoring a sensational 19th round knockout over Fred Bullions, he suffered four consecutive defeats. A hand injury forced him to retire after 11 rounds against Johnny Curley, points and disqualification defeats to Billy Palmer were followed by a 15-round point loss to Bullions.

The run of defeats had a psychological effect on the youngster. Disillusioned he decided to leave England and join his brother in Montreal where they ran a successful physical culture establishment and also managed a number of Canadian boxers. It was the opportunity Al needed and once settled into the new environment, he regained his appetite for fighting although it was not easy. Nine months out of the ring had left him rusty and not surprisingly he lost two of his first three contests in Montreal. Yet with the help of his brothers he gradually got back into his stride and built up a steady string of victories.

At the end of 1924, Al moved to the United States and although little was heard of him in the United Kingdom during the next five or six years, his career really blossomed. He joined the US army and in 1926 won the combined American Services featherweight championship. In the professional rings of New York, Washington, Detroit, Chicago and Philadelphia, he was devastating. By May 1928 he had lost just two of 38 contests since moving there with 24 victories by way of knockout.

Returning to Montreal, Foreman set a world record for the quickest ever ending to a fight by knocking out Ruby Levine in 11 1/2 seconds, including the count. He went on to win the Canadian lightweight title by knocking out Leo 'Kid' Roy in two rounds and during the next 12 months ran up five more victories and a draw. One of those successes was at the Canadian Hockey Club Arena in Montreal against former world featherweight champion Johnny Dundee, a veteran of more than 300 contests.

To the delight of his fans, Al out-boxed the American from the start and won every round but the ending was not without controversy. In the tenth and final round Foreman cut loose causing his opponent to wilt badly. A series of knockdowns followed, but each time the proud and gallant Dundee struggled to his feet. Twice the Briton sportingly appealed to the referee to step in but was ignored. Realising he had to end matters conclusively himself, Al measured his man and put him out of his misery. A vicious right hook sent Dundee crashing to the canvas. Although he was out cold the referee took up the count but at 'six' suddenly ordered Forman to his corner where, amid confusion, he was declared the winner by knockout. It later transpired that the bell had interrupted the count thus technically saving Dundee from being counted out for only the second time in his career. The official ruled, however, that as he could not have possibly have risen by 'ten', Foreman was entitled to victory by knockout.

Although Al surprisingly lost his Canadian title to Billy Townsend at Vancouver in December 1929, he was anxious to press his claims to a shot at the world title held by Sammy Mandell. The stumbling block was that Jack 'Kid' Berg was also progressing well in America and had better connections to secure a championship fight ahead of him.

Realising he needed to establish himself as an outstanding contender, Foreman decided to focus his attention on winning the British title. He and his brother Maurice therefore booked their passages and headed for London early in the New Year. Before leaving America, Al entered into a contract with prominent sports goods company *Everlast* to use their gloves in all of his contests in the UK. As he had very small hands it suited him to have his gloves specially made thereby increasing his punching power. He also secured agreement for the company to provide a supply of standard size gloves to be used by his opponents.

On arrival in London, the brothers approached Premierland boss, Victor Berliner and offered to fight for basic expenses on condition that the *Everlast* gloves were used by Foreman and his opponents. The economics of the proposal suited Berliner perfectly and he immediately installed Al as a Sunday matinee top-liner.

Foreman's impressive Canadian record and his reputation as a devastating puncher were sufficient to make him a major attraction. He was given three fights in as many weeks and won them all in impressive style, knocking out Roy Beresford in four rounds, Douglas Parker in two and Len 'Tiger' Smith in nine. After despatching Harry Brooks, a leading London lightweight and British title contender, in just 80 seconds four weeks later, Al issued a challenge to British champion Fred Webster. This, however, did not meet with the approval of the stewards of the newly formed Board of Control with whom Al had become extremely unpopular. No matter how things were shaping, his instant success at Premierland had clearly upset their championship eliminating plans. Furthermore, his *Everlast* sponsorship deal and persistent demands for recognition caused several members to view him and his brother as disturbing influences.

Despite there being hundreds of boxers in every weight division in Britain, the championship situation was poor. The lightweights in particular were in disarray. No fewer than six men had been nominated by the Board to try and establish a worthy challenger for Webster. Much to the annoyance of the governing body, Foremans's sudden arrival on the scene upset those plans.

Determined not to be side-stepped, the brothers found a solid supporter of their cause in John Murray, editor of the trade paper *Boxing*. A frequent critic of the Board, he helped them embark on a campaign designed to bring Al the British lightweight title. Fred Webster had been champion for almost a year but had not defended the title during that time. This was due largely to the fact that the leading contender, Jack 'Kid' Berg, was campaigning in America.

Foreman was so confident of beating Fred that he re-issued his challenge stating that he would fight for expenses only and leave the bulk of the purse money to the champion. In the meantime, and with the press firmly behind him, he announced that he was willing to fight any of the men nominated by the Board as contenders.

Incensed by what they considered an intrusion, the stewards promptly ordered Webster to defend his title against George Rose of Bristol. The Foremans realised that if such a contest went ahead it could be months before Al got a championship fight. He had spent a great deal of money travelling to Britain, fought basically for just expenses and delayed a return to Canada where several lucrative engagements awaited. Something had to be arranged quickly, so with Maurice acting as manager, Webster was offered his own terms to defend the title against Al.

After some hard-bargaining agreement was eventually reached for the contest to take place on Wednesday 21 May. Fred had signed a contract on 12 May just two days before the deadline set by the Board of Control for acceptance of purse offers to stage a fight with Rose. The champion's proviso, however, was that his purse money was handed over in full before he entered the ring.

Despite contracts having been signed, promoters were reluctant to stage the fight at such short notice. There was also the fear of disciplinary action by the Board for staging a bout it had not approved. The Foremans therefore decided to promote it themselves and hired Premierland where shows only took place on Thursdays and Sundays. Knowing that the Board would not recognise the contest as being for the British title they advertised it as for the lightweight championship of the British Empire on the basis that Al was Canadian champion. They omitted to disclose that he lost that title in December the previous year.

Furious at the audacity of the Foremans, the Board stewards met on the Monday before the fight with a view to banning it. By this time, however, it looked like being a sell-out so in order to save face, they relented. Not only did they sanction it, they also approved of it being for the British title although no championship belt would be at stake. The Board's only proviso was that the winner defended his title against George Rose

The fight was a massive attraction and the streets around Premierland were heavily congested a couple of hours before the doors even opened. By the time the contestants were called to the ring, the grand old arena was bursting at the seams. In announcing the fight, Master of Ceremonies, Buster Cohen, stated that it was the first championship contest ever fought in the East End. He had obviously overlooked the fact that several were contested at Wonderland and that Ted 'Kid' Lewis beat Paul Til of France for the European featherweight title at Premierland in February 1914. It was nevertheless, the first title contest which had been approved by the new British Boxing Board of Control to be fought east of Aldgate. On that account, it was notable enough.

At the weigh-in, Foreman had scaled three pounds inside the 9st 9lbs limit. He looked extremely fit and lean when he stripped off as the announcements were being made. Determination was written all over his face as he bounced up and down on his toes anxious to get into action.

At the opening bell, he went straight on the attack and slammed a left hook to the champions jaw. He was badly shaken and despite trying to box his way out of trouble a terrific right to the temple sent him crashing to the floor. He rose at 'six' but was on unsteady feet and a vicious right under the heart made him gasp. A rapid burst of hooks to the chin followed and Fred again fell heavily to the canvas. Although he was on his knees at 'six', that was as far as he got, and referee Jack Smith counted him out. It was all over in less than two minutes.

Foreman was mobbed by excited fans and carried shoulder high back to his dressing room. His venture to Britain had cost him £800 of his own money, but he considered it to be worth every penny. As British and Empire champion, he intended to return to America and press his claims for a shot at the world title.

Immediately after the Webster fight, however, Al received a lucrative offer from William Glass, the promoter at Ilford Skating Rink, to meet British featherweight champion, Johnny Cuthbert, in a non-title bout over 15 rounds at 9st 4lbs. It was a fascinating contest between the dynamic punching Foreman and the extremely skilful, but lighter punching Yorkshireman.

A huge crowd assembled for the contest but went away disappointed because as soon as Foreman's *Everlast* gloves were produced Cuthbert refused to wear them. Although some previous opponents had protested, all eventually agreed to wear them, but Johnny was an exception and would not yield. There was a violent argument in the ring during which the Foremans produced their contract which stipulated the use of *Everlast* gloves. Cuthbert insisted that his contract contained no such clause and flatly refused to wear them.

After 20 minutes of wrangling, referee, Sam Russell intervened: 'Boxers use the gloves supplied by the promoter in this country' he told Foreman sternly.

'In that case, there won't be a fight' snapped Al.

At that point Russell ordered the Foremans from the ring. Within a few minutes, Len 'Tiger' Smith stepped up to face Cuthbert. It was a clear indication that everything had been set up to break Al's monopoly of the gloves.

Angry and disillusioned, Foreman immediately returned to Canada where he scored four victories within the space of seven weeks. He was then ordered by the British Boxing Board of Control to defend his British title against George Rose. Despite previous hostility with the Board, he accepted a purse offer for the fight to take place at Belle Vue, Manchester, on 20 October. A brand-new Lonsdale belt would be at stake.

Giving away five pounds in weight, Foreman was out-boxed from the start although he did floor Rose for a short count in the third round. George was down again just before the bell to end the fifth from the only serious punch the champion landed in that round, yet it proved to be the turning point in the fight. Going to work at the start of the sixth, Al needed only one deadly right hand to bring proceedings to an end.

The National Sporting Club had been co-promoters of the fight and when it was suggested that the champion should face Johnny Cuthbert on their show at Olympia in December, he was delighted. Having won the featherweight belt outright, Johnny was confident he could also rule the lightweight division, but Foreman had other ideas. He had never forgiven the Yorkshireman for his antics at Ilford earlier in the year and was determined to make him pay in the ring.

Intent on finishing it quickly, Al smashed Cuthbert to the canvas within 15 seconds of the opening bell. He was down again in the second and third rounds but managed to avoid the champion's follow-up attacks. Although the Yorkshireman was floored again in round eight, the power appeared to have gone from Foreman's punches. He looked the more tired of the two and as the fight continued, Cuthbert had the better of the exchanges. At the end the referee called it a draw, a decision which most spectators thought flattered the challenger.

After a break of a couple of months Al scored three knockout victories over continental opponents within the space of three weeks in February 1931. Intent on pursuing a challenge for the world title he then returned to Canada where he was backed by the Canadian Boxing Commission. Tony Canzoneri had become champion, but to Foreman's annoyance agreed to defend against Jack 'Kid' Berg. Although he was beaten in three rounds in April, Berg's connections secured a return five months later. He lost that one as well, but still Canzoneri's people showed no interest in a fight with Al.

Despite eight months of inactivity whilst attempting to get a world title shot, the Canadian Boxing Commission recognised Foreman as world junior lightweight champion. He was also voted best boxer at that weight for 1931 being rated above recognised champion 'Kid' Chocolate.

Angry and disillusioned, Al returned to England towards the end of the year and boxed up and down the country. Between October 1931 and February 1932, he won nine consecutive contests, six by knockout. Still a great attraction he was then persuaded to meet skilful featherweight champion, Nel Tarleton, who had relieved Johnny Cuthbert of the title the previous year. It was one of the few occasions that Foreman's big punches failed to have any effect on an opponent and Tarleton took a good points decision.

Shortly afterwards Al received a letter from the Board of Control notifying him that they had accepted a purse offer for him to defend his title against Cuthbert at Sheffield. The promoter was Johnny's father, but his offer was so low it would have barely covered the champion's training expenses. Foreman promptly refused to take the fight whereupon the Board advised him that by way of his actions he had forfeited the British title and ordered him to return the Lonsdale belt.

Al was furious, so rather than give into the Board he pawned the belt instead. 'I was not prepared to let them get away with it', he later remarked. 'They never forgave me for messing up their plans by becoming champion'

Knowing he was finished as a top-line fighter in Britain, he booked a passage aboard a liner to Australia. Although his followers were disappointed, he left them with the memories of three more victories in as many months before departing in July 1932, never to return. He was well received down under and quickly notched up a trio of victories. As he still held the British Empire title, he agreed to defend it against Jimmy Kelso at Melbourne in April 1933 but was outpointed. In a return the following month he regained the title when Kelso was disqualified in the third round.

Returning to Montreal in September that year, Foreman regained the Canadian title, but was just a shadow of the man who, three years earlier, was pressuring for world honours. In his next fight he was beaten inside the distance for only the second time in over 160 contests. The curtain finally came down on his career the June the following year when he was outpointed by the promising American Petey Sarron, in Washington.

For a while Al worked in Canada as a photographer before joining the Royal Canadian Air Force at the outbreak of war. As an observer, he flew on bombing raids over Germany and was later decorated with a flying medal.

His unexpected death in 1954 at the age of forty-nine came as a great shock. Al was a likeable character both in and out of the ring and one of the hardest punching British champions. No fewer than 65 of his victories came by clean knockout. His career was colourful and tempestuous, and he thrilled packed arena's in Britain, Canada and Australia.

Traceable Record
164 Contests
133 Won
11 Drew
20 Lost

13

DANNY FRUSH

(Aldgate)

A London Jew born at Aldgate in 1899, his real name was David Thrush but due to a slight speech impediment he pronounced it Frush. He also preferred Danny than David, so this was how he became known. Like so many other fistically inspired Hebrew boys he got into boxing by joining the Brady Street Jewish Working Lads Club. He quickly showed that he was a natural fighter of no mean ability by winning an all-England schoolboy championship.

It was at the Working Lads Club that he became close friends with another Jewish youngster, Harry Levene. Their conversations were generally about boxing and one day during the spring of 1916, they were drinking tea at an Aldgate café when Harry asked Frush how old he was. He replied that he had just had his seventeenth birthday, adding that he had not long turned professional. He had in fact started fighting for pay a year earlier, all of his contests being in the small halls of the East End.

Levene was already a sharp, ambitious and adventurous young man and with the First World War into its third year suggested that they went to America to avoid getting called up for military service. After discussing the pros and cons they set off to start a new life across the Atlantic with

Danny, already an aspiring young featherweight doing the fighting and Harry as his manager.

On arriving in the States, Frush trained hard and quickly adapted to the aggressive two-fisted style of fighting which impressed the fans and promoters thereby guaranteeing himself plenty of work. He scored an impressive number of victories and it was not long before news of his progress reached the United Kingdom.

Danny and his young manager were a good partnership and Levene, for his part, knew how to hustle and negotiate terms. He quickly acquired a convincing line of chat, something which he became known for as a leading promoter in later years.

Frush averaged about a dozen fights a year and after his first on American soil in May 1917, lost only four of 48 by July 1921, including an unbeaten sequence of 24. It was at this stage that Levene believed he was ready for a shot at the world featherweight title. Johnny Kilbane was the undisputed champion having held the title for nine years during which time he had defended it on seven occasions. As a professional for 14 years he had lost only a handful out of about 140 contests and suffered only one inside the distance defeat. Despite such impressive credentials, Levene believed at thirty-two years of age, the champion was ready for the taking.

With Danny's agreement, Levene travelled to Cleveland, Ohio, for discussions with Kilbane's manager. He was quickly informed that although a fight was a possibility, it could only take place in the champion's home town of Cleveland. A further proviso was that Frush would first have to take on a contest there because local fans would want to see him in action before any agreement could be reached.

Danny duly impressed, knocking out Eddie Wallace in three rounds. A week earlier Kilbane had a no decision 10-rounder against another Aldgate boxer Freddie Jacks who was also based in America. Frush, having beaten Jacks on points over 12 rounds at Baltimore a year earlier, so impressed the fans with a dynamic showing against Wallace, that he was booked again a month later and knocked out Kid Texas in seven rounds.

Before Frush and Levene left Cleveland, a contract was signed for Danny to meet Kilbane over 12 rounds on 17 September, a Saturday afternoon. Although on paper it was to be a world championship contest, the odds were stacked heavily against the Aldgate man from the start. The champion was guaranteed $60,000 plus a further $3,000 for expenses while Danny would only get $2,500 to cover training expenses plus the title if he could win it. To do that he would have to knock Kilbane out.

On the day of the fight there was more skulduggery. Although Danny made the championship weight, Kilbane refused to go to the scales. During the introductions, however, it was announced that Frush scaled 125 ½ pounds (8st 9 ½ lbs) and the champion as being 'inside the stipulated weight of 126.' Despite wet weather, the crowd was 22,000 with the box office clearing $100,000. There was heavy betting on the fight and although Kilbane was a slight favourite, many people wagered that the Londoner would win by knockout.

When they stripped off the champion was noticeably heavier but Frush seemed unfazed by the obstacles he faced. He started quickly, intent on putting the ageing champion under pressure. His tactics seemed to be working when Kilbane went into a clinch and appealed to the referee that he had been hit low. Ignoring the ploy, Danny fought to get away, but was kneed in the groin and fell to the floor in agony.

There was uproar around the arena as the referee ordered Kilbane to a neutral corner whilst he helped Frush's seconds to lift him from the floor and get him to his corner. Levene was furious and yelled vigorously that his man had been fouled. Clearly flummoxed by the situation, the official pushed Harry away and leaned over the ropes and conferred with the State Commissioners. On returning to the centre of the ring he held up his hand to call for silence and then announced that it had been ruled that Kilbane's action was unintentional and the fight would continue once Frush had recovered.

There was a mixed reception to the ruling, but in reality, had Kilbane been disqualified in front of his own fans in his home town, serious crowd disorder would most likely have resulted. Yet as far as Danny was concerned the damage had been done and despite him having the better of some wild exchanges when the fight resumed, much of the strength had gone out of him.

He did floor Kilbane with a hard right in round three, but the champion was up without a count. He also had the better of things in the fourth, but after an even, yet free-hitting fifth, he looked destined for defeat. After taking a count in round six and being in trouble at the bell, the end duly came in the seventh. He was floored for a count of 'three' and bravely tried to carry on despite the reserves of strength having been drained from his body. After taking another count, this time of 'nine', Frush was there for the taking and the champion finished it with his next flurry of blows.

Although it was a bad set back to their aspirations, Frush and Levene still believed the world title was within their grasp. Remaining in America, Danny scored six knockouts in an unbeaten run of eight contests in the first five months of 1922 and was then given another title shot, this time against Johnny Dundee at Brooklyn on 22 August. The chance arose due to the complicated situation in America regarding world titles. Although Kilbane was officially still champion, he had refused to meet Dundee who was therefore recognised as champion by the New York State Athletic Commission. As Frush was considered to be next best at the weight he was given the opportunity to make up for his misfortune at Cleveland.

Dundee was a highly skilled fighter with a record of over 260 contests in 13 years as a professional and was the reigning world junior lightweight champion. Frush again was unfazed by the quality of opposition he faced and put up a terrific battle for eight rounds. In the ninth, however, the American landed a hard right to the head followed by a left to the body which many onlookers claimed was low. The referee overruled protests from Danny's corner and counted him out.

Frush returned to London and was given a wonderful press. Within three months faced Bill Handley at The National Sporting Club and he won by a knockout in five rounds. The following month he knocked out Johnny Curley in one minute forty seconds of the opening round at The Ring, Blackfriars.

Being extremely well respected in the United States, Danny went back in May the following year and took on young prospect Louis 'Kid' Kaplan. A professional for only two years, he lived up to his reputation, knocking out the Aldgate man in six rounds and going on to become world champion two years later.

On returning to Britain, Frush knocked out former British featherweight champion, Mike Honeyman, in the first round. He had two clear objectives: get some good paydays and win a British title. The quick victories over Curley and Honeyman excited the fans and confirmed reports they heard about his progress in America. The situation certainly impressed promoters at The Ring who matched him with Billy Matthews, already established as a leading contender. It was announced that the winner of what was a mouth-watering fight, would get a direct shot at British title holder Joe Fox from Leeds, who was also campaigning in the States.

It was standing room only when the contest took place on New Year's Eve 1923. A large majority were from the East End to support Frush but Billy, having been born in St Georges, had plenty of followers from West London.

On paper, it was anybody's fight because Matthews had also built an impressive record. A former pageboy at The National Sporting Club, he turned professional at the age of fifteen and although not a big puncher, had an aggressive two-fisted style. He reached the top of his game in 1922 when he outpointed European featherweight champion Arthur Wyns of Belgium, over 15 rounds at Liverpool. Wyns was furious and demanded a return over 20 rounds with his title at stake but Billy again outpointed him. His reign only lasted six months with Eugene Criqui stopping him in 17 rounds in Paris, yet Matthews remained an extremely popular figure.

The fight with Frush was a tempestuous affair with a clear element of needle. There were plenty of incidents which aroused the passion of supporters of both men and rounded off by one of the most confusing conclusions to a contest in the history of boxing in that the fans went home not knowing who had actually won.

Although Matthews attacked from the start, Danny had far greater skill and clearly knew more about fighting. In reality there was only one man in it as he floored Billy in round two and twice more in the third.

There was much of the same in the fourth when a hard right to the chin sent Matthews down again. He looked in distress, but after remaining on his knees for several seconds was at the point of rising when Frush stepped forward and slammed a hard right to the chin. As Billy was technically still down there were screams of 'foul' from his corner which were loudly endorsed by his fans. Danny's supporters remained dumbstruck expecting their man to be disqualified.

As the whole arena erupted into a frenzy of protest and counter protests, referee Charles Barnett, who had been officiating from a seat outside the ring, climbed through the ropes and ordered Frush to his corner and appealed to Matthews to get up. Overruling claims of a foul, he eventually persuaded Billy to get on with it, but before another blow could be struck the bell ended the round.

Yet more controversy followed as they commenced round five. Still showing the effects from the last blow he had taken, Matthews backed around the ring with Frush in close pursuit determined to achieve victory. Things then became messy when Billy went into a clinch. As they wrestled, Frush held with one hand and hit with the other, yet the referee who remained inside the ring did nothing to break them up. It was a shamble but then Danny suddenly fell to the floor clutching his lower abdomen with both hands and dramatically indicating that he had been fouled. Again, there was uproar among the fans with opinions divided as to whether Billy should be disqualified or Frush counted out.

The referee, however, had lost control and took no decisive action prompting a further storm of booing. Eventually, he sent Matthews to his corner and called Danny's seconds into the ring to render aid to their man who was still writhing on the canvas. Crowd dissatisfaction intensified as he was carried to the dressing room while Billy walked around the ring appealing for support.

Meanwhile, the referee left the ring and was replaced by the Master of Ceremonies who waited patiently for the noise to subside before announcing that no decision would be made until Frush had been examined by a doctor.

Several fights then broke out between rival supporters as everyone waited for the news but when no further announcement was forthcoming, the arena gradually emptied with only members of the press remaining. Eventually, there was an announcement that no decision would be made until the following day.

Back at The Ring next morning it was disclosed that the management's own doctor explained that when he examined Frush there was ample evidence to show that he had been struck low. Matthews handlers, however, were not satisfied and asked that they be permitted to call a doctor of their own. This was agreed but on examination of the boxer he confirmed the opinion of the official doctor.

Press representatives present were advised that following further consultation with the referee the official result of the contest was that Matthews had been disqualified for striking at least one low blow. During that period a disqualified boxer did not get paid and years later Billy confirmed that he never got a penny. Nor did he ever box at The Ring again.

The amazing state of affairs was aired in most national newspapers and sporting publications for some days with a variety of differing opinions. Matthews, who felt unjustly treated, demanded a return but fortunately common sense prevailed and the two went their separate ways.

Frush didn't get the promised shot at the British title and after six months out of action travelled back to Paris for two fights. The first was against former World and European featherweight champion, Eugene Criqui, still a huge attraction in the French capital. He had become world champion in June the previous year by knocking out Johnny Kilbane in six rounds but was beaten by Johnny Dundee the following month.

It was predicted that Danny had a huge obstacle to overcome in Criqui but it turned out to be quite the opposite. From the second round, he was the master in all quarters, flooring the former world champion five times, three of which were in the seventh. In round eight he was able to hit Criqui at will and even pleaded with the seconds to pull him out. It was a relief when Frush ended the contest with a terrific right uppercut later in the round.

Afterwards Criqui and his seconds paid tribute to Danny on his performance and sportsmanship, the Frenchman declaring that he was to retire from the ring. The masterful performance by Frush endorsed the fact that the obstacles stacked against him when he fought Kilbane three years earlier undoubtedly deprived him of becoming world champion.

Danny quickly established himself as an idol in Paris and remained there after beating Criqui. He gave exhibitions while promoters clamoured to match him with other French stars, Charles Ledoux and Edouard Mascart. Yet with International Boxing Union authority he was matched with Fred Bretonnel for the European lightweight title in Paris on 24 June.

Despite the Frenchman having a four-pound weight advantage, Frush started favourite. In a furious toe-to-toe battle, he won the opening three rounds, flooring the champion in the second. Gradually, however, Bretonnel took over, eventually battering Danny to defeat in round eight. Victory would have guaranteed him another world title fight but instead he returned home and rested for a few months.

He eventually got back into action in December 1924 with two quick wins at Premierland. After knocking out Billy Sheppard in one minute of the opening round in a match made at 9st 4lbs with £50 side stakes, he returned six days later to face Roelof Kool, advertised as the featherweight champion of Holland. He had no defence to the powerful punches of Frush who floored him nine times before administering a knockout in round three.

On returning to Paris the following month, Danny was knocked out in two rounds by Edouard Mascart, a former European featherweight champion. More troubles were heaped upon him when his manager, Lew Burston, had his purse money stopped, claiming Frush was boxing in Europe without the managers consent and was therefore in violation of his contact.

By this time Frush's career was reminiscent of a roller coaster ride – all ups and downs. After two knockout victories at Premierland, he became so frustrated that he went to Australia where the inconsistency continued. After two defeats and a victory he moved on again, this time back to America where his punching power was still good enough to score three knockouts.

In what proved to be his final contest in a British ring he tried desperately to avenge a defeat suffered against Battling Van Dyk but was disqualified in round eleven. It was 13 months before he boxed again.

Returning to New York in December 1927, he wound up his career with four consecutive victories of which three came by knockout. In his penultimate contest, however, he had just enough to take a six-round points victory from a mere novice who floored him twice.

Frush was a sensible man and quit before he got badly hurt. He spent the rest of his life in Cleveland, Ohio and died on 21 March 1961. A talented East Ender, it is no exaggeration to state that unsavoury tactics almost certainly deprived him from becoming world featherweight champion.

Reference to his career summary does, however, highlight the inconsistency regarding records of fighters during the early 1900's, particularly those performing in America. During that period, many results were shown as being of no decision whilst others were determined by newspaper opinion. One respected British source credits Frush with 65 victories, 32 of them by knockout, 15 losses, four draws and one no contest in a career of 85 contests. An American publication, however, summarises his record as being 88 contests of which 60 were wins, 24 of them by knockout, 10 defeats, one draw and 17 no decisions. Whilst the aforementioned details, in no way detract from Danny's overall achievements which were extremely credible, they do emphasise the difficulty in obtaining accuracy regarding records of particular boxers.

14

JACK GREENSTOCK

(Aldgate)

Although born at Bethnal Green in 1894, Jack was generally recognised as being from Aldgate. Very similar to many other Jewish boys, he came from a poor background and was often subjected to bullying at school and in the street. Being a bright youngster, he took to boxing at a very young age and won a Boys Federation competition at seven stone when he was fourteen, making him the first Hebrew lad to do so.

Within two years he embarked on a professional career and like so many other East End youngsters, cut his teeth at the Judean Club. At first, he was billed as 'Kid' Greenstock before graduating to 'Young' and eventually Jack.

If records are to be accepted as accurate, he began his ring career with two contests against the irresistible Ted 'Kid' Lewis, already an established competitor with the experience of 19 fights behind him. Yet at the end of a lively six-rounder on 17 July 1910, in which Greenstock impressed the knowledgeable audience, honours were even.

Always looking for attractive pairings, Sam Kite immediately booked them for a rematch the following week and again they couldn't be separated. They met again the following year by which time Lewis had engaged in 53

Jack 'Kid' Berg (Aldgate) former World Junior Welterweight champion and British Lightweight champion

Aldgate Featherweight
Young Jack Greenstock

Harry 'Kid' Farlo
(Whitechapel)

Moe Moss
(Stepney)

Aldgate Middleweight
Harry Mansfield

Young Jack Cohen
(Aldgate)

Phil Lolosky
(Aldgate)

Welterweight, Sid Burns,
(Aldgate)

Johnny Quill
(Stepney)

Harry Brooks
(Aldgate)

Former British & European Welterweight champion, Young Joseph (Aldgate)

Former British Light-heavyweight champion, Harry Reeve (Stepney)

Stepney, St. Georges, Featherweight, Young Johnny Brown, poses with his wife prior to leaving London for South Africa in 1924

Al Phillips (Aldgate) shakes hands with Ronnie Clayton (right) at the weigh-in for their 15 rounds non-title bout at Earls Court on 11 April 1950, which Clayton won on points.

Lew Lazar (right) & Sammy McCarthy chat with trainer Snowy Buckingham after a sparring session, watched by Yolande Pompey (far left)

Trainer, Jack Goodwin (right), with former British Bantamweight champion Johnny Brown & his dog, take a break whilst out for a training run at Shoeburyness during early 1925

contests as opposed to Jack's nine, yet again the result was a draw.

With an upright stance and good left hand, Greenstock had undoubted talent yet could not get regular ring work. Although he took contests at the Judean, Wonderland, the National Sporting Club, Marylebone, The Ring, Premierland and Hoxton Baths, a total of 14 during 1911 was by far his busiest year. By February 1912 his record was four defeats from 24, all on points.

Although similar in many respects to hundreds of other young Jewish boxers Jack surprisingly attracted the attention of French promoters. In January 1912, aged just seventeen, he went to Paris where he outpointed Leon Truffier over 10 rounds. The French fans appreciated his style, so the promoter persuaded him to stay and fight Georges Gallard the following week. Again, he took a points decision earning two further contests with Truffier which resulted in a victory and a draw during the next three weeks.

The Parisian fans loved Greenstock and this was never more appreciated than when he returned in May that year and faced Charles Ledoux who would become European bantamweight champion the following month. Despite the difference in class Jack showed immense courage withstanding ceaseless vicious attacks before being knocked out in round eight. In defeat he was the hero of the night and as he left the ring a society lady pressed a 100 franc note into his hand. Georges Carpentier added his admiration by squeezing a gold piece into his fist.

After sensibly taking a few months break, Jack got back into training, determined to force a fight with fellow Aldgate bantam Nat Brooks who had compiled a credible record of just six defeats from 53 contests. In doing so he had busily gone about wrecking the reputations of aspiring champions. With Greenstock being accepted as a boxer of exceptional talent following his victories in Paris and his courageous stand against Ledoux, a contest between them was a mouth-watering prospect for the East End fans.

Confident that he had the beating of his adversary, Jack deposited £25 with the trade paper *Boxing* as an enticement to promoters to put it on. Unfortunately for the local working-class fans, the National Sporting Club were quick to match the pair and it went ahead at the club on 4 November.

Although he put up a great display Jack lost narrowly on points at the end of the 15-rounder. His effort and determination, however, impressed the club promoters and following victories in Dublin and at The Ring, they wanted him back. After outpointing Harold Walker (Salford) over 10 rounds, he was matched with Alec Lambert in a British featherweight title eliminator three weeks later.

In reality, it turned out to be a step too far and Greenstock was comprehensively beaten by a more experienced man. Lambert had won the ABA featherweight title back in 1909 and simply knew too much. Although Jack tried desperately to rough him up, he was always on the end of an accurate left jab. The nearest he came to victory was in round 11 when, following a collision of heads, Lambert sustained a badly bruised left eye and was very dazed. Yet with great defensive skills he survived and came back strongly. By the end of the 14th Greenstocks teeth were embedded in the flesh of his mouth and the fight was stopped.

Lambert's reward was a fight against Ted 'Kid' Lewis four months later for the vacant British featherweight title. Despite being a slight favourite, he found Lewis far superior and was knocked out in round 17.

Greenstock, meanwhile, remained convinced that he was good enough to win a title. After a points victory at Plymouth, he was back at the National Sporting Club in October against another former ABA champion, Con Houghton, from Bethnal Green, with side stakes of £25. It was a hard, close contest and there was little between them going into the 10th and final round. As both went for victory, Jack paid the price for having removed his teeth protectors a few rounds earlier. There was a clash of heads and the impact forced his teeth through his lips in similar fashion to when he was beaten by Alec Lambert. Despite blood cascading from his mouth, he desperately wanted to continue, but his chief second, Arthur Gutteridge, insisted on pulling him out.

Realising that he had no chance of winning a British title, Jack decided to chance his arm in America where purse money was far greater than in the UK. Basing himself at Philadelphia where contests were generally decided by newspaper decisions, he had five contests in as many months starting on Christmas Day 1913, with a draw against Tommy O'Keefe who had the experience of 111 contests. Three weeks later he outpointed Willie Moody who had taken 134, of which he had lost 38. After winning his next bout Jack was adjudged to have lost the final two.

On returning home Greenstock was welcomed back to the National Sporting Club where he had two contests against Frenchman, Marcel Dennis, winning both on points. He later claimed that the second victory, two nights before the 1914 Derby, gave him more satisfaction than any other.

Between November 1914 and December, the following year, Jack boxed almost exclusively at The Ring, Blackfriars, winning just five of 14 contests during that period. By late 1916, he had lost his way having been outpointed by former triple British champion, Johnny Summers and stopped by Australian, Hughie Mehegan in Liverpool.

His only other fights were abroad after the war. With just two in 1920 and 1923 at Belgium and Germany, both of which ended by knockout defeats, he did not box again until 1926. He then had five in Poland within the space of six weeks, winning only one. He then finally retired.

Even when he was still boxing Jack helped train a number of other professionals including Al Foreman when he fought as Bert Harris in his early career, Harry Mason and Alf Simmons.

Despite his lack of success during the latter part of his ring career, Greenstock earned good money which he put to use in later life. Apart from setting up a successful millinery business in Bethnal Green, he also promoted small hall shows at Slough, Colchester, Ilford Ice Rink and other venues in the East End.

Jack was devoted to boxing and in 1930 opened a top-class gym at Mile End Road where he ran weekly Sunday morning shows with the bills consisting of mainly local East End youngsters. It was in some respects similar to the activities of the Judean Club some years earlier albeit on a much smaller scale. For some years he also instructed 18-year-old lads on the principles of the sport prior to their call-up for National Service when boxing would be a must-do sport.

Traceable Record
63 Contests
30 Won
26 Lost
7 Drew

—.15.——

JACK HYAMS

(Aldgate)

SOUTHERN AREA MIDDLEWEIGHT CHAMPION 1936 – 1938

SOUTHERN AREA LIGHT-HEAVYWEIGHT CHAMPION 1938 – 1939

SOUTHERN AREA LIGHT-HEAVYWEIGHT CHAMPION 1941 (retired undefeated)

One of the most liked and respected men in boxing, Jack Hyams was a professional for 19 years taking part in almost 200 fights. He started as a bantamweight and over the years went up through the weights to light-heavyweight, meeting reigning champions in each division at some stage in his career. Despite his class, he got only one shot at a British title and had to wait 11 years for it.

Born in Aldgate on 8 February 1909, Jack went to Myrtle Street school with Jack 'Kid' Berg and learned his boxing at the same gymnasium; Victoria Boys Club in Commercial Road. Most youngsters of the day with ambitions to earn money from boxing made their way to Premierland and Hyams duly followed Berg there to commence his professional career just three weeks short of his seventeenth birthday. It would be the first of almost 40 bouts he fought at the venue.

It was Joe Goodwin, the whip at Premierland, who gave Jack his start by entering him for a featherweight novices competition. Although he could easily make the bantamweight limit, he did not seem surprised when he won it after three contests at weekly intervals.

At the start of his career, he boxed as Kid Froggy, a similar pseudonym to that used by an older brother who called himself Young Froggy. Dispensing with it in 1927, he fought as Jack Hyams for the rest of his career despite his real name being Issie.

Although only seventeen, he boxed his first 10 round fight within three months of making his debut and moved up to 15 round contests in June the same year. These were hungry days and possessing great skill Jack was generally able to avoid heavy punishment or serious injury. Boxing predominately at Premierland, usually at fortnightly intervals, he gradually met better quality opponents and in his first year as a professional engaged in 24 contests dropping only one decision, that being to Johnny Curley who was British featherweight champion at the time.

In his previous contest Jack had beaten Young Johnny Brown (Stepney) at bantamweight so it was a massive step up to take on the champion of the higher weight. Predictably, he received a boxing lesson, but profited from the experience - he was a youngster always ready to learn.

The setback merely made him all the more determined to succeed and after taking a decision over Mick Hill he tackled Harry Corbett (Bethnal Green) who had given Curley a hard and close fight for the title. Hyams was again outpointed, but to demonstrate just how much he enjoyed battling the top men in the division, he had two successive 15 round contests with Johnny Cuthbert who, by that time had taken the featherweight title from Curley.

Still a growing lad, Jack decided to move up to lightweight and was soon facing some of the top men in the higher division. A good run of victories earned him a fight against Sam Steward at The Ring, Blackfriars, in July 1928 with the winner guaranteed a contest for the championship vacated by Harry Mason. Sam had outpointed Jack twice over 15 rounds during the preceding six months and did it again over 20 rounds after a hard battle. He went on to win the British crown by knocking out Ernie Rice in 12 rounds.

Hyams again put his defeat down to inexperience. Still full of determination he regrouped and built an unbeaten run of seven contests which included a points victory over Harry Corbett and draws with Ernie Izzard and Fred Webster, all of whom won British titles at one time or another.

Still only twenty, he had taken part in almost 50 contests, mostly over 15 rounds and decided to try his luck in America. It was a brave, but mature decision guaranteeing him an abundance of experience. Between November 1929 and May, the following year, he lost only one of seven contests and also spent some time sparring with World welterweight champion Jackie Fields, who spoke well of him. Although he could have earned plenty more money in the States, Jack decided to return home at the end of his contract because he wanted to get married.

Once back in the East End he was trained by Dave Phillips and got straight back into action as a welterweight outpointing George Brown over 15 rounds at Premierland but lost over the same distance to Archie Sexton (Bethnal Green) three weeks later at The Ring, Blackfriars. Again, experience was the deciding factor, Archie having crammed in well over 100 fights since turning professional in 1925.

Only the best was good enough for Jack and when The Ring management wanted British champion Jack Hood, to top a bill at their arena, he agreed to face him. Despite conceding ten pounds in weight, the Aldgate youngster gave his best but found Hood in devastating form. Punching extremely hard he knocked Hyams out in the fourth round, the only time in his career that he failed to beat the count.

Jack got married during the summer of 1930 and was on his honeymoon when the chance came to meet Sexton again. Needing the money, he agreed to leave his bride and face Archie at Premierland. Although floored twice in round seven, he rallied magnificently to take a close decision. Five years later they met for a third time in what was classed as an eliminator for the British light-heavyweight title which Hyams won on points.

After settling down to married life Jack continued to box regularly and following his defeat of Sexton in 1930, took part in 47 contests up until November 1935. The names of many top-quality men appear on his record including Harry Mason, Alf Mancini, Jock McAvoy, Jerry Daley, Seaman Harvey, Del Fontane, Johnny Summers and Glen Moody.

Passing the 100-fight mark in 1935, he had his first championship shot in November that year but was outpointed by Frank Hough for the vacant Southern Area middleweight title. It was the first of six meetings between them and the only time Jack lost. He took the title from Frank in a return in March 1936 and defended it against him twice the same year. He also won the Southern Area light-heavyweight title beating Bill Hardy in 1938, but subsequently lost both although he did regain the light-heavyweight crown beating Eddie Maguire in 1941.

Despite his undoubted ability and success, Hyams got only one shot at a British title. His chance eventually came in 1937, when he faced Jock McAvoy for the middleweight championship. They had met twice before, the first occasion being in 1931 at Leeds when Jack was disqualified somewhat harshly for persistent holding in round eight. Their second encounter was two years later at The Ring and on this occasion the East Ender put up an incredible fight only to lose on points, a decision that met with considerable dissent.

Although Jack had put on a credible performance, his hopes for a shot at McAvoy's title were forlorn ones. Instead, the champion faced other challenges, went after the European title and then went to America where he had a series of fights culminating in an unsuccessful challenge for John Henry Lewis's World light-heavyweight title.

It was not until the autumn of 1937 that Hyams finally got the chance he had been waiting for, for over four years. During that time, he had battled on and eventually the Board of Control nominated him as a contender and entered him in a series of eliminators. In the final in February 1937 he beat Welsh champion, Dai Jones and was duly matched with McAvoy.

The fight was scheduled to take place at Belle Vue, Manchester in July, but the champion sustained a spinal injury after being thrown from a horse. They eventually met on 25 October in what was a gruelling affair. McAvoy attacked viciously from the start, but Jack more than held his own. He scored well, hurt the champion on several occasions but the turning point in the contest came in round seven when Hyams sustained a bad cut beneath the left eye. The injury worsened during the ensuing rounds and by the 11th the eye was completely closed. After taking a battering in that round, the corner pulled him out. Despite his anger at the time Jack subsequently acknowledged the wisdom of his seconds action. McAvoy later commiserated with him and insisted on personally taking him to hospital to have the injury treated.

Following a break of almost four months, Hyams returned to action and carried on very much as before until 1943. He faced more than a score of good class opponents including Ben Valentine, McAvoy; twice, both of which he lost on points over ten rounds, Charlie Knock, Ernie

Woodman, Dave McCleave; twice, and Freddie Mills; also twice, one of which he won on a disqualification.

Jack was serving as a gunner with the British Army in the Orkney Isles when he retired in 1943. He had taken out a manager's licence in 1939 and during the ensuing years his best boxer was another Aldgate man, Lew Lazar. Like Lew, Jack was also a taxi-driver but later became a clothing manufacturer and moved from the East End to live in Bushey, Hertfordshire.

He was a member of the Southern Area Council of the British Boxing Board of Control for 36 years and when Board Chief Inspector, Harry Vines passed away, Jack took his place on the Grants Committee. He also wrote a boxing column in the popular publication, *Weekly Sporting Review.*

Jack was never a devastating puncher during his career but had a great defence. Consequently, the majority of his fights went the distance. Although he lost quite a few, they were usually to men of championship class. It was a sign of the times that after being a professional for only six months he was regularly boxing 15-rounder's. He featured mainly on London promotions with over 60 of his contests taking place at The Ring, Blackfriars.

It was generally accepted that Jack Hyams was one of the best boxers never to win a British championship. He died in November 1982 aged seventy-three after a long illness.

Traceable record
161 Contests
107 Won
12 Drew
42 Lost

—.16.—

FREDDIE JACKS

(Aldgate)

Only the most ardent boxing fans and historians would know anything about Freddie Jacks, yet he was one of those extremely tough East End fighters who warrants inclusion in any boxing history of the region. In his heyday he was known as 'The Aldgate Iron Man' not just because of his amazing durability but also the destructive power of his punching. He never became a champion or fought for a title most probably because he was considered too dangerous.

Born at Aldgate on 12 February 1893, the son of a second-hand furniture dealer, Freddie's first taste of freedom was running around the streets of the East End with a gang of mates. One day when the most mischievous of them ran into a local boxing gymnasium, the others followed just for a lark. The man in charge invited them to "have a go" and, pointing at Jacks, held out a pair of boxing gloves. Urged on by his mates, he reluctantly slipped them on and climbed into the ring to face another boy. Only then did the group discover how well he could fight. Excited by his performance, Freddie went back to the gym the following day and soon became a regular. He was well and truly hooked on boxing and following sessions of proper instruction entered and won several novice competitions.

In 1910, at the age of seventeen, Jacks decided to embark on a career as a professional. Having been to the fights at Wonderland he knew it was there that he wanted to perform. Full of confidence, he went to the arena and met Jack Woolf who was impressed by his muscular physique. Always seeking new local talent, the promoter gave him a six-round contest on his next bill. Although he lost it on points, Freddie showed enough aggression and promise to get the fans on his side. In his next fight six weeks later, he won in the second round and the East End had another promising young star.

Jacks was an adventurous youngster and the following year joined the navy as a stoker. Although it was hard, dirty work, shovelling coal developed his arms and shoulders considerably. By the time he was discharged from service, he weighed just over nine stone despite being only five feet three inches tall. Biceps measuring 11 ½ inches and a chest of $36\frac{1}{2}$ inches, (expanded 38 inches) completed his powerful physique.

Still keen to continue boxing he seized an opportunity when his ship put into a French port one day. Shortly after going ashore, he saw a poster advertising a promotion in Paris. After making his way to the venue he was lucky enough to get a substitutes job. He performed well enough to impress the crowd and promoter, the result being that he was offered further contests during his time in the service and later in civilian life. Early in 1913, Jacks knocked out good class Frenchman, Rene St Didier, in two rounds, then a fortnight later fought a terrific 10-round draw with Paul Dorguille. His last contest in Paris was against French featherweight champion, Paul Til, who outpointed him over 10 rounds after an exhilarating battle.

Til was another top-class fighter who, in 1909 had boxed a draw with Georges Carpentier. In February 1914, he was matched with Ted 'Kid' Lewis for the European title at Premierland, and during his preparation for the contest Lewis engaged Jacks as a sparring partner. 'Fred has fought

Til and knows all there is to know about him', Lewis told the press. Although it took Ted 12 rounds to beat the Frenchman, courtesy of a disqualification for persistent holding, he admitted that the knowledge Freddie shared with him was crucial.

By this time Jacks was back in civilian life and keen to resume his ring career in London. As Wonderland had been burned down he went to Premierland where, in 1914 he fought six consecutive contests and became another East End favourite. He also made his debut at The National Sporting Club where he lost on points over six rounds to 'Kid' Black who nobody else would fight.

Freddie did not return to the navy after the First World War started. Instead he volunteered for the army but was not sent to France until 1916. In the meantime, he was granted service permission to accept ring engagements and during 1915 had 20 contests, all in London. He won 12, twice knocking out Alf Wye, (Hoxton) and held Charlie Hardcastle to a draw over 20 rounds. Charlie became British champion two years later knocking out Wye in the opening round.

During the first six months of 1916, he made the most of his remaining opportunities by taking another 20 contests of which he won 12. He drew with Young Joe Brooks whom he beat in a return, but twice lost to Louis Ruddock, a top-class boy from Leeds. He was also outpointed by Tommy Harrison, who in 1921 won the European bantamweight title and the British and British Empire titles the following year.

Freddie was then posted to France as a Sergeant Instructor with the British army. He was married by this time, but whilst at the front he received a letter from his wife stating she was short of money. Keen to rectify the situation he wrote to his manager stating that he was coming home on leave and asked that he fixed up a fight for him, which he did. When introduced from the ring the Master of Ceremonies announced him as 'Fred Jacks on leave from His Majesty's Armed Forces'. Before the fight had gone many rounds, however, word reached the ringside that a group of military police were on their way into the building. Jacks quickly left the ring, darted to the dressing room where he bundled up his uniform and whilst still in his boxing kit, was pushed into a car by some mates and driven to the docks. There he boarded a steamer bound for France, made his way to his unit and reported for duty. At his subsequent 'Absent without Leave' hearing the fact that he had given himself up was taken into consideration and helped reduce the sentence which he served with ease.

Posted back to England during the summer of 1917, Fred immediately resumed boxing and trained under Jack Goodwin who had shaped his career when he was quite young. Anxious to keep busy, he was prepared to take on anyone put in front of him, one of which was up and coming Frank Moody from Pontypridd who he faced at The Ring, Blackfriars, in 1918. There was no stipulated weight for the 20-round contest and although Jacks knew his trainer was aware of Franks reputation in Wales, neither had seen him until he ducked under the ropes. To their amazement, he looked huge.

'That's a nice nine stone man' snapped Fred, 'He's a welterweight'.

'Well, what are you going to do?' asked Goodwin.

'Fight him of course' was the prompt reply.

Although Moody was too big and strong for him, he lasted 17 rounds before being disqualified for using his head. He protested bitterly at the decision because being shorter meant the top of his head reached the Welshman's chin and therefore frequently made contact whenever they were in clinches. Once he had calmed down, however, he raised a glove and addressed the crowd saying, 'Gentlemen, I came here to fight a featherweight not a welter'.

Despite the setback, Jacks continued to impress his followers. Amongst his successes was a knockout victory over British featherweight champion Tancy Lee in Scotland during 1918 but as the contest was not under the auspices of The National Sporting Club, the champion did not lose his title. The success proved beyond doubt that he was a genuine title contender, yet it did nothing to enhance his chance of a championship contest. One of the main problems was that he was proving a stumbling-block for top class men at this weight.

Fred eventually joined the same stable as Mike Honeyman, but it failed to improve his chances. They trained at the same gym, sparred regularly together but despite possessing similar talent, the manger favoured Mike. As a result, he was given the opportunity to progress towards a title. Had Fred been based elsewhere he may well have been matched with Honeyman.

Jacks was an ambitious man with great self-confidence and always believed he could beat Mike, but the manager kept them apart. Failure to get a title fight convinced him to try his luck in America. Furthermore, he knew it was the only way he could get out of the contract with his manager. Having taken his wife and two children with him, Fred had his first American contest in Detroit on 1 March 1920. The fans loved his aggressive non-stop style and durability and he was constantly in demand in all the small fight towns. Win or lose, he always gave value for money.

On reaching New York, Jacks put himself under the management of Joe Woodman, who had looked after the famous black fighter, Sam Langford. He soon became busy, Joe quickly recognised his style was well suited to American audiences. In 1921 alone, Fred engaged in 24 contests and although he lost 13, he was never stopped. It was an indication of his extreme toughness and believing he could stand up to most men of his weight, Woodman sought out World featherweight champion, Johnny Kilbane.

At first Kilbane was hesitant, but after watching Jacks fight in New York, he agreed to meet him on condition that the contest took place in his home town of Clevedon. It would be a no decision affair over 10 rounds and made 125. pounds. In effect this meant that the only way Fred could win was by knocking the champion out.

Kilbane had held the title for nine years having won it in February 1912. In those days, many top American professionals made fighting their sole means of livelihood. They thought nothing of taking as many as 20 fights a year, but as most were of no decision, the chance of being beaten was minimal and therefore there was no need for a fighter to over exert himself. Johnny was no exception to this situation and rarely took risks with his title.

When the contest took place on 25 May 1921, the World champion held no fears for the aggressive Jacks who gave it everything by crowding Kilbane from the opening bell. He almost caused a sensation in the second round when a terrific right to the chin sent the champion heavily across the ring. Only his great experience saved him from going down. Most of the newspaper men had Freddie as the winner but that did not make him a champion. When he demanded a rematch with the title at stake, Kilbane insisted on a $20,000 purse for himself. It was such an outrageous demand that one paper published a cartoon emphasising on the unsporting gesture.

Jacks had eight further contests during the next five months, losing three and was then matched with Louis 'Kid' Kaplan over 12 rounds in Connecticut on 19 November. Despite being a novice, he would go on to win the World featherweight title in 1925. Although he gained the decision over Jacks, newspapers described the margin of victory as scant. The local favourite was said to have out-punched the Londoner, but Freddie landed the cleaner wallops.

Five days after meeting Kaplan, Freddie faced Jimmy Goodrich in New York, but was outpointed over 12 rounds. They met again the following February in Toronto with the American gaining a split decision over 10. Three years later he would claim the World lightweight title.

During the same period of time Jacks twice fought Joe Dundee, later to become World welterweight champion. Their first contest was in January 1922 at Baltimore in which he put up a tremendous battle flooring the American heavily in round three. He was on one knee at the count of 'six' but did not straighten up until a second after the referee had called 'out'. Dundee's seconds jumped into the ring and began remonstrating with the official. With things looking ugly both inside and outside the ring, the local Boxing Commissioner ruled that the bout should continue. It went the full 12 rounds at the end of which Jacks was awarded the decision of a contest he had realistically already won. They met again at the same venue two months later and the American took the decision albeit a close one.

Throughout his spell in American rings, Fred continued to fight top class men. He faced Rocky Kansas on three occasions, losing the first two on points over six rounds in 1923 and '24. The first, which took place at Buffalo, was a real war with the home-town fans protesting loudly when the referee awarded the decision to Kansas. The last took place at Tampa in 1926, in what was Rocky's first contest since becoming World lightweight champion by beating Jimmy Goodrich three months earlier. On this occasion Jacks was stopped in six rounds.

He faced Jack Bernstein in New York in July 1922 but was beaten on points. They met again in Philadelphia three years later and Jacks was knocked out in five rounds just four weeks after the American had become World junior lightweight champion.

Although Fred had fought mainly in the United States since 1920, he took the occasional contest in Canada and towards the end of 1922 went to Australia, where he was contracted for five 20 round contests in the space of five months. Two of these were against National champion, Bert Spargo, who outpointed him in both at Melbourne Stadium. Although his only success was a good points victory over Stanley McBride, Fred thrilled the crowds and left Australia with a host of newspaper clippings which gave glowing accounts of his battles there.

He returned to America in mid-1923 where he continued to face good-class opposition, one of which was another East End fighter, Al Foreman, who was also on a lengthy fight campaign. They met at Washington in May 1925 and Jacks was beaten on points. By this time, he was past the age of thirty and whilst still extremely durable, was very much in the category of a journeyman. When he finally retired in 1928, he had won only one of his last 27 contests, but stopped just three times in that period, two of which were in his last five contests.

Although he never became a champion Freddie Jacks contribution to the ring should never be forgotten, particularly in the East End. It was there, in the smoky halls, that he learned his demanding trade before moving to the United States. There he battled for a further eight years facing some of the best men in the world at his weight in the rings of Brooklyn, Philadelphia, Buffalo and Louisiana to name just a few. During that time (there) he had about 80 fights, a large majority of which were wars. The fans on both sides of the Atlantic loved his aggressive style and admired his durability.

Freddie loved America and its people and after retiring from the ring, made his home there and lived happily with his wife Ray until he passed away on 3 August 1961, in Brooklyn, aged sixty-nine. The 'Aldgate Iron Man' was an accurate description of him.

Traceable Record
176 Contests
79 Won
82 Lost

15 Drew
(Includes newspaper decisions in the United States)

—.17.—

YOUNG JOSEPH

(Aldgate)

BRITISH WELTERWEIGHT CHAMPION 1908 – 1911

EUROPEAN WELTERWEIGHT CHAMPION 1910 – 1911

The story of Young Joseph, one of the most popular boxers to have come from the East End, effectively starts on the streets of Whitechapel. Born in Aldgate on 12 February 1885, as Aschel Joseph, he was known as Harry Joseph amongst the dozens of youngsters that gathered outside Wonderland on fight nights during the late 1800's and early 1900's. He was a bright lad who always had plenty to say for himself and from an early age he had the burning desire to become a professional boxer, and in due course, a champion. He thought nothing of running alongside a fighter who left Wonderland after a gruelling fight and firing a host of questions at him.

Full of confidence, he pestered Jack Woolf to give him a chance to fight at the arena. Eventually after incessant pleading and harassing, Jack agreed to give him some trial bouts for which he was given a few shillings' reward. A flyweight at the time, Joseph was too fast on his feet to run into trouble during one-minute rounds. He also had good hand speed. The promoter loved what he saw and calling him Young Joseph which stuck throughout his career, gave him his first contest on 28 February 1906, just sixteen days after his eighteenth birthday. By the end of the year he had lost only one of his 18 contests and won a flyweight competition for which Harry Jacobs presented him with a belt.

Boxing exclusively at Wonderland, Joseph made great strides and before he had completed his first year as a professional, was invited to box at The National Sporting Club. Although beaten on points in his first two fights there, he won the third and became quite a favourite. His modest personality and skilful, spirited boxing proved a delight to the members.

In those early years, Joseph rarely ventured outside London but his chance to seek recognition beyond the capital came in 1907. Approaching the age of twenty-three and having had about 70 fights, but none over 15 rounds, a Sheffield promoter offered him a 20 rounder against local man, Billy Gordon. The pay being good, Aschel accepted it and was rewarded with a knockout victory in 18 rounds.

Returning home, he felt extremely proud and walking around the East End one day, met up with businessman and close admirer, Edward Emmanuel, who asked him who he was going to fight next. Joseph said he was waiting for a fight, where upon Emmanuel suggested he challenged Jack Goldswain, who had won the British lightweight championship in 1906, but had reportedly vacated it due to weight difficulties. 'He is a big name in Bermondsey but a shake past his best' remarked Emmanuel. 'If you beat him, which I reckon you can, you will have done yourself a power of good'.

The idea appealed to Aschel so he and his admirer went to Wonderland to put it to Jack Woolf. It was agreed that if Goldswain was willing, a fight would be made at 10st 2lbs over 20 two-minute rounds for side-stakes of £50 which Emmanuel immediately covered. Being much more experienced, Goldswain willingly accepted, telling his friends that he intended putting 'Flash Harry' in his place.

The fight took place at Wonderland on 21 October and boxing as well as anytime in his career, Joseph won clearly on points, but as it was such an intense struggle a return was inevitable.

Woolf put them on again at catch weights three months later for a purse of £165 and side-stakes of £200. Wonderland had seating for 2,000 but twice that number crowded in and it was estimated that more than 1500 disappointed fans milled about in the street outside awaiting the result. Again, Joseph's superior speed and boxing skill earned him the 20-round decision, and such was the attraction that moving pictures of the fight were taken by the Warwick Trading Company and shown at Holborn Empire the following evening.

Joseph continued to progress and laid claim to the British welterweight title following his victory over Lance Corporal Baker at the National Sporting Club in October 1908. The Club, however, did not support the claim as they had not advertised the fight as being an official eliminator. Elsewhere however, Joseph was hailed as champion.

It was not until March 1910, that The Club put up the first of the newly launched Lord Lonsdale belts for the welterweight division. Joseph and Jack Goldswain were duly matched to contest it and, being rivals from opposite sides of the River Thames, the Club was absolutely packed.

The Aldgate man had lost only one of his last 18 contests, that being to the redoubtable Freddie Welsh at Mountain Ash in July 1909, when he was disqualified in the 11th round. Yet the fight with Goldswain was the least attractive of their three meetings because Joseph was well on top from the opening bell. Only gameness and persistent holding allowed Jack to survive until round 11 when the referee threw him out after issuing numerous warnings.

Goldswain did not get his end of the £200 purse, a decision taken by The National Sporting Club because both men had signed a contract stipulating that in the event of a disqualification no part of the offender's purse would be paid. Despite this, Jack sportingly turned up at the club the following day to see Joseph presented with the new belt.

In a subsequent court action taken by Goldswain against the Club, Aschel gave evidence insisting that his opponent had tried his best during their fight and should not be penalised financially. The court, however, found against Jack and ordered him to pay costs.

Even as British champion, Joseph remained faithful to Wonderland and Jack Woolf rewarded him in the best way possible by matching him with Harry Lewis of America over 20 rounds for the welterweight championship of the world.

Joseph had always been immensely popular at Wonderland and the East End fans had no intention of staying away as their hero was about to get the chance of his life. Even with increased admission prices, crowds swarmed into the building hours before the programme commenced and continued to do so until shortly before the main event was due. Although the seating capacity was far from adequate to deal with demand, this was a gala occasion for the grand old arena. Not having to abide by the health and safety regulations of modern times, Woolf therefore allowed as many people as possible to stand. It was just as hectic outside, and the police were kept busy because Whitechapel Road and surrounding streets were jammed.

Sadly, the hopes of the fans were virtually shattered in the opening round when it was apparent that the American was by far the heavier puncher. Joseph was floored in that round and again in the third and only avoided disaster by desperately ducking and weaving on the ropes. For six rounds, he made a tremendous effort, exhibiting great skill but his blows had no effect on his aggressive and rugged opponent who always looked to have the edge.

After being floored again in round six, Aschel looked very weary and in the seventh Lewis went for the finish. Attacking viciously, he put the British champion down for a count of 'nine' and when he rose a chopping right put him down again. He climbed bravely to his feet but was on the end of a vicious body attack before a right to the chin sent him back to the boards. As he clambered up Lewis swung his right sending Joseph to his knees and only the bell saved him from being knocked out. He was in a bad way as his seconds carried him to his corner where they told the referee that he couldn't continue.

Despite the shattering defeat, Joseph was back in the Wonderland ring within five weeks. By the end of the year he was undefeated in 13 further contests, his only blemish being a 10-round draw with old foe, Jack Goldswain, at The Ring, Blackfriars. In the meantime, he had fallen out with The National Sporting Club and was considering a fight with Freddie Welsh for an alternative welterweight belt offered by Jack Woolf. When things didn't materialise, he travelled to Paris where he beat Battling Lacroix to secure the European title.

When called upon by The National Sporting Club to defend his Lonsdale belt against Arthur Evenden, Aschel refused stating that it was beneath his dignity to accept the derisory purse offered. Instead he agreed to a subsequent offer from The Ring to meet Evenden on 23 January 1911.

Aschel felt no loyalty to The National Sporting Club and returned the belt he had so proudly carried everywhere with pride and displayed it wherever he fought. The Club had already found that he could be a handful when he gave evidence in court against them on behalf of Jack Goldswain.

Against Evenden, Aschel was a huge disappointment being hammered for three rounds before referee, Eugene Corri, disqualified him for persistent holding. The decision caused an uproar amongst members of the betting fraternity, many of whom crowded around the ring creating an almost riotous situation. Joseph had been a firm favourite to win, but as soon as he realised the hostility he took the microphone and shouted for quiet. Loudly and concisely he addressed the simmering gathering. 'Gentlemen,' he said 'there is no squarer or straighter sportsman in the world than Mr Eugene Corri. All over the world he is respected and though I am sorry that he has given the decision against me, I know he must be right and I abide by that decision'. His diplomatic words quietened the crowd and they gradually retreated from the ringside. With order restored it endorsed the respect the Wonderland regulars had for Joseph.

Despite the conclusive defeat to Evenden, Aschel continued to claim the welterweight title insisting that the contest had not been under championship conditions. Furthermore, he refused to accept that his career was over and went undefeated in 10 fights in as many months during 1911 as he tried to swell his bank balance. Amongst his successes was a points victory over French champion, Robert Eustache, in Paris, in defence of his European crown. Five months later he accepted a purse of £200 to defend it against a young Georges Carpentier at Kings Hall.

Aschel's loyal friends and followers packed the South London arena, but despite putting on his usual game and determined display, he was no match for the brilliant Frenchman who won almost every round. In the tenth, after being floored three times, he wobbled back to his corner where upon his seconds threw in the towel.

Until he faced Carpentier, the Aldgate man had only lost to Evenden in 23 contests, so in his mind he was far from finished. Within six months he faced Johnny Summers in Liverpool in defence of the British title which he still claimed despite not being recognised as champion by The National Sporting Club. He lost a clear 20 round decision and from that point, although continuing to box, the gaps between contests lengthened and the purses began to dwindle. By November 1914, when he had failed to win any of his last seven fights, he wisely decided to call it a day at the age of twenty-nine. His career spanned 12 years, during which he had over 150 contests, almost 70 of which were at Wonderland.

Joseph remained in the sport, managing fighters and even promoting at small shows - particularly the Whitechapel Pavilion. Some years earlier whilst still boxing he acted as a referee on a number of occasions at The Judean Club. He was at the heart of a newly formed Boxers Union in 1910 and elected president the following year.

In September 1911, he was one of a number of respected boxing personalities selected to attend at court and support the sport in legal proceedings to ban a proposed world heavyweight championship fight between Jack Johnson and Bombardier Billy Wells at Earls Court on 2 October that year.

No matter what Aschel did, he retained his immense popularity. At one time after retirement from the ring, he kept a clothing shop in the East End. Unfortunately, by the mid 1930's he had been struck down by a form of paralysis and as a result was virtually crippled. He spent most of his time sitting in the saloon bar of his son-in-law's public house, the Rose and Crown, at Burns Street off Edgware Road hoping that someone would come in for a chat with him. Eventually, with his speech difficult and having almost lost the use of his limbs, he had to rely on his relatives for support.

One of his last public appearances was at a Parade of Champions held in the East End during 1938. One by one they were called to the stage, but when it came to his turn, Aschel could not make it alone and had to be supported on both sides by white sweater clad seconds. He had the twisted figure of an elderly man and his hands, once the tools of his trade, were now fragile claws. His feet dragged painfully across the carpet with a hideous shuffling sound and his face had the expression of a death mask. The lines of pain were etched deeply into it through suffering. He was a pitiful sight. Much of Joseph's disability was claimed to have resulted from a fight with Freddie Welsh at Mountain Ash in July 1909. Although he was beaten on a disqualification it was reported that he was subjected to repeated kidney punching, which the powers subsequently decreed should be outlawed. Boxing, however, should not be blamed for all of Aschel's troubles - rheumatics and arthritis came to fighters and civilians alike as they grew older.

In the late 1940's Joseph lived at Blenheim Crescent in the Notting Hill area of West London and could only walk with the aid of sticks. At one stage when he was in dire financial trouble, a committee was formed to run a testimonial event for him. When he died in 1952 he was virtually confined to a wheelchair. It was a tragic ending for a man who gave so much to boxing.

Traceable Record:
154 Contests
98 Won
29 Drew
27 Lost

—.18.—

SAM KELLER

(Aldgate)

Born to the east of Aldgate Pump, of Jewish parents, in 1885, Sam Kellar began boxing at the age of fifteen. On appearance, he was a frail looking young man who would surely be unwise to become involved in the tough demands of the ring. Yet appearances frequently count for nothing, particularly in sport, and he soon proved that he was well able to look after himself against the onslaughts of more robustly built opponents. His skill was such that he was comfortable engaging in 10-round contests in his second year as a professional.

A number of his early fights took place at the Alma Grounds, Canning Town before he became a favourite at Wonderland where he was rarely beaten. His style and skill also caught the attention of the matchmakers at the National Sporting Club where he was given a number of contests during 1905 and 06.

Despite his apparent frailty, Sam had massive enthusiasm and ambition and following a win and draw against highly regarded Jim Kenrick, a veteran of about 120 contests, he crossed the Atlantic in search of fortune and fame in the United States. He spent over 12 months there during 1907 and 1908, and engaged in 16 battles, mostly in

New York, losing only four, all on points courtesy of newspaper decisions.

On returning home he took a good 20-round points victory over respected flyweight, Curley Osborn but then lost over the same distance to Digger Stanley at the National Sporting Club in October 1908. Kellar's performance in this contest confirmed his quality and standing in the eight-stone division.

Stanley, a professional since 1899, had claimed the British title in 1903, but was not accepted as champion by the National Sporting Club which controlled British boxing at the time. It was not until 1911 that the first belt, presented to the club by Lord Lonsdale, was contested under their auspices. Stanley was a top-class fighter and later won the British bantamweight title and claimed the British version of the World title.

The highlights of 1909 for Sam were two victories over Bill Fielder, the defeat of French title holder, Paul Til, another draw with Jim Kenrick and a draw with north country hope Ike Bradley. In December the same year he outpointed Alf 'Spider' Stewart over 15 rounds at Celtic Park, Belfast in a contest billed as being for the Irish 7st-10lbs / 7st-12lbs title despite neither man having been born in Ireland. That month he also refereed a fight at the Judean Club.

After beating Bill Ladbury on points over 20 rounds at the National Sporting Club and drawing with Ike Bradley over the same distance at Liverpool in early 1910, Sam decided to return to the United States where earning capacity was far greater. In a 14-month period between August that year and October 1911 he had almost 30 contests of which he only lost six.

It was a confusing situation because in many States, the winner of a fight lasting the distance was generally decided by a newspaper decision. In many fights the result was recorded as 'No Decision.' What was clear, however, was that in two tours of America, Sam was never stopped or knocked out which in itself was a remarkable achievement.

Following the first contest of his second tour, against Willie Canole in San Francisco, in which one of his seconds was former World featherweight champion, Owen Moran, it was reported that local fans believed Sam was talented enough to do well against good class opponents. This proved to be the case because once he was settled he boxed regularly, often three times a month. He won and lost against Jimmy Carroll, described as one of the best men in California. Against Harry Dell he was on the wrong end of a split decision which upset many in the crowd. *The Oakland Tribune* claimed he was robbed.

In his sixth contest in just two months, Kellar met Harry Forbes, who held the World bantamweight title between 1901 and 1903 and had the experience of almost 130 contests. He had also challenged unsuccessfully for the featherweight title and again for the bantam crown. The class of the Londoner was clear for all to see as there were times when he out-boxed the veteran and lasted the 10-rounds in a no decision contest.

Against hard-hitting Joe Shugrue on 2 January 1911, one reporter described Sam as 'boxing like a Jim Driscoll' as he easily handled his hard-hitting opponent throughout ten rounds in what was said to have been one of the best fights in New York that week. They met again at the same venue three weeks later when the American was given a newspaper decision. Again, Kellar put up a great fight, adding to his increasing popularity.

Four months later, again at New York, Sam outpointed Willie Jones in a bad-tempered fight in which they often traded blows head to head. The Londoner had a good points lead by round six, but after one exchange on the bell, the needle between them showed. After landing heavily in the next round Jones asked: 'How do you like it so far?', Kellar ignored him and continued to jab with his left giving the audience at the Olympic Boxing Club an exhibition.

Whilst in New York, Sam teamed up with another Aldgate fighter, Joe Shears and they eventually agreed to return home together, but it never happened. Shears, another flyweight, developed into a good prospect and during July, World featherweight champion, Abe Attell, took him under his wing.

That month Kellar faced Charlie Harvey at Albany, New York and the British publication *Boxing,* subsequently reported that he was beaten. When Sam discovered this, he wrote to the editor and expressed his dissatisfaction, enclosing two cuttings from an Albany newspaper which both confirmed that he had in fact won. 'I shall be greatly obliged if you will correct your earlier report,' he wrote. 'As you know, a boxer loses his reputation when he is called a loser. I have to depend on boxing for my living so I try to win every time I fight.'

The editor subsequently confirmed that Kellar had won the 10-rounder on points and apologised for any injustice but added that the paper had to rely on American sources which, on this occasion, had been incorrect.

Sam also sent details of other boxers he claimed to have met and defeated in America. These too, were not completely comparable with records held in the UK and highlight the difficulty regarding accuracy during this period of time. In his article the editor of *Boxing* pointed out that from the locality of the majority of contests, to which Kellar referred, the likelihood was that the vast majority would have been No Decision affairs. It would therefore have been valuable and most interesting to have been sent cuttings regarding all of them. *Boxing* confirmed that it knew Sam was a fine boxer, but not fully aware of his true capability due largely to the lack of information contained in American reports.

Sam's final contest in the States was in Cleveland, Ohio, on 10 October 1911 against old foe Harry Forbes. Again, he fought brilliantly against the vastly experienced veteran, but yet again there was conflict over the result. One source had Forbes as the winner while *The Ring Encyclopaedia* recorded it was a draw. In reality it is now irrelevant because whichever was correct, it confirmed the class of Kellar and he returned home having always heard the final bell.

Meanwhile, back in London the National Sporting Club nominated Sam to meet Sid Smith (Bermondsey) for the British flyweight title. As soon as he was contacted he sacrificed some excellent prospects in the United States, gave up his home and all his affairs in the hope of winning the championship and the first belt for the division which was being donated to the club by Lord Lonsdale. On arriving home, he and Smith signed articles and the fight was set to take place at the club on 4 December.

Kellar had a group of wealthy backers and observed by British lightweight champion, Matt Wells, he embarked on a strenuous preparation programme, but with two weeks to go he was forced to pull out of the fight with appendicitis. The subsequent operation meant he would be side-lined for several months. It was a tragedy especially as Christmas was approaching but Wells and Sam's backers organised a benefit night to help his wife and family.

Kellar's misfortune presented tough Stepney flyweight, Joe Wilson, with the opportunity to take his place. Although he put up a magnificent display, he was narrowly outpointed, thereby depriving East End fans of a mouth-watering fight with Sam once he was fit.

Kellar returned to the ring in April the following year and billed from Mile End, he boxed a 10-round draw with promising Joe Fox from Leeds at Premierland. In a return at the same venue four months later, the result was the same after a thoroughly disappointing contest in which both men seemed anxious not to spoil their reputations by getting knocked out. There was an abundance of holding and very little exciting action and as a result both men were booed from the ring, action almost unheard of at the East End arena. Two weeks later, however, all was forgiven as Sam was involved in a thriller against promising Aldgate youngster, Nat Brooks who outpointed him over 10 rounds.

The following month Kellar looked to be back to his best as he outpointed Tommy Harrison at Sheldon Drill Hall in Staffordshire. After a thrilling contest, one newspaper report said, 'The Jewish boy gave an exhibition of boxing which is rarely seen in the provinces'.

Despite his return to top form, Sam lost more fights than he won from this point in time, but he ducked nobody. Those who beat him had been, were or would have become champions at flyweight or bantamweight. Between 1912 and 1916 he faced Bill Ladbury (lost on points over 20 rounds), Sid Smith, who by this time had compiled an impressive record, losing only five of over 70 fights, (L.Pts.20), Curley Walker (L. Disq 10), Percy Jones (L.Pts.20), Joe Symonds (L.Pts.15 & W. Disq 6), Tommy Harrison (L.Pts.20) and Tommy Noble (LTKO.8 & L.Pts. 6).

Apart from his two extended trips to America, Sam rarely fought outside London, but whenever he did he was afforded generous receptions from fans who appreciated his skills. A typical example was when he faced Alick Lafferty at the Scottish National Club in Glasgow, in September 1913 and hundreds of ticket-seekers were turned away to prevent overcrowding. Kellar was a natural flyweight and better exponent of finer points of boxing but the Scot was a husky bantam with several pounds advantage in weight. Having been out of action for five months, Sam was set too hard a task and was stopped in the 12th round, but only after putting up a crowd-pleasing performance.

Towards the end of his career he faced World flyweight champion Jimmy Wilde in a non-title contest at the West London Stadium, Marylebone. The fight was made at 8st-2lbs to protect the champion's title, but although Kellar scaled almost two pounds over the limit, it made no difference. Wilde had lost only one of over 100 fights by this stage of his career and although he fought with his customary pluck Sam was no match for the world champion and retired in round eight.

After two defeats to Tommy Noble in June and August 1916, Sam announced his retirement, but a good money-match in Paris three years later was too tempting to resist. His opponent was the brilliant French featherweight, Eugene Criqui who, three years later, would become European champion and later world title holder. His record of only 14 defeats from about 100 contests confirmed his ability. Facing a fighter of this quality after three years out of the ring was too much for Kellar and he was stopped in five rounds never to lace a glove again.

In retirement, Sam opened a gym at Walworth Road in South East London and amongst those he instructed in the basic skills of boxing were his two sons, Dave and Sam junior. In later life he often spoke proudly of his ring career, particularly his trips to America. He even kept a host of newspaper cuttings of his battles out there. He was extremely proud of his sons, especially Dave who won a Southern Area Championship.

Sam later moved to the Midlands and by 1947 had built up a prosperous business in Hinkley, Leicestershire where he remained until he passed away in 1976, aged ninety.

Traceable Record
114 Contests
63 Won
32 Lost
19 Drew
(Includes 33 newspaper decisions in the United States)

——.19.——

TOM KING

(Stepney)

Born in Silver Street, Stepney on 4 August 1835, Tom King was regarded as the last legitimate champion of the British Prize Ring. Along with his brother Sam, he joined the Royal Navy while in his teens and served on ships on both the east and west coasts of Africa helping the suppression of the slave trade. Upon discharge of service he took employment in London's Victoria Docks where he become a foreman.

Working amongst a very rough class of man, he was involved in his share of hard scraps, one in particular, with a ruffian known as 'Brighton Bill.' In or out of the drink he was a foul-mouthed quarrelsome individual who most of the other workers were intimidated by.

One day Tom had to remonstrate with him and after work told him that if he persisted using such language he would be out of a job. Bill reacted by throwing off his coat and yelling that he would 'knock the hell' out of Tom who, despite his mild manner, was no coward having experienced plenty of fights in the Navy. Confidently slipping off his jacket he told the bully to go ahead. Keeping calm, Tom avoided his opponent's crude rushing tactics and repeatedly knocked him to the ground. After about 15 minutes his blooded antagonist surrendered.

News of King's performance reached the ears of former champion, Jem Ward, who kept The George Inn on Ratcliffe Highway. They soon became friends and after giving him a workout with gloves, Jem convinced the youngster that he had a future with his fists. Ward was so impressed that he issued a challenge that his man would 'take on any 'big 'Un' in England for £50.'

The challenge was taken up by Joe Clamp, known as the Newgate Butcher and the necessary £5 was deposited to bind the match. Unknown in London, Clamp decided to visit Ward's sparring-room to have a look at King and even accepted the gloves for a spar with him. King had no idea who his adversary was but after five minutes Clamp surrendered, and the £5 bond was forfeited.

After several successful contests, Tom's backers considered he was good enough to face any man in the country, including recognised champion Jem Mace. A challenge of £200 was issued and duly accepted by the champion on condition that King deposited a £200 side-stake.

After a series of false trails to avoid the authorities the fight was staged at Godstone, Surrey, on 28 January 1862. The experience of Mace, however, proved crucial and Tom was beaten in 43 rounds which lasted 68 minutes. It was an incredible fight described as a credit to both men and although eventually beaten, King proved beyond doubt that he was a man of some merit. A return was therefore natural.

They met again on the banks of the River Medway, in Kent, on 26 November the same year and this time King dominated proceedings. He stopped Mace in 21 rounds, (38 minutes) giving him the championship of England, but afterwards said he wouldn't defend it because he was getting married. The following year, however, he was induced out of retirement having received a challenge of £1,000-a-side to fight John Carmel Heenan of America.

The situation arose after Heenan arrived in England hoping to get a second fight with Tom Sayers. He made friends amongst the betting fraternity and put it around that he wanted a fight with King for no less than £500, adding that he had friends who would make it £1,000-a-side if required. This was published by the editor of *Bell's Life* and Tom's backers took up the challenge. Agreements were drawn up for the fight to take place within 100 miles of London on 8 December 1863. The venue eventually decided upon, was a field in Wadhurst, Kent and although the American out-weighed King by 23 pounds he did not have the class or skill of the Londoner who won in 24 rounds lasting 35 minutes.

Following action by the local squire and the owner of the field where the fight took place, all parties appeared for trial at Lewes Court Spring Quarter Sessions. King's counsel told the court that he was retiring from the prize ring and would not therefore commit further offences of prize fighting. Tom was bound over in his own recognisance of £100.

He didn't fight again. Instead he became an accomplished oarsman, developed an interest in horse racing and became a successful bookmaker. Yet he was a quiet reserved man who loved to exhibit flowers at horticultural shows. Married to the daughter of a ship owner he amassed a considerate fortune before his death at Stockbridge, Hampshire, on 3 December 1880, aged fifty-three. His fight with Heenan at Wadhurst was regarded as the last great prize-fight in England.

20

LEW LAZAR

(Aldgate)

SOUTHERN AREA MIDDLEWEIGHT CHAMPION
1955 TO 1958
(RETIRED UNDEFEATED).

Born in Aldgate on 3 February 1931 Lew, real surname Lazarus, was one of 22 children in the family. His older brother Harry was a good welterweight who, during the early part of the Second World War was of championship class. During that period one edition of *'Boxing'* featured him on the front page claiming he was the 'modern day Jim Driscoll'.

In a professional career of over 100 contests between 1938 and 1950 he beat many good quality men including Dave Crowley (twice), Johnny McGrory, Bob Ramsay, Harry 'Kid' Silver, Dave Finn, Harry Mizler, Laurie Buxton, Henry Hall and Jake Kilrain to name just a few. Yet the nearest he came to championship contention was in 1948 when he outpointed Jim Wellard in an eliminator for the South Eastern Area welterweight title. Despite his victory a title fight never materialized.

Greatly influenced by his brother's success, Lew soon became involved in the sport and as an amateur, boxed on the East End club circuit, winning 59 of 60 contests. During the course of his national service, he twice won BAOR championships in Germany two years running.

After leaving school at the age of fourteen he started work at an East End upholstery company owned by relatives. Some years later when he was contemplating turning professional he sought their advice. They gave him every encouragement but stressed the importance of getting a good honest manager. After lengthy discussions with former professional boxer Jack Hyams, also from Aldgate, by this time a pipe smoking part-time taxi driver, contracts were signed.

Jack would become Lew's manager and experienced Snowy Buckingham his trainer. Hyams was an excellent choice because having been a good class middleweight, with the experience of over 160 contests before retiring in 1943, he had taken out a British Boxing Board of Control managers licence, four years earlier. He was also an established member of the Board's Southern Area Council.

Lew made his professional debut in June 1951 out pointing Freddy Bird over six rounds at Mile End Arena. By the end of the year he had won 11 of 12 contests, eight of which were inside the distance. The only blemish on a perfect record was a draw with tough Nigerian Santos Martins. One of his victories was a third round knockout of fellow East Ender Charlie Kray at the Royal Albert Hall in December.

The run of successes continued with Lew winning all of his 12 contests during 1952. His victims included Santos Martins, Southern Area champion Alf Danahar (Bethnal Green) and Dougie du Preez of South Africa. The following year, after being unbeaten in 27 contests, he suffered his first defeat when Terry Ratcliffe from Bristol narrowly outpointed him over eight rounds on a charity show promoted by Jack Solomons at Manor Place Baths. In a great fight, Lazar won the early rounds but then elected to mix it and lost a close decision. Many critics were of the opinion, that it could have been voted 'fight of the year'.

A return was inevitable, and the following month Lew gained revenge with a third-round stoppage at the Empress Hall. Having floored his man twice in the opening round, he then inflicted a bad cut to Terry's left eye in the second. When this worsened in the next round the referee called a halt.

A rubber match was a natural and when the Board of Control nominated it as a British welterweight title eliminator, promoters clamoured for the right to stage it. Freddie Mills won the bidding and put the fight on at The Empress Hall in October the same year (1953). After a terrific battle in which Lazar outboxed and outpunched his opponent, he was declared the winner when the referee called a halt in round 10 to save Ratcliff unnecessary punishment.

Lew had to wait a further 12 months for a championship shot and then in October 1954, after five further victories, he challenged Wally Thom for the British and European titles at Harringay Arena. It was to be his last contest at welter because struggling to make the weight, Thom knocked him out in round six.

After moving up to middleweight the following year, Lew got back to winning ways with nine victories from 10 bouts, his sole defeat being on points to Billy Ellaway. After victories over leading contenders Gordon Hazell and Johnny Read, he faced old foe Terence Murphy (Canning Town) at Shoreditch Town Hall. They had boxed a draw the previous year but this time the Southern Area middleweight title was at stake and the fight broadcast live on ITV. After another extremely close battle Lew got the decision which put him back into British championship contention

Five weeks later he beat Les Allen on points over 10 rounds in an eliminator and followed that with victory over another good man, Martin Hansen. These were solid performances which earned Lazar a final eliminating contest with Billy Ellaway in Liverpool in April 1956.

His 12 rounds points victory earned him the right to challenge British and Empire champion, Pat McAteer, and they met in Nottingham in October that year. Unfortunately for the Londoner, Pat produced one of the finest performances of his career. Having floored his challenger three times in round four, the champion retained his titles when referee, Ike Powell, called a halt thus ending Lazar's hopes of winning a major title.

Although he carried on for another two years Lew had seen better days. Two wins, two draws and two defeats were the best he could manage. One of the defeats came in Harringay at the hands of an up-and-coming Terry Downes effectively meaning the Aldgate man had reached trial horse status. His final contest was in Harringay in January 1958 against another promising fighter, Welsh middleweight champion Phil Edwards. After Lew had been floored three times the bout was stopped in round five and compassionately recognising that his man was well past his best, Jack Hyams announced that he was to retire.

Throughout his career Jack spoke highly of his young protege in press interviews. 'When I first took him on he was already a natural. I just helped smooth out the rough edges', he told one reporter. 'He is a dream boy to manage and never any trouble. He trains whenever he is told and listens to every bit of advice'.

There was a small consolation for Lazar during the summer of that year when he became one of a very small number of boxers to have the unique honour of sparring in the grounds of Buckingham Palace. The others were Jack Gardner, Johnny Williams and Freddie Mills. The occasion was before an invited audience at an open-air function on behalf of the Not Forgotten Association.

Lew Lazar was a dedicated professional, easy to manage and train and was extremely game. He never spoke badly of other fighters or boasted of his own success. He received a great deal of hero worshipping from his many Jewish admirers in the East End and could always claim to be a credit to the sport he loved.

A fitting tribute to him appeared in an edition of *Boxing News* whilst he was still fighting. It said:

> Few fighters get the crowd on their toes as does Lew Lazar of Aldgate. Few fighters make every fight look as hard as Lazar and few fighters get blood stained as often as he. Lew Lazar is a promoter's dream fighter and his raw battle with Dennis Booty of Stepney was a crowd pleaser that thrilled everybody

In retirement, Lew eventually did the knowledge and became a London taxi driver for many years. In 1981 he was living in Basildon, Essex and died April 2010 aged seventy-nine.

Traceable Record
60 Contests
48 Won
4 Drew
8 Lost

21

MARK LESNICK

(Stepney)

Had Mark Lesnick been around in modern times he would never have been granted a licence to box because he had extremely poor eyesight from birth, but with no Board of Control or stringent medical controls in his day, anything went.

Mark was born in Stepney on 10 December 1906 of a poor Jewish family. As a lad, he lived with his father, Jacob, his mother, Leah, brothers, Aaron and Morris and sister Bessie in squalid surroundings.

Although no previous member of his family had boxed, he loved the sport from an early age and joined the Brady Street Club when he was age fourteen. He had about 80 amateur contests, his major successes being London Federation of boy's club's junior and senior championships in 1922 and 23 at 6 st 7 lbs and 7 st. He had barely reached seventeen when he turned professional to help support his family, his manager being Morris Gordon and his trainers Harry Goodman and George Carney.

Mark made his debut at Premierland on 23 March 1924. Although there was a tram and bus strike that night it had little effect on the attendance, with the new famous arena being packed as usual. Despite weighing barely 7 st, he had an all action, come forward style and was unfazed by the new surroundings. Showing immense talent, he stormed into action at the opening bell attacking his opponent, Kid Martin from Queens Park with heavy hooks to the head and body before knocking him out in the opening round.

The Premierland faithful quickly took to Lesnick who had a large following. He had his first 37 fights there and a total of 48 during his career. Progressing rapidly, he was soon established as the 'house fighter', being matched over 15 two-minute rounds in only his fifth contest. From that stage all were made over the same distance with just two exceptions, one over 20 rounds and the other over 10.

By the end of 1924, Mark had won all of his 12 contests in only nine months, but it was not all plain sailing and he nearly came unstuck in the last fight which was against Harry Hill from Birmingham, who pushed him to the limit. At the end he was extremely lucky to get referee, Sam Russell's, decision which many in the crowd thought was harsh on his opponent. Afterwards, however, it was discovered that the Stepney youngster had severely damaged his right hand during the early rounds.

Mark's all-action style enabled him to win against good-quality opponents and his winning streak lasted 14 months. It eventually came to an end in his 19th contest as a professional against Dod Oldfield from Leeds at Premierland on 21 May 1925 in what was the first of six meetings between them. Four would take place that year, all at the same venue.

The decision in favour of Oldfield caused uproar and the following week the trade paper *Boxing* stated:

> There certainly seemed perfect justification for the packed house going off at the deep, when Charles Barnett gave Oldfield the decision. It was the Stepney boy's first defeat and how on earth the official arrived at his verdict is a thing to be wondered at.

A return was inevitable and took place 10 days later. It was made over 15 three-minute rounds at 7st 10 lbs with side stakes of £50. Intense from the opening bell, it was incredibly close as the two great, little men battled for supremacy. The referee's decision of a draw was, on this occasion, a popular one.

With both sides keen to establish who was the better man, a third meeting was staged two months later. Again, it went all the way and this time the Stepney boy got the decision after what *Boxing* described as 'a rattling good bout'.

Their fourth meeting was in September and ended in another draw after which *Boxing* commented 'Lesnick was doing all the forcing, Oldfield the boxing, but Lesnick was the stronger at the close'.

In between the last two contests Mark had a tear up with Frankie Ash from Plymouth. He had the experience of almost 100 contests behind him and in 1924 had gone the distance with Pancho Villa in a challenge for the world flyweight championship in New York. The ending to the contest, however, was disappointing because after eight gruelling rounds the referee declared it a no contest because both men were continually using illegal tactics.

They met twice more, firstly in October 1925 when Ash was disqualified for illegal use of the head and again in January the following year when the Plymouth man got the decision. All three contests were staged at Premierland over 15 three-minute rounds.

Although he had not conclusively beaten Ash in three contests, Lesnick was confident of his own ability to take on the best men in his division. With that in mind he issued a challenge to fellow East End star Teddy Baldock of Poplar. Clearly accepting that the Stepney man posed a threat, Teddy's people wanted the fight to be made at 8 st 2 lbs, well above Marks natural weight. As it was too much to concede to a man of Baldock's ability, a contest between them failed to materialise.

After losing to Ash in January 1926, Mark's form appeared to drop. Although he managed to draw with former European champion, Michael Montreuil of Belgium, he had to wait almost two years for his next victory. In the meantime, he lost eight out of 11 contests. Among those who beat him were Young Johnny Brown (Stepney), Young Jackie Brown (twice) and Phil Lolosky (Aldgate).

A fight with Johnny Hill at Premierland in August 1926 was one which Mark always remembered because of the controversial ending. By this stage of his career he had engaged former Stepney flyweight, Joe Wilson, as his trainer. Joe knew the game inside out and during his career pushed Sid Smith close in a fight for the British flyweight title in 1911. During their preparations for the Hill fight he tried to change Mark's style to that of a straight left boxer, as opposed to that of an out and out cyclone type fighter.

Despite carrying out the trainer's instructions, Mark was no match for the Scotsman so in round 11 when Wilson told him he was behind on points, he reverted to his usual aggressive style. With just 20 seconds of the final round to go, Hill's seconds already had his stool in the ring and during a set-to in the corner the stool caught Mark's ankle severely damaging a tendon. He fell to the floor in pain and hung on to Hills legs until the bell ended the contest.

There was pandemonium as his seconds screamed at the referee for Hill to be disqualified, while on the opposite side of the ring Johnny's cornermen were making identical demands because Lesnick had been holding his opponent whilst lying on the canvas. The referee was left with little choice other than to rule a no contest, a decision which infuriated the crowd and prompted a free-for-all at the ringside. Apart from sustaining the bad ankle injury, Mark was hit by a chair thrown into the ring by an irate spectator.

The injuries he sustained kept the Stepney boxer out of action for 12 months. Johnny Hill meanwhile, went on to win the British title the following year and the European crown in 1928.

When he returned Mark was disqualified in round six against Billy James but two months later squared up yet again to Dod Oldfield, this time at Forest Gate Skating Rink. Like their previous encounters it was a crowd-pleaser, which Lesnick lost on points and *Boxing* described it as 'blood and thunder all the way'. They met again for the sixth time two months later at the same venue and again the man from Leeds got the nod.

During 1928, Mark's form improved considerably, and he lost just three of 15 contests, one of which was to Oldfield. There were two during that period which stood out for different reasons. At Premierland in March against Nipper Pat Daly, a brilliant fifteen-year-old who had already engaged in almost 50 contests, referee, Jack Hart, called a halt after 11 rounds and ruled it a no contest. He considered that both boys were guilty of too many infringements which were creating an extremely poor contest. In view of that ruling a steward of the Board of Control ordered that both contestants purses be withheld pending an enquiry.

At Premierland six months later, Lesnick faced Ernie Jarvis from Millwall, a grand little battler with over 140 bouts behind him, a high percentage of which were victories. The result was a draw after 15 absorbing rounds and was Mark's best performance for some considerable time.

Although he was still difficult to beat, Mark was coming towards the end of his career. Despite beating and drawing with Kid Rich (Aldgate) within the space of three weeks, the problems with his eyesight had worsened. Having kept matters very much to himself, the extremity was first noticed by the wife of his manager, Morrie Gordon. He decided to put his man to the test and holding up his hands asked Lesnick how many fingers he could see. Mark guessed wrong. 'That's it' said the manager. 'You're finished'.

Lesnick, however, was booked to fight at Liverpool the following night and pleaded to be allowed to go through with it. He had originally been due to fight an Italian, but when he pulled out Evan Lane, a young Welshman having his first contest over 15 rounds, deputised. Mark was confident he could handle the new opponent and pleaded with his manager not to pull him out unless he was in serious trouble.

Despite being much lighter than Lane, who scaled 8st 4 lbs, Mark won clearly on points after giving an aggressive performance. That victory represented his last ring appearance after a five-year career in which he was never stopped. He had known about his eyesight problem throughout and in later years told a *Boxing News* reporter: 'After every fight I would go home and cry myself to sleep because of my bad eyes, something I succeeded in keeping to myself until the end of my career'.

Having been compelled to retire from the ring, Mark underwent an operation during the summer of 1929, but with no other occupation to turn to, was soon in desperate need of financial help. On hearing of his plight, referee and former boxer Sam Russell, well known for his ever-ready generosity, got together with a group of local sportsmen and staged a concert for his benefit at the People's Palace. It was a huge success and news of Mark's difficulties spread throughout the East End.

A highly respected young man both in and out of the ring, Lesnick desperately wanted to remain in the sport that he loved. Again, it was Russell and his colleagues who were on hand to help him by forming the Stepney Social Club at 52a Bancroft Road, close to Stepney Green Station where they put Mark in charge. He wasted no time in setting up a small well-equipped gym where, after taking out a Board of Control trainers licence he developed and managed a number of young East End boxers. He also became an agent acting on behalf of those from the continent wanting to fight in Britain.

Apart from regulars Moe Mizler, Kid Farlo, Moe Moss, Dave Finn and others, plenty of big name fighters used his gym from time to time. They included George Cook, Eddie Phillips, Archie Sexton, Harry Mason, Harry Mizler and Jack Kid Berg who was particularly supportive towards Mark. At the beginning of February 1930, when he arrived back from America for his fight with undisputed world junior lightweight champion, Mushy Callahan, he told a group of press reporters that he was going straight to Mark's gym to do a public workout and raise some money for him.

Within a few months of taking over the club, Lesnick obtained a promoter's licence and staged his first show in early March. The seven-fight bill produced some exhilarating scraps and his programmes of short distance contests, which he call Sprint bouts, proved extremely popular, attracting ever increasing audiences. Staged on Friday evenings and Sunday mornings each week, they ran for several years. He even had a full house on Christmas day 1931.

Support for Lesnick came from all quarters with Primo Carnera and Young Stribling making guest appearances. On a special evening in May 1931, Panama Al Brown, in London to defend his title against Teddy Baldock, was a guest of Sam Russell and sat through the entire programme.

In 1936, Mark married Vickie and they had three sons, Barry, Malcom and Jeffrey. When war broke out he joined the Royal Army Ordnance Corps and later explained that he only got in because 'They were taking anybody'. After nine months, however, his eyesight problem was identified, and he was discharged.

The family moved to Hitchin in Hertfordshire after their London home was blitzed during the war and he became a market trader. After retiring he assisted one of his sons in a children's clothing business. Even in the later years of his life, Mark remained a fitness fanatic, carrying on many of the routines he learned while boxing.

Throughout his career Lesnick was a rough, tough, muscular little fighter with a reputation for breaking the rules. During his career he was disqualified on four occasions and involved in three other bouts which were ruled 'no contest' because of what went on between him and his opponent. He had no regrets about never getting the chance to contest a championship but was extremely proud when his photograph appeared on the front cover of *Boxing,* now *Boxing News,* dated 5 November 1924 bearing the caption 'The consistently successful paperweight cyclone'.

Marc Lesnick was a typical brave little East End crowd-pleaser from a poor background. He had a huge following and it was a tragedy that his career was cut short. He died in November 1992, aged eighty-five.

Traceable record:
55 Contests
30 Won
8 Drew
13 Lost
4 NC

22

TED 'KID' LEWIS

(Aldgate)

BRITISH FEATHERWEIGHT CHAMPION 1913 - 14
UNDEFEATED

EUROPEAN FEATHERWEIGHT CHAMPION 1914
UNDEFEATED

BRITISH AND BRITISH EMPIRE WELTERWEIGHT
CHAMPION 1920 – 24

EUROPEAN WELTERWEIGHT CHAMPION 1920
UNDEFEATED

WORLD WELTERWEIGHT CHAMPION 1915 - 16 AND
1917 -19

BRITISH MIDDLEWEIGHT TITLE CLAIMANT 1920 – 21

EUROPEAN MIDDLEWEIGHT CHAMPION 1921 – 23

BRITISH MIDDLEWEIGHT CHAMPION 1921 – 23

BRITISH EMPIRE MIDDLEWEIGHT CHAMPION 1922 – 23

It is no exaggeration to refer to Ted 'Kid' Lewis as arguably the greatest pound-for-pound fighter Britain has ever produced. In a professional career between 1909 and 1929 he took part in 42 championship contests between featherweight and light heavy, 29 of which were in America.

Whilst there could never be any doubt about his talent and ability there was, however, always some dispute about his age. The record books give his date of birth as 24 October 1894 but in his book *'The Big Punchers'* the late Reg Gutteridge, OBE, insisted that Lewis was a year older. Ted himself claimed he was born in October 1896 which if true would have made him only sixteen when he beat Eric Lambert for the British featherweight title at the National Sporting Club on 6 October 1913.

Yet more confusion arose in 1990 when Ted's son published an in-depth biography of his father entitled *'Ted Kid Lewis - His Life and Times'* and stated that he was in fact born on 28 October 1893. Whichever date is true matters not one iota, because it takes nothing away from the overall achievements of the great man.

His true name was Gershon Mendelhoff and he was born in the basement of 56 Umberstone Street, Aldgate. His parents, Solomon and Leah, had fled from Russia some years earlier and his father, a cabinet maker by trade, set up a business in the East End and brought up his family of eight children on £2 a week.

Gershon, the third child, experienced extreme poverty as a youngster often having to make do with a slice of bread and dripping for his daily nourishment. His health was also a problem and necessitated frequent visits to hospital which was a constant source of worry to his mother.

He attended the Jewish Free School but was frequently admonished by his teachers for preferring fighting to regular classroom lessons. With times being so hard he had to rush home after school to help his father at the workshop. In 1906, Gershon left school to start an apprenticeship with his father, who lied to the school authorities by saying his son was fourteen when in fact he was only twelve. By the age of fourteen, despite being virtually skin and bones, the young Mendlehoff was the leader of a gang of about 20 other Jewish lads for whom fighting became an obsession. They were frequently involved in scraps with other local East End gangs at a time when there was a great deal of anti-Semitic feeling in the area. It was as a result of one such scrap in August 1906 that led to him becoming involved in boxing.

The fight in the street with a local rival was well underway when a policeman intervened. He pulled the two youngsters apart and without too much fuss suggested that if they wanted to fight they should go along to the Judean Club just off Cable Street where they could do so and get paid. Although Gershon went straight there his rival failed to turn up, but it made no difference because the prospect of being paid meant a great deal to him.

Asked by Club secretary, Sam Kite, for his name, he did not say Gershon Mendlehoff for the fear of his father finding out. He was a very strict man and although he had an intimate knowledge of the fight game, he was totally set against people doing it for money. Thinking quickly, he said his name was Lewis, which was the surname of American boxer, Harry Lewis, whose photographs he had seen in a newspaper. 'Kid' was added because of his tender age and the Christian name of 'Ted' would feature some years later.

When he started boxing, he was a mere slip of a boy, white faced, frail and underdeveloped with nothing but his fiery enthusiasm. On one occasion as he climbed into the ring, a worried spectator shouted for 'heaven's sake don't let this poor kid box he'll be killed'.

Kid Lewis had his first recorded contest at the Judean Club on 29 August 1909 against Kid Da Costa, a lad of similar age and height from Mile End who beat him on points over six rounds. The fight was refereed by Young Joseph. Two weeks later he suffered a similar defeat to Johnny Sharpe, another East End lad, later to become a successful boxing trainer and manager. Ted was paid sixpence for his efforts and given a cake but afterwards Sharpe told him to join the Judean Club, as did Sam Kite, who offered him another fight the following weekend

That's when it all really began, but times were hard. Ted was in fact so poor that he arrived at the club one day without boxing shoes. He was prepared to box in his socks, but another boy who had been beaten took pity on him and gave him his. In the fight, which he won well, Lewis showed all the courage that would characterise him throughout his career.

By the end of 1912 he had crammed in an incredible 122 bouts, losing just a handful. Despite scaling little over seven stone he became a real favourite at the club where he had the majority of his fights until the end of 1911, 73 in all.

His regular hunting ground then became Premierland, having boxed there on the opening show on 11 December 1911, outpointing Billy Taylor (Bethnal Green) over eight rounds. It was the first of his 48 contests at the new venue, 35 of which took place between January and December the following year.

Fighting almost weekly since he began Lewis' progress was incredible. Although he lost the occasional contest on points, the only serious setback was against Duke Lynch from Camberwell who he had outpointed at Premierland in February 1912. It had been an extremely controversial verdict which infuriated a member of the National Sporting Club who was present at the East End arena. Afterwards he told Lynch to go to the club the next morning and tell the matchmaker Peggy Bettinson, that he the member would back the boxer for £25 in a re-match with Lewis. Bettinson duly made the match for purses and side stakes totalling £80, to go on at the club on 1 April. It was an important break for Lewis who despite being unbeaten in his last 50 or so contests, had rarely boxed away from East End venues, but was due some top-class exposure.

Although Ted was a 2-1 on favourite few could have anticipated what occurred. Caught by a hard right to the chin in the opening 15 seconds he took a count of 'eight' and on rising on shaky legs, was hammered down again for a count of 'nine'. A final right resulted in him taking the full count and it was all over in 55 seconds. Such a devastating defeat had no effect on Lewis and two days later he travelled to Paris where he outpointed Leon Truffler over 10 rounds. He rounded off a hectic week by knocking out Gus Venn in seven rounds at Premierland. A knockout defeat followed by two victories all in the space of five days was a clear indication that the teenager was a very special talent.

Midway through the following year the class of Lewis was officially recognised, and he was matched with Joe Starmer at the National Sporting Club in an eliminator for the British featherweight title. He won clearly on points and after more successes, one against Duke Lynch, he faced Alec Lambert for the vacant British and Empire titles. Lambert, the son of the club whip, outboxed Ted for 16 rounds, but could not match his pace and slumped to a stoppage defeat in the next session. A few months later, Lewis added the European crown to his honours beating Paul Til of France on a disqualification in round 12.

A triple champion at such a young age brought him to the attention of promoters overseas and in 1914 he accepted an offer for fights in Australia. Almost a welterweight by this time he packed in five 20-rounders there in a hectic 63-day tour, losing just one. He then moved to the United States where, based in New York he put himself under the guidance of Charlie Harvey who specialised in handling English boxers.

Although the majority of Ted's early contests in America were of no decision, he quickly endeared himself to the fight fans. He became so at home there that he didn't box in Britain again until December 1919 almost 100 fights later.

At the time, the world's welterweight championship was going through one of its spells of confusion, but the claim of champion most widely accepted was that of Jack Britton. When he and Lewis first met in March 1915, the Londoner had the better of a no decision 10-rounder. A string of good performances followed including a decision over highly rated Mike Glover and earned Ted a rematch with Britton in the American's hometown of Boston in August that same year.

Unlike New York, points decisions were permissible in Boston and Ted's 12 round victory there completed the long road from being a Judean Club novice to world champion and universally accepted as such. The experience he gained at the East End club proved far more valuable than the sixpenny and one shilling purses he was paid.

Despite the importance of the contest there were a series of disputes raised by Britton's handlers over a number of issues. Although these were eventually resolved, further trouble flared up once they were in the ring. No sooner had the first bell sounded than the champion suddenly dropped his hands and returned to his corner refusing to fight because Lewis was wearing a mouthpiece.

A violent argument followed between the boxers, their seconds and the referee, who eventually ordered Ted to remove it. When he refused the hostilities continued before Lewis suddenly realised he was playing into Britton's hands. Pulling the object from his mouth he flung it at Jack's feet shouting: 'Alright then, lets fight.'

It was later claimed that Lewis was the first British boxer to wear a gumshield in a world title fight. It was relatively new in boxing with much of its technology being credited to another Aldgate boxer Jack Marks a professional from 1909 to 1919 with almost 200 fights to his name.

Ted repeated his success over Britton four weeks later and when he got the better of Willie Ritchie in New York in December, albeit in a no decision contest, he was universally accepted as champion.

Over the next four years Lewis met the best welter and middleweights in the world, earning himself a fortune as probably the best and most consistent European ever to fight in America. He faced Jack Britton an incredible 20 times between March 1915 and February 1921 with the title being contested on 15 occasions. He lost it to Jack in New Orleans in April 1916 but regained it from him in Ohio 14 months later before Britton ended his reign with a ninth-round knockout at Canton on St. Patrick's Day 1919.

Realistically, Ted should have been nearing the end of his career because, despite only being in his late twenties, he had already engaged in about 240 recorded fights. Instead he returned to England in late 1919 and embarked on another phase of his incredible career which saw him win British, European and Empire championships at welter and middleweight as well as making an audacious challenge for the world light-heavyweight crown.

Jack Britton failed his final bid to regain his old welterweight crown in 1921 but victories over Johnny Basham and Jack Bloomfield confirmed that Ted was still unbeatable in two divisions at British and European level. When he beat Bloomfield for the British middleweight title in June 1921, Lewis scaled one and a half pounds inside the welter limit. Then, five months later he built himself up to 11st 9lbs to tackle light-heavyweight champion, Noel 'Boy' McCormack, who he stopped in 14 rounds at the Royal Albert Hall, although his victory was not officially recognised as being for the title.

Ted's next performance was even more remarkable because at Brighton in February the following year, weighing only 11st 6lbs he took on Tom Gummer, a useful heavyweight scaling in 13st 10lbs and knocked him out in the opening round. On the strength of those last two contests he was matched with charismatic Frenchman, Georges Carpentier, for the world heavyweight crown at Olympia on 11 May 1922. Again, he gave away considerable weight scaling just 10st 12lbs, 23lbs lighter than the Frenchman.

In reality it was a fight Lewis could never win by conceding so much weight to a man of Carpentier's class. Yet, Ted's reputation ensured that the promotion was a huge success with receipts of £43,000 breaking the record for an indoor boxing event. The contest had created so much interest that it was arranged for flares to be fired to signal the result to the huge crowds gathered outside the arena. Green would indicate a Lewis victory and red for defeat.

Within two minutes red lights lit up the sky because Ted had been knocked out in the opening round. The ending, however, was very controversial with furious arguments that the Frenchman should have been disqualified. The fight had started at breakneck speed as Lewis tore into Carpentier who, although fighting back furiously, could not keep him off. He hung on grimly and twice threw punches dangerously low. Barely half a minute had elapsed before Lewis complained bitterly to referee, Joe Palmer, about his opponent's tactics. As the third man pulled them apart, Ted threw himself back into action and hurt the Frenchman who, perplexed and anxious, grabbed and held again.

'Stop' shouted Palmer who then admonished Lewis who dropped his gloves and protested that he was trying to fight. The referee was still holding his wrist when Carpentier unleashed a deadly straight left to the jaw. Ted fell heavily to the floor where he stayed on his knees to be counted out.

There were thunderous protests from all parts of the arena as everyone except those in the French corner shouted 'foul'. Lord Lonsdale led the contemporary opinion that Lewis had been cheated. By the fact that Palmer was still in physical contact with him when the fatal blow was landed meant that Carpentier should have been disqualified. His sportsmanship was also questionable.

Despite his anger and disappointment, Ted regrouped and quickly moved on. Five weeks later he knocked out hard-hitting Australian, Frankie Burns in 11 rounds at Holland Park to reclaim the British Empire middleweight title. In November he successfully defended the British, European and Empire titles by outpointing Roland Todd but in a return at the Royal Albert Hall three months later, Todd relieved him of the titles with a 20-round points victory.

By this time Ted was playing the music halls and even travelled to South Africa performing in Cape Town, Durban and Johannesburg. When he returned to England in July 1923 he faced Augie Ratner at the Royal Albert Hall but was outpointed over 20 rounds. In October, however, he got back into more regular action taking a fight a month well into 1924 and remaining undefeated in bouts at Premierland, Milan, Paris, Hamburg and Berlin. In July he successfully defended his British and Empire welterweight titles with a points victory over Hamilton Johnny Brown, but lost them to Tommy Milligan who outpointed him in Edinburgh in November.

Although Ted fought for many years on the big stage in America, he wound down his career mainly back in the East End including eight further contests at Premierland. After the occasional contest in South Africa, America and Canada he brought the curtain down on an incredible career with a third-round knockout victory over Johnny Basham at Hoxton Baths in December 1929.

Lewis had an incredibly full life, doing and achieving so much. In America he fought the legendary Benny Leonard, sparred with Jack Dempsey and Jack Johnson and in 1964, thirty-five years after he retired from the ring, was honoured by being elected into the Hall of Fame.

Following his retirement, he continued to serve boxing in capacities from trainer to manager, promoter and referee. Even while still fighting he was involved in the running of Premierland for a short while but found it too complicated. He was also matchmaker at Collins Music Hall, Islington and Ilford Skating Rink for a while and had his own stable of young boxers in the late 1940's. He spent time in Hungary where he was employed by the government as a 'tutor of boxing'. An articulate man, he wrote a weekly column in the paper *Boxing, Racing and Football.*

Outside boxing he owned clubs in Soho, played the music halls and had parts in films. His kindness was incredible, especially for the ill-kempt kids of the East End where he was lionised. Children frequently filed behind him as he walked the streets of Whitechapel. He organised coach trips for them all to the seaside each summer absorbing all the costs personally.

Ted was always willing to attend fund raising events and contributed generously to the individual charities even after he had given away most of his hard-earned fortune. Yet, he always remained in touch with his sport and was constantly in demand for the role of guest of honour at boxing related functions. He was a massively popular and respected figure and remained so until he passed away on 20 October 1970. At his funeral at East Ham Cemetery, the rabbi spoke of the honour he brought to the Jewish people by his skill in so many countries all over the world.

Because different publications quote varying figures, it is impossible to compile a concise ring record for Lewis. It is therefore reasonable to accept that which is contained at the rear of his biography as being the most accurate;

Traceable Record
299 CONTESTS

193 WON
14 DREW
28 LOST
64 ND

23

SAMMY McCARTHY

(Stepney)

BRITISH FEATHERWEIGHT CHAMPION
1954 - 1955

'The nicest man in boxing' is the phrase which has for years been used to describe former British featherweight champion, Sammy McCarthy. It is moving that despite some serious setbacks in his life this genuinely nice guy has remained in such high esteem.

An extremely polite, quiet and well-mannered man, he has remained as popular in modern times as he was back in the 1950's when he packed boxing arenas particularly in the East End. Warmth has radiated from Sammy throughout his life and he has always retained the familiar smile that earned him the affectionate title of 'Smiling Sammy' when he was a young amateur boxer.

Born in Stepney on Guy Fawkes day 1931, Sammy was the sixth child of a family of ten; six girls and four boys. 'As far as I can say, I am half Irish and half Jewish', he once remarked. 'Both my grandmothers were Jewish, and my grandfathers were from the Emerald Isle'.

Following the outbreak of the Second World War, Sammy, along with many other youngsters from the East End was evacuated to Egham in Surrey where he remained for five years. Only when he returned to Stepney did he become involved in boxing. His elder brother, Freddie, a good amateur who won a junior ABA Championship in 1938, persuaded him to join the Stepney and St Georges Club and learn to look after himself.

An extremely popular and well-run club which originally had its headquarters at The Highway, it eventually moved to Smithy Street. It did a tremendous amount to keep East End kids off the streets and regularly staged successful boxing tournaments before full houses at Poplar Baths and East India Hall.

Sammy's grandfather had also been a capable performer in his day and with boxing in the family blood he progressed well. His trainer was Johnny Mann, a good featherweight out of Stepney and St Georges during the 1920's and early 30's who also had a successful amateur career with Limehouse and Poplar ABC.

Sammy had an abundance of natural talent and desperately wanted to follow in Freddie's footsteps. He had incredible enthusiasm and after his first amateur contest in early 1946 always believed he would become a champion.

His dream was not long in coming and in 1947 he won the North East London Divisional junior title at 7st. In February the following year he won a London Youth Clubs 'B' championship at 7st 7lbs. That success progressed him into the Junior ABA semi-finals at Wembley where, after a close and thrilling contest, he was beaten on points.

Although he was a good junior, Sammy really came to notice in his first senior bout when he outpointed Norman Watts (Fitzroy Lodge) in January 1949. Watts was a proven competitor having won the North West London Divisional Bantamweight title the previous year and was being tipped to win an ABA title. Yet the packed audience watched in amazement at the youngster's skill and maturity as he strode to victory. He beat Norman again three weeks later at Mile End in what *Boxing News* described as one of the finest bouts seen in London that season.

From that moment Sammy's following grew rapidly and the Sammy McCarthy Fan Club was formed. Whenever he boxed at least a dozen coach loads of fans would leave from the Hope and Anchor public house at Watney Street to support him. Throughout the East End, billboards were set up advertising 'McCarthy fights tonight – fare 2/6d.'

Throughout his amateur career Sammy worked for his father who had a greengrocery business. Every morning he was up at 5.30am and caught a bus to Spitalfields market where he loaded a barrow with vegetables which he then pulled the two miles back to Watney Street. After helping his father set up his own barrow he took the empty one back to the market before returning home and accompanying his father on their regular round of the Stepney Streets.

With this demanding daily routine Sammy did not need to do any roadwork, but four evenings a week he trained at the boxing club with Johnny Mann anxious to perfect his style and remedy faults. Injury, however, prevented him from pursuing ABA titles in 1949 and 1950, but when finally fit in 1951 he was narrowly outpointed by Ron Hinson (West Ham) in the North East London Divisional Championships.

Although he failed to win a major amateur title, Sammy was nonetheless extremely successful in the unpaid ranks. The fact that he lost only seven of about 90 contests and boxed for England on four occasions is testimony of his undoubted ability.

McCarthy was just nineteen when he turned professional with Jack King although before anything was agreed Jack asked trainer, Snowy Buckingham, to look him over. When Sammy arrived at Jack Solomons' gym at Windmill Street, Snowy couldn't believe he was a boxer. 'He looked so smart and acted like a gentleman', the trainer recalled years later. When the young boxer opened his bag, the trainer got another shock: 'I'd never seen a bag more neatly, cleanly or carefully packed,' he remarked.

The East End lad made a perfect start to his professional career, knocking out Hector Macrow in just 57 seconds of the first round at Earls Court on 30 April 1951. During the next five weeks three more quick victories followed, but Sammy's first real test came against Freddie Hicks of Bermondsey in November. There were two occasions during the contest when it looked as though he had been overmatched and although the referee called it a draw, general opinion was that the Stepney youngster was very fortunate. Sammy always retained a vivid recollection of that fight and in one interview years later remarked; 'Perhaps the referee was rather kind to me that night. I wouldn't have complained if I had lost'.

McCarthy's popularity was incredible and increased with every contest. It was not just confined to the East End because in February 1952 readers of *Boxing News* voted him the best British-born boxer of 1951. Although just a shy twenty-one-year-old barrow boy, he had aroused a fight frenzy in the East End just like Teddy Baldock, Jack 'Kid' Berg and Ted 'Kid' Lewis had years earlier. He punched harder than in his amateur days and his exciting style ensured that whenever he boxed the venue was sold out.

On 27 July 1952, Mile End Arena was packed for what Sammy always referred to as the hardest fight of his career. His opponent in an eight-rounder was Johnny Molloy of St Helens, who had been a professional for nine years. During that time he had faced Ray Famechon of France and most of the top men in Britain including Ronnie Clayton whom he beat in 1948, but lost to in a title fight the following year.

Molloy took everything that was thrown at him and by round five looked well in command. In the following round Sammy bled from the nose and was cut over the left eye. He was in serious trouble but hit back viciously only to play into Molloy's hands. Heavy rights put him down for a count of 'nine', the first time he had been floored as a professional. On rising he was put under immediate pressure and driven across the ring before going down again for a count of 'eight'.

Sammy, however, never lacked courage and with wonderful fighting instinct fought back bravely. His tremendous attacking skills and determination turned the fight around and frustrated all of his opponent's efforts to end it. He kept it up until the final bell and was rewarded with an extremely close decision.

The popularity of McCarthy and the intensity of the fight were condensed in a moving report by the *East London Advertiser* a few days later:

> Magnificent Sammy McCarthy, the boyish-looking boxing idol of the East End, fought his greatest, grandest and most gruelling fight of his short career at the Mile End Arena on Tuesday when, in an eight-round contest packed with explosive excitement, he sensationally outpointed Johnny Molloy of St Helens in spite of being floored twice in the sixth round. The following that this modest and quiet young boxing hope has in the East End today must equal that of any boxer in by gone years. The arena was jammed tight with fans 15 minutes before the programme started and notices that only ticket holders would be allowed in, were posted outside.

After stopping his first overseas opponent, Jan Maas, the featherweight champion of Holland in three rounds, Sammy became a leading contender for Ronnie Clayton's British title. Promoter, Jack Solomons, matched them at catchweights over 10 rounds on a charity show at Harringay on 10 December in the presence of his Royal Highness, The Duke of Edinburgh. Again, Sammy put on a brilliant display to narrowly outpoint the champion. As he was putting on his dressing gown and preparing to leave the ring he heard a voice suddenly call out; 'Stay where you are son, The Duke wants to see you!'.

McCarthy and Clayton were then taken to the ringside and introduced to the Royal Guest. 'That was a good fight,' he told them. 'I enjoyed every second of it. You boys will have to box again, and I'll see if I can get a night off and come and see it'.

For his success against Clayton, Sammy was awarded a *Boxing News* Certificate of Merit for the best performance of December 1952. He was also presented with a silver belt having been voted by readers of the publication, as the fighter who did most for British boxing in 1952.

McCarthy continued to progress in 1953 with a series of victories over Continental opposition and eventually in September, the Board of Control ordered Clayton to defend the British title against him. Jack Solomons wanted to stage the fight before Christmas, but the Board extended the champion's period of grace to enable him to fulfil an engagement in South Africa.

Anxious to keep busy, Sammy faced Hogan Bassey of Nigeria who, since arriving in the UK less than two years earlier, had a record of 19 victories from 26 contests. Not much was known about him in London as he had only boxed in the capital twice, winning one and losing the other. He was therefore not expected to pose McCarthy too many problems.

The fight turned out to be full of brilliant boxing. It was one for the connoisseurs and everything rested on the final round which Bassey took much to the dismay of the London fans. Although it was his first professional defeat in 29 contests, Sammy had no complaints because he had learned a great deal from it.

The following month he suffered another setback, being outpointed by former European Champion, Ray Famechon. More disappointment was to follow because when Ronnie Clayton withdrew from a British title fight, Sammy was matched with European Champion, Jean Sneyers of Belgium. Again, he found the step up in class too great and lost on points over 15 rounds.

The British title fight with Clayton eventually took place at the White City on 1 June 1954. When they came together in the centre of the ring for the referee's final instructions the champion said, 'Evening Sammy, let's have a nice fight.' With his usual courtesy Sammy replied, 'Yes of course Mr Clayton'.

Having belatedly got his chance, McCarthy made no mistake. He boxed brilliantly, and the contest became very one sided. The end came when Ronnie retired at the end of round eight suffering loss of vision.

Sammy insisted on being a fighting champion and by the end of the year was unbeaten in a further four contests, the last of which was a brilliant 10-round points victory over Gold Coast star, Roy Ankrah. In the new year however, he unwisely agreed to defend his title in Belfast against Billy 'Spider' Kelly. Whilst training in Brighton he sustained a recurrence of an injury to his right hand initially picked up during the fight with Ankrah. Stupidly, he made no mention of it to his manager or trainer as he knew they would call off the fight.

It was set for Belfast on 22 January 1955, but adverse weather seriously affected the journey. All planes were grounded due to fog which resulted in Sammy and his handlers spending 19 hours travelling from London by train and then boat and depriving him of a hotel bed for the night before the fight.

Kelly gave a fine exhibition of boxing and took a wide points decision. It was one of Sammy's worst performances and only in the final round did he slug it out in a desperate attempt to hang on to his title. Typically, he made no excuse for his defeat, despite the fact that he could have put forward a number of reasons including the fact that his damaged hand gave way during round four and that he had struggled to make the championship weight of nine stone.

Sammy's attitude was affected badly by the defeat and he became confused and disinterested in boxing. It was five months before his old zest came back and he wanted to become a champion again. He returned to the ring in June and ran up a string of six victories, five inside the distance but then in November was narrowly outpointed by old foe, Jean Sneyers.

Moving up to lightweight, he faced British champion, Frank Johnson, over 10 rounds at the Royal Albert Hall in January 1956. Being more comfortable at the higher weight he gave the champion a real beating by winning every round. It was McCarthy at this very best but just when it seemed he was heading for another title everything came apart.

During April, in a fight which attracted tremendous betting, he was narrowly outpointed by the young up-and-coming Dave Charnley. It was a wonderful fight and although he was on the floor for long counts in the second and third rounds, Sammy attacked for all he was worth. His biggest obstacle, however, was the fact that he was facing a southpaw for the first time in his career.

Dave was still not twenty-one and not eligible to fight for the British title, so McCarthy was matched with the champion, Joe Lucy (Mile End) over 15 rounds at Wembley on 26 June. Although it was an all East-End affair, it was very tame. Sammy was floored for a count of 'seven' in the opening round and quickly fell a long way behind. When referee, Ike Powell, went to his corner at the end of round 12 and enquired how he felt, Sammy replied; 'I am alright, thank you Mr Powell'. In the next round, however, the official decided he was too far behind to have a realistic chance of winning, so he stopped the fight.

Although he was in no physical difficulty, the decision deprived Sammy of his extremely proud and credible record of having never been stopped. Convinced that he still had plenty to offer he regrouped and beat Midlands Area champion, Johnny Mann, twice on points over 10 rounds and stopped Johnny Miller and former French champion, Jaques Dumesnil, in six and four rounds respectively before the end of the year.

Sammy's final contest was on 22 January 1957 when he was outpointed by Frenchman, Guy Gracia, who had already beaten Charnley and Lucy. Again, McCarthy sustained damage to his right hand and sensibly accepted he was past his best and announced his retirement.

Two months later the BBC honoured him with a *This Is Your Life* programme. It was a fitting end to the career of one of Britain's most popular champions. Among the guests were former opponents Hector Macrow, Jean Sneyers and Ronnie Clayton. Another celebrity was Terry Spinks who as a young schoolboy idolised Sammy and often sat on his doorstep at Commercial Road waiting for him to come home. Three months earlier the youngster had won the Olympic flyweight championship and gold medal at Melbourne. During the programme he told Sammy that he was about to turn professional and wanted him to become his manager. The request was immediately accepted.

McCarthy took out a manager's licence and apart from Spinks also handled Canning Town boxers, Terry Gill, Terry Brown and Brian Bissmire amongst others. Spinks was by far the most successful, winning the British featherweight title while Gill became Southern Area welterweight champion.

All of Sammy's boxers trained at the Thomas A'Beckett gym in the Old Kent Road. Whilst they were dedicated to their work, he was constantly on his guard. 'They were young lads who liked the beer,' he remarked in one interview, 'So I had to make sure they trained properly'.

Although he experienced several serious brushes with the law during later life, it made no difference to Sammy's incredible popularity. He always retained an interest in boxing and a special affection for Spinks. When Terry was seriously ill during the 1990's, he was a frequent visitor to both hospital and clinic over a 21-month period. When Spinks was awarded the MBE in 2002, Sammy was one of the three guests invited to accompany him to his investiture at Buckingham Palace.

Throughout his retirement from the ring, fans retained their love and respect for him. Another honour bestowed upon him was for his success in the 1950's, when an effigy in wax was exhibited at Madam Tussauds. In later life he underwent a hip replacement, but this did little to curtail his activity especially the visiting of friends and colleagues in hospital or attending funerals.

Sammy McCarthy remains one of the nicest men ever to have climbed into a boxing ring and is a shining example of the sport.

Traceable Record
53 CONTESTS
44 WON
1 DREW
8 LOST

—.24.—

CHARLIE MAGRI

STEPNEY

BRITISH FEATHERWEIGHT CHAMPION 1977-1981
(undefeated)

EUROPEAN FLYWEIGHT CHAMPION 1979-1983
(undefeated) 1984-1985 (undefeated)
and 1985-1986

WORLD FLYWEIGHT CHAMPION (WBC version) 1983

As an amateur, Charlie Magri was talked about as the best flyweight to come out of the East End since Terry Spinks in the 1950's. Carrying his skill into the professional ranks he was undoubtedly the best little man from the region in modern times.

Born in Tunisia on 20 July 1956, but always billed from Stepney, only Latin and Oriental eight-stone men could beat him in the paid ranks until, when well passed his best, Duke McKenzie stopped him in four rounds of a contest with the British and European titles at stake.

Charlie boxed for Arbour Youth as a schoolboy and senior amateur, winning junior ABA titles in 1972 and 1973 as well as NABC titles in the same years. As a senior he won the ABA light-flyweight title in 1974 and was flyweight champion in 1975,'76 and '77, and a Young England, England Senior and Great Britain International representative. At European level he won a silver medal in the under-21 championships at Kiev in 1974 and bronze in the senior championships in Poland the following year.

Having such a successful amateur career, in which he lost only three of 56 senior contests, none of which was to an Englishman, there was considerable pressure on him to turn professional. In reality it was the most sensible course to take because having been eliminated in a preliminary round of the 1976 Olympics at Montreal, he could not progress any further as an amateur. Consequently, he had a number of attractive offers to consider.

He eventually decided to go with Terry Lawless whose training headquarters were at the Royal Oak at Canning Town. Yet, telling his amateur trainer, Jim Graham, with whom he had been for 10 years, was the most difficult task partly because Jim was no lover of the pro game.

Magri's first paid contest was at the Royal Albert Hall on 25 October 1977 against Northern Ireland bantamweight champion, Neil McLaughlin. Some critics considered it risky as the twenty-nine-year-old from Derry had an amateur career at least as successful as Charlie's, also being a European bronze medallist. As a professional he had drawn with British title contenders, Johnny Owen and Dave Smith and hit solidly enough to earn the Londoner's respect. The Stepney lad, however, showed sheer class, winning by a knockout with a devastating left hook to the body towards the end of the second round.

After disposing of Welshman, Bryn Griffiths, in two rounds at York Hall, Bethnal Green, three weeks later Magri was matched with Dave Smith (Eltham) for the vacant British flyweight title at the Royal Albert Hall on 6 December. Having beaten Smith in two rounds as an amateur, it was a fight Charlie was expected to win, which he ultimately did but only after resisting brave and determined opposition. Despite boxing competently and intelligently, Dave lacked the power to keep the Stepney man away. He was floored five times before referee, Roland Dakin, intervened with 10 seconds of the seventh round remaining.

Magri's victory equalled a statistical record set by Dick Smith back in 1914, when winning the British light-heavyweight title after only three contests. Charlie did, however, set a record of his own by becoming a British champion having been a professional for only two months.

There were light-hearted scenes in the new champion's dressing room afterwards, as he clutched the Lonsdale belt which looked three times too big for him. The champagne corks popped and as Charlie took a swig, he was interrupted by a lady in tears as she shook hands with him and wished him luck. It was Dave Smith's mother and Magri gave the impression he was apologising for beating her son. It was a moving moment.

After a two-month break, Charlie embarked on a learning course by facing a string of imported opponents over the next 14 months. Only one, Manuel Carraso of Spain, lasted the eight-round distance. He had come to London with a reputation of being a skilful boxer, having only been beaten once in his 14-fight career. He was also Magri's first southpaw opponent with advantages in height and reach and proved durable, game and awkward. Yet, Charlie coped well with the obstacles and won all eight rounds on referee Harry Gibbs scorecard. Although it was a valuable learning fight, it was not without an injury setback as the British champion sustained a damaged nose which kept him out of action for almost five months.

After 18 months of careful grooming Charlie faced Franco Udella of Italy in a challenge for the European title at Wembley on 1 May 1979. Udella, a former WBC light-flyweight champion had an impressive record with only four defeats from 41 contests with only two, against world champions in title bouts, unavenged.

In what was only his twelfth professional contest, Magri boxed brilliantly and executed a mature 12 round points victory which would elevate him into world class. The only sour note was that he had to settle for a split decision because a Swiss judge scored it to Udella by one round. The other two had it 120-116 and 120-115 meaning that the British champion had not lost a round on either card.

There was no resting on his laurels for Magri and alternating between the Albert Hall and Wembley Arena promotions he secured three stoppage victories over Mexican opposition before being called upon to defend his European title against Manuel Carraso on 4 December. Although he didn't lose a round on any of the three judges scorecards, he never looked like stopping the tough Spaniard. On the plus side, he got more rounds of experience under his belt for when he faced the tougher world rated opponents.

After knocking out Aniceto Vargas of the Philippines in three rounds at the Albert Hall in January 1980, Charlie had to wait five months for his next contest. It was his longest break since turning professional and when he returned on 28 June, it was in defence of his European title against Italian Champion, Giovanni Camputaro.

Although the Italian had never been stopped the contest developed into a farce as the challenger clinched and held on grimly at every opportunity. Even the ending was confusing with Magri utterly baffled when the Dutch referee intervened during the second minute of round three, with the majority of onlookers believing he had disqualified Camputaro. Only when the Master of Ceremonies gave the official verdict did it become clear that the contest had been stopped to save the challenger further punishment, despite the fact, that he did not appear to be in any trouble.

It had become clear by this stage that there were no continentals at the weight capable of testing Magri, so, with that in mind, his promoters matched him with former world champion, Alberto Lopez of Panama over 10 rounds at Wembley Conference Centre on 16 September. In what was by far the toughest fight of his career, he won a comprehensive 10 round decision but it was far from being one way traffic as Lopez put him under severe pressure.

Four weeks later Charlie stopped Enrique Castro of Mexico in the opening round at the Royal Albert Hall before facing tough Argentinian champion, Santos Laciar, over 10 rounds at the same venue. Despite being just twenty-one, Laciar was a typically rough product of the Argentinian fight school having crammed 46 contests into his three-year professional career, losing just four, all on points.

In what was another extremely tough battle, Magri was floored by the first punch of the contest and knocked almost to a standstill in round nine. After the initial drama, he landed the cleaner punches. His driving, damaging uppercuts in the eighth had Laciar almost out on his feet. It was a mature and controlled performance by the British champion who displayed immense courage and skill to put the decision beyond doubt. The final round was, in the opinion of most critics, one of the finest seen in a ring that year.

Next up for Charlie was a defence of his European title against Enrique Rodriguez Cal from Spain who, although twenty-nine, had an impressive record of 19 consecutive wins. He had also been a formidable amateur winning bronze medals at the 1972 Olympics and 1973 European championships, a bronze at the 1974 world championships and silver in the 1975 Europeans. He had also competed at the 1976 Olympics.

Despite his impressive credentials the Spaniard was no match for Magri and it took the champion just four minutes to dismiss his challenge. Cal was floored four times before the referee intervened. Despite the one-sidedness of the event no blame could be attached to the promoters, Micky

Duff and Mike Barrett, because it was made on the orders of the European Boxing Union.

The next step in the progression of Charlie's career was what his promoters expected to be a difficult test in Juan Herrera of Mexico in a 10-rounder on the Jim Watt – Alexis Arguello bill at Wembley on 20 June 1981. Herrera was ranked at number eight by the WBC and nine by the WBA, but failed to justify either, being floored twice and knocked out in the opening round.

Continued success had elevated Charlie to the position of leading contender for the WBC title, so in August he relinquished the British title to concentrate on achieving world honours. Whilst awaiting his title shot he took on Mexican, Juan Diaz, at the Albert Hall. With a record of 22 victories and a draw from 39 contests he was not regarded as being world class yet considered as an opponent adequate to keep Charlie ticking over.

Mexican's, however, have always had reputations of coming to fight and Diaz was no exception. Although Magri won most of the early rounds it all went wrong in the sixth when two short right hooks had him in trouble. Backed against the ropes, another right to the side of the head sent him to his knees for a count of 'seven'. He was still badly dazed when he rose and two more short, but powerful shots sent him back to the floor. Despite frantically struggling to rise, referee, Roland Dakin, counted him out as he slumped back.

Charlie's immediate future was wrecked and despite efforts of Mickey Duff to persuade Diaz into a rematch, he was having none of it, arguing that he should now get a world title shot. It was Magri's first setback in 24 contests since turning professional exactly four years earlier. Yet it could have been so different because he had comprehensively outboxed and outpunched the Mexican and but for his gameness might have been won by a stoppage.

After a four month break during which time he and his wife Jackie became parents to baby daughter, Emma, the re-building process began. Facing Los Angeles-based Mexican Cipriano Arreola at Albert Hall on 2 March 1982 it was expected to be a routine job, but again he was unimpressive and came within seconds of another disaster. Although he won comprehensively on points, Magri was dumped on the seat of his pants by the left hook at the end of the ninth round. Had it not been for the bell he would most certainly have been stopped or knocked out.

Despite the victory, it was clear that he was not ready for a world title shot so it was back to the Albert Hall six weeks later against Ron Cisneros of Colorado. It was a sensible match because although the American had lost only one of 18 contests he was not a recognised puncher. Knowing that if he lost, all hopes of a world title fight would be gone, Magri did his job quickly and efficiently. Cisneros took a fearful beating, including three counts before being stopped 50 seconds into round three.

It was imperative that Charlie kept busy if he was to regain the position he held prior to meeting Diaz. With that in mind he was matched with another Mexican, Manuel Leal at Wembley six weeks later. Whilst being a decent-grade opponent he was not regarded as being particularly dangerous at this stage of the re-building process. Yet again, however, the best laid plans fell apart and Leal pulled out and was replaced by unranked and unknown Jose Torres, a Mexican from Tucson, Arizona. He had a modest record and was not expected to trouble Charlie.

Although Magri always held a commanding lead, Torres often threatened to tear up the script and in round nine did precisely that. A chilling left hook swept the Stepney man off his feet and dropped him for a count of 'four'. He was hurt and confused as he rose, and the Mexican swarmed all over him before flooring him again, this time for 'three' and Magri rose too early and as he reeled into the ropes, unable to keep his balance, referee Roland Dakin stepped in.

Charlie's career looked in tatters but after a five month break he returned to action on 18 September with a European title defence against old opponent, Enrique Rodriguez Cal. It took place in a converted cattle market in the Northern Spanish town of Aviles. The trip was a new experience which took Magri and Terry Lawless 25 hours from the UK.

They flew to Bilbao and then began a journey exceeding 200 miles by car which was first complicated by an ancient car ferry which held them up on the outskirts of Bilbao for more than an hour. They then endured the discomfort of huge lorries which belched out thick smoke and slowed their progress on narrow, winding roads. The journey became so torturous that they stopped halfway and booked into a hotel at Santander and completed the journey the following day just 24 hours before Magri was due in the ring.

Despite Charlie's one-sided victory over Cal 18 months earlier, the contest had been ordered by the EBU, raising eyebrows in the media, particularly in Britain. As expected, Magri won quickly, the Spaniard being knocked out in round two. It was extremely one-sided, Cal being floored twice early in the opening round and cut badly over the left eye. He lasted just 97 seconds longer than in their first meeting.

Magri's handlers knew there would be nothing to be gained from taking on European opposition and arranged a return with Mexican conqueror, Jose Torres at Wembley in November. After a bitterly hard-fought contest the Stepney man triumphed on points, but it was extremely close and considered by some reporters as the hardest fight of his career. Both men were guilty of infringements, but the crowd loved it. At one stage, in round five, it threatened to get out of control when Torres blatantly butted Charlie after taking a hard right. The Stepney man promptly yelled an expletive at him whereupon the referee called a halt and told them to calm down.

The verdict in Charlie's favour was of huge importance and four months later he faced Eleoncio Mercedes of the Dominican Republic, at Wembley Arena, for a long-awaited challenge for the WBC flyweight title. That night the dream came true as the little man from Stepney turned in a masterful performance to halt the champion in round seven. Although the stoppage was due to an inch long cut on Mercedes left eyelid, that in no way detached from Magri's triumph. From the opening bell he never stopped going forward, relentlessly pounding out punches and only occasionally showed hints of the weakness which threatened to wreck his career in the preceding 18 months.

The success quickly brought a host of challenges including one within a week from rival promoter, Frank Warren. He offered to put up a purse of £110,000, winner take all, for Charlie to meet his fighter, Commonwealth champion, Keith Wallace. The antipathy which existed between the two camps, however, made it unlikely that such a match could ever be arranged.

After a break of six months, during which time he vacated the European title, Magri was matched with Frank Cedeno of the Philippines in the first defence of his title. A professional since 1976, the challenger had lost five and drawn three of 39 contests and had been stopped only once. A Magri victory was expected but once again disaster struck. Although he started brightly, Charlie was floored three times in round six and in serious trouble again in the seventh causing the referee to intervene. It was later discovered that he had sustained a nasty cut on the knuckles of his right hand which required six stitches.

Charlie's career looked over but after almost 12 months out of the ring he returned in August 1984 and travelled to Cagliari to face unbeaten Italian champion Franco Cherchi for the vacant European flyweight title. What was expected to be a test for him fizzled out after two minutes 10 seconds of the opening round when the Italian was ruled out with two deep gashes along his left eyebrow sustained by a clash of heads. Although the EBU ordered an immediate rematch it never took place and Magri remained inactive for a further six months.

Then came a chance he could never have dreamt of when he was matched with Sot Chitolada of Thailand, holder of the WBC title. Promoter of the contest, set to take place at Alexandra Palace, was Frank Warren who, a few months earlier would have been considered unlikely to promote a contest involving Magri and those handling him.

As it was always going to be a tough task Charlie vacated the European title to concentrate on his preparations, but it was all to no avail. Despite starting quickly, the powerful and accurate Thai soon moved up a gear and was in control when a nasty cut on the left eyelid led to Terry Lawless pulling his man out at the end of the fourth round.

Although it was generally felt that Magri would hang up his gloves, he travelled to Alessandria, Italy eight months later to challenge old foe Franco Cherchi, who had captured the vacant European title. Proving that he still had the class to beat anyone in Europe, Charlie quickly disposed of the Italian, knocking him out in the second round to recapture the title he never lost in the ring.

After a break of eight months, he returned to Wembley Arena on May 20, 1986 to face Duke McKenzie in a 12-rounder which involved the defence of his European title and a challenge for the British title held by his opponent. It was generally accepted that Charlie was near the end of his career and having had only seven rounds of competitive boxing since losing to Cedeno almost three years earlier, faced a tough assignment against the twenty-three-year-old from Croydon.

Realising a long fight was not a sensible option, Magri threw everything he had at Duke in the opening two rounds, but to no avail. The pattern changed in the third as McKenzie took the initiative. By the end of the session, the end looked in sight as Charlie returned to his corner with blood seeping from a cut below his right eye. It duly came in the fifth after two good rights put him to the floor for 'nine'. As he rose, Lawless, having already recognised the inevitable threw in the towel.

It was a sad ending to the career of the man who had been the best flyweight in Britain for 20 years. Despite two titles being up for grabs, Wembley was devoid of big-fight atmosphere and it was the worst attended show there for many years. For his courage and achievement over the years Magri deserved to go out on the bigger stage.

Despite holding the British title for almost five years he was never able to make a coveted Lonsdale belt his own property due purely to the fact that there were no suitable contenders in the flyweight division to challenge him. The British Boxing Board of Control subsequently decided to honour his outstanding contribution by presenting a belt to him. The last time a boxer had been so honoured was Walter McGowan, also a flyweight back in the 1960's.

In retirement Charlie eventually took out trainer and manager licences for a few years but eventually drifted away from the boxing scene.

Traceable Record:
35 CONTESTS
30 WON
5 LOST

—.25.—

ALF MANSFIELD

(Aldgate)

Born at Aldgate in the late 1800's, Alf, real name Issac Hyman, like many other youngsters of the time, got involved in boxing to earn some extra pennies. Boxing regularly at the Judean Club where he appeared almost exclusively for the first two years of his career starting in late 1910, he crammed in almost 40 contests with an equal spread of wins, draws and defeats.

A short, broadly built young man who was easy to train, he soon made a name for himself as a good flyweight prospect in London, although an injury to his right arm during mid-1912 curtailed his appearances somewhat. Once he had recovered he ventured to Scotland where he faced Johnny Best over 20 two-minute rounds at the National Athletic Club in Glasgow in September. Although he lost the decision he received good press with one reporter describing him as 'the coolest-headed boxer' seen at the venue with the exception of fellow East Ender, Sam Keller.

Alf continued to develop as a stylish boxer and showed his quality in November 1912 when he drew with Eugene Criqui over 10 rounds in Paris. It was a remarkable achievement and when they met again at the same venue eight weeks later they still could not be separated. Those results said much for the ability of Mansfield because Criqui, already a rising star, became the scourge of European boxers from flyweight to feather. He went on to have a glittering career, the highlights of which were winning the European featherweight title in 1922 and the world crown the following year.

Having established himself as one of the best flyweights in Britain, Alf faced a better quality of opponents. A week before his second contest with Criqui, he lost a 15-round decision to Joe Symonds at Plymouth. The following year Joe would become British champion. They met again two months later at The National Sporting Club where Joe won a six-round decision.

Promoters clamoured for Alf's services and during 1913 he had 16 contests and was only beaten by top men, Joe Wilson on points over 10 rounds at Premierland and Percy Jones twice. At Tonypandy in June he forced Mansfield to retire in five rounds and in November at Liverpool Stadium forced another retirement, this time after eight. Both contests had been scheduled for 15 rounds. Jones, a Welshman, became British champion the following year.

During the next two years Mansfield boxed at a variety of venues including the National Sporting Club, The Ring, Blackfriars, and West London Stadium. A non-drinker and non-smoker, he always trained enthusiastically and never shirked or cut corners. Such was his progress that his supporters began to clamour for a fight with Jimmy Wilde from Tylorstown, who was undefeated in about 80 contests and, pound-for-pound, was the most outstanding prospect around.

With both men willing, a 15-round contest was staged at Leeds in September 1914. Although he faced a massive task, Alf boxed confidently and put up a tremendous fight, but with the edge in class, the Welshman earned the decision. They met again five months later during the early days of the Great War on the opening of the new West London Stadium at Marylebone. Again, Wilde was by far superior and forced Alf to retire in round 10. Despite the defeat he still got good press, not only in the newspapers, but from Wilde himself who remarked 'Elsewhere, I have given my sincere opinion of Alf and in this bout he showed his incredible courage almost too well'.

Despite going their separate ways Mansfield and Wilde met again in May 1919 at Holborn Stadium. In between times Jimmy had won British, European and World flyweight titles and lost just once in almost 130 fights. The amazing little Welshman again proved superior to Alf and knocked him out in the 13th of a 15-rounder. Despite suffering three defeats, Mansfield always proved a worthy opponent to Wilde, especially in the last contest when he was at the height of his career.

Between the second and third fights with Wilde, Alf received an offer to go to America. After signing a contract, he boxed mainly in Pennsylvania, taking 17 contests between August 1915 and July 1916, losing just five. He got off to a slow start with a ten-round draw at St Nicolas Arena, New York and then two months later was disqualified in the final round against Abe Friedman at the same venue for persistently hitting on the break.

After a victory and two draws he was disqualified again at the same venue, this time against Jimmy Tolard amid controversial circumstances before a crowd of 1,500, in what was the main event of the evening. Following a skirmish in one corner of the ring, Alf claimed a foul but was over-ruled by the referee. He was so incensed that he refused to continue whereupon the fight was awarded to his opponent. When they met in a rematch three weeks later Alf won a ten-round decision.

Amongst his fights during the next five months Alf faced Billy Bevan on three occasions, winning the first and losing the second. A rubber match took place on 8 May 1916 after which there was a wild gulf in reporting as well as controversy in the ring. During round six a sponge was thrown into the ring from Mansfield's corner whereupon the referee stopped the fight. Not having been in any trouble, Alf protested that it had not been intentional. Showing good common sense, the official, having consulted the fight supervisor and the seconds in each corner, ordered the boxers to continue. At the end *The Reading Times* had Alf winning every round except the fifth in which he was floored. The *Reading Eagle* had him winning seven of the 10 rounds but neither mentioned the sponge incident or the fight being stopped. Some records even show Mansfield losing by a technical knockout in round six.

Reports of Alf's progress in America clearly impressed the National Sporting Club who invited him to return home and meet Jimmy Wilde for the British flyweight title. The terms of his contract, however, made this impossible but when he did return, the club matched him with George Clark over 15-rounds at 8st 2lbs with side stakes of £100.

The club had high hopes for Alf and his backers asked respected trainer, Jack Goodwin, to prepare him. After setting up camp at the Black Bull at Whetstone, Jack quickly realised it was a bad match because despite Alf usually doing 8st 2lbs in America, his natural fighting weight was 7st 12lbs. He told the backers in no uncertain terms that the boxer had been badly prepared in the past.

Although Goodwin got Alf into prime condition, he was badly out of range during the early rounds of the fight. When he returned to his corner at the end of one round he told the trainer he could not see his opponent clearly enough. There was no improvement as the fight progressed with the consequence that Mansfield was widely outpointed.

In the dressing room afterwards, Alf confessed to Jack that his eyesight was bad. Being the ultimate professional, Goodwin immediately told National Sporting Club boss, Peggy Bettinson, to get a doctor to examine the boxer. This was done without delay and they revealed that Alf had cataracts which required urgent treatment. Bettinson immediately gave him a letter to take to a hospital.

Unfortunately, the boxer did not act responsibly because being at the height of his career during the desperate years of war, earning money was his main priority. Instead of listening to medical advice, he proceeded to take three further fights in as many months, all at Hoxton Baths. After a no contest affair with Kid Davis just three weeks after being told he needed an operation, he engaged in two 15-rounders being outpointed by Bill Ladbury and then taking a decision from Johnny Moran. Only then did he take steps to have the necessary operation which kept him out of action for almost five months.

Following his recovery, Alf had two great fights with Scottish flyweight, Walter Ross. He lost the first on points over 20 rounds at Holborn Stadium in what was described as one of the best flyweight contests ever seen in London. As a result, they were re-matched over 15 rounds at 8st 2lbs at the National Sporting Club two months later with side stakes of £100. Jack Goodwin again took him to the Black Bull to prepare and he won the bout comfortably on points.

The match however, was not without an element of kidology a few hours before it was due to commence. Despite Ross being a 6-4 on favourite during the morning, it was rumoured that he was not able to make the weight. Word had reached Goodwin that he had spent an hour in a Turkish bath prior to the weigh-in. When Jack saw that Mansfield was gloating over the story he was quick to put him straight, 'Don't you take any notice of those rumours,' he warned 'Ross' supporters are not betting 6-4 on a man who has just come out of a Turkish bath' he continued. 'You get into that ring and box him and you'll soon find out whether it's true after a couple of rounds.'

Alf did as he was told and after a few rounds returned to his corner and whispered, 'I should say so, he's had no

Turkish Bath, he's as strong as me. I can tell when I'm inside with him'.

Despite having regular treatment Alf's eye problems recurred and curtailed his career considerably. Things went from bad to worse and he eventually lost the sight in one eye. Shortly after the other one started to deteriorate as well. They were desperate times as the eye treatment was expensive and had eaten into his savings. He had not made a great deal from the ring but boxing was his main and often only source of income. In order to hang onto his licence, the eye trouble had to remain an absolute secret.

After a no contest bout with Lewis Williams at National Sporting Club in March 1918, Alf was out of action for almost a year. When he returned he beat Williams on an eighth-round retirement at The Ring, Blackfriars. London promoters had no more idea of Mansfield's condition than the boxing public and after two distance fights in early 1919 resulting in a loss and a victory, a third fight with Jimmy Wilde was an attractive proposition especially from a financial point of view. Promoter, C.B Cochran who was staging shows at Holborn Stadium saw the box office potential and made Alf an offer he couldn't refuse. Moreover, he still believed he could beat the Welshman.

The match was made at 8st 4lbs to take place on 16 May just three weeks after Mansfield had beaten Young Baker at the National Sporting Club. Jack Goodwin again took Alf to the Black Bull and by this time he was well aware of his eye problems. Before each sparring session he had to put a drop in the better eye and adopt the same procedure immediately before the fight.

Despite his handicap, Mansfield fought with immense courage throughout what was an incredible contest and going into round 13 it was level. Only then did Wilde begin to realise that there was something wrong with his opponent. Playing on his blind side he caught him with a good punch which sent him to the floor but instead of taking a count Alf jumped straight back up. Knowing that he had not recovered from the effects of the blow, Jimmy refused to let him off the hook. He let fly with heavy punches which sent his man back to the canvas. This time he was badly hurt and failed to beat the count.

Despite the conclusive ending, it had been one of Alf's best performances and earned him an eliminator for the British flyweight title. Promoters at the National Sporting Club had long been impressed by Mansfield, featuring him on seven occasions before he went to America, again in his first contest on returning to the UK and on the subsequent occasions prior to the Wilde fight. In the eliminator they matched him with Arthur Bishop over 15 three-minute rounds. The fight was to take place on 2 June, just 16 days after he had been knocked out by the Welshman.

On reflection this was an amazing, even irresponsible decision as Alf was given far too little time to recover from what had been a demanding contest. It was a dangerous ploy, but permissible in those days because a boxer suffering a knockout defeat was not subjected to a period of suspension as in modern times. Desperately needing money, Alf was unlikely to refuse the fight, but in reality, he was being pushed back into the ring far too early, mainly for the benefit of the promoters. Alf, of course, gave it everything as he always did but his efforts were not enough to get the decision, therefore depriving him of a well-deserved title shot.

With his eyesight continuing to worsen, he had just three more contests, losing them all. During a seven-day period in July, he lost on a disqualification to Jack 'Kid' Doyle and was then stopped by Billy Green, both fights taking place at The Ring. After 16 months out of action, the curtain finally came down on Mansfield's career when Walter Ross forced him to retire after five rounds at Hoxton Baths in November 1920.

Alf had been a wonderful competitor, willing to face anyone. Quality fighters appear throughout his record and apart from Eugene Criqui, who failed to beat him twice and

Jimmy Wilde who he faced three times, he met Joe Symonds, Percy Jones, Bill Ladbury, Joe Wilson, George Clark and Tommy Harrison, all of whom were or had been champions or challengers for titles.

By the early 1930's, Alf was totally blind and to help ease his financial hardship he used to sell embrocation which he called 'Mansfield's Rubbing Oil'. Claiming to have created the substance personally, he sold it at boxing shows in London, particularly the East End. Promoters never refused him admission because they appreciated his massive contribution to the sport.

With tremendous effort and determination Alf established a successful business with a line containing seven oils: olive, caster, mustard, linseed, eucalyptus, camphorated and winter green. As it developed he frequently ventured outside London to sell his products. Always accompanied by his escort, another little ex-boxer from the East End who had been his lifelong friend, he was a regular visitor to promotions in Manchester where Alf had many regular customers. They would travel from London by rail and catch the mail-train back in the early hours of the next morning.

Alf eventually moved to Leeds, by which time his business had expanded. His products were extremely popular with many boxers particularly within the Manchester stable of champions consisting of Jackie Brown, Jock McAvoy and former bantamweight title holder, Johnny King. Yet they were not only used by athletes, they were also used by people who suffered back pain and other bodily pains.

Alf Mansfield was an extremely jovial and popular little man and irrespective of his blindness, always managed to stay cheerful. Boxing followers in the North loved him and showed him respect wherever he went. His sales pitch was always the same; 'Come get a bottle while stocks last. Only a few left'. A leaflet bearing a boxing pose of Alf and instructions how to use the product was attached to each bottle.

Mansfield's situation highlighted the hardships many young men were prepared to put themselves through to survive and provide for their families. Taking almost 20 contests over a four-year period whilst partially blind was sheer madness yet done out of desperation. Whilst extremely dangerous, only his immense skill and bravery backed by a huge helping of good fortune surely prevented him suffering a worse fate.

Despite his handicap, Alf never hesitated to help others. In 1947, he told journalist Charlie Rose an incredible story about how he once actually had the temerity to conduct two fellow blind sufferers across a motor congested thoroughfare in the West End of London.

Eventually, he was admitted to the Dolly Ross Home for the Blind at Southbourne, Hampshire, where he remained until late October 1962 when he passed away aged seventy. His funeral took place at Kinson Cemetery, Bournemouth, on 6 November that year.

Traceable Record
174 CONTESTS
67 WON
66 LOST
39 DREW
2 NC

—.26.—

HARRY MANSFIELD

(Aldgate)

Born in Aldgate in the late 1800's, his real name was Harry
Ginsburg but when he started boxing in 1905 he adopted
the name Jack Jones. One theory was that, like a number
of Jewish youngsters, he didn't want his parents knowing
that he was fighting for pay.

The majority of his early contests took place at
Wonderland where he entered several novice
competitions at 122 pounds (8st 7lbs) winning one. On 16
March 1907, he fought twice at the venue winning six-
round contests on the afternoon and evening promotions.

Towards the end of 1908, Harry went to America and
based himself in Philadelphia where, like other States,
contests lasting the distance were generally decided by
newspaper decisions. One of his first fights was a six-round
no decision affair against veteran, Jack Blackburn, who had
the experience of approximately 100 contests. In effect it
became the last of his main career because the following
month, January 1909, he lost his temper during an
argument and shot three people. He was sentenced to 15
years imprisonment but being a model prisoner was
paroled after just four years and eight months.

The fact that Mansfield stood up to Jack was early
evidence of his incredibly toughness and guaranteed him

regular fights. He maintained it throughout his stay in America which lasted until April 1911, during which time he was never stopped or knocked out in over 40 contests.

Philadelphia was a tough breeding ground for fighters, but Harry settled in and matured quickly. He developed physically and moved up to welterweight and then middle. With a good straight left and a hefty wallop in his right hand, his style of fighting was ideal for the American ring. The fans warmed to him and whoever he fought they were assured of a great battle. Averaging approximately two fights a month he faced some of the best men around.

Although reports of his progress filtered back to the United Kingdom, they were far from complete. It is known, however, that between March and September 1909 he had 13 contests losing only three to world class fighters; Frank Klaus, Harry Lewis and Joe Thomas. In the fight with Thomas who had previously faced Stanley Ketchell on three occasions for the world middleweight title, Harry put up a tremendous battle only to lose the six-round contest on a newspaper decision.

Three weeks later he faced Lewis, a veteran of about 140 contests, who had claimed the vacant world welterweight title in 1908. It was their third meeting, the first of which was three weeks after Harry faced Jack Blackburn and was of no decision. This time, however, he was the master and received a 10-round decision by the *Boston Globe* newspaper.

Buoyed by success and demand Mansfield took two more contests in September beating Kyle Whitney and Billy West within the space of four days. Still referred to as Jack Jones of Aldgate, he then lost four consecutive decisions before getting back to winning ways. More big names appeared on his record as he again faced both Harry Lewis and Joe Thomas as well as Frank Mantell who would progress to claim the world middleweight title in 1912.

In July 1910, Mansfield stepped in as a late substitute against Willie Lewis at the New York National Sporting

Club. It was an extremely tough fight for the Londoner against a hardened veteran of over 120 contests. Yet despite taking to the ring at extremely short notice, his performance was remarkable. He outboxed Lewis throughout the first seven rounds but then tired badly and was floored three times in rounds eight and nine. Although he survived to hear the final bell, the *New York Times* awarded the decision to Lewis much to the annoyance of many in the crowd who thought Harry deserved to win.

Six weeks later Mansfield faced Harry Lewis at the same venue for what was their fifth meeting. According to the *New York Times* it was a very poor contest and newspapers were divided as to who should get the decision. It was therefore called a draw.

The following month when Joe Grim, known as 'The Philadelphia Hard Man', failed to appear at the Bastian Athlete Club to face Mansfield, Eddie Haney substituted. Harry won the first six rounds but had to withstand heavy punishment during the final two. During the contest Haney became irritated by the Londoner's tactics and at the end they purposefully hit each other after the final bell. Within a few seconds, however, they smiled and shook hands. Then words were passed between them and they started an ugly brawl, which also involved their respective seconds. It took the help of police to restore order. Although two Philadelphia newspapers gave the decision to Hanley, British publication *Boxing* claimed Mansfield won a narrow but popular verdict.

Harry added another American scalp to his belt when he outpointed former United States Navy champion, Dennis Tighe, on the opening show at the Keyhole Athlete Club of Allentown the following week. Again, referred to as Jack Jones of Aldgate, he claimed to be the real welterweight champion of England. It was a vicious fight from start to finish in which Tighe held his own despite being 15 pounds lighter. Both men were continually applauded throughout the fight with one report subsequently claiming it would go down in history as one of the greatest ever contests at Allentown.

Mansfield dished out systematic punishment, but the former sailor refused to yield and was still on his feet at the final bell when the Londoner was awarded the decision by the *Allentown Democratic* newspaper. After the fight he stated that it was his intention to return to England during the latter part of November to seek contests with the likes of Tom Thomas, Jim Sullivan and other leading middleweights. It is doubtful whether the trip was actually made because there were no reports of contests or negotiations for such in the UK. Instead, Harry was back in action in Pittsburgh on 2 January 1911.

In the meantime, victory over tough-as-teak Joe Grim at Easton, Pennsylvania, was no mean feat and endorsed public opinion that Harry had climbed the fistic ladder considerably since arriving in America. Although newspapers called the contest a draw, *Boxing* claimed Mansfield won. In a return three weeks later, however, Boston and Philadelphia papers were in agreement that the Londoner won.

Many boxer's records during this period of time are known to be incomplete and Harry was no exception. The only traceable record in the UK credits him with having had 36 fights in America of which he won 12, drew 8 and lost 13 with three deemed no contest. Yet following his defeat of Dennis Tighe in October 1911, *Boxing,* in its column 'American News and Notes', refers to him having beaten Mike Donovan, Joe Walcott, Jimmy Carroll, Charlie Hitte and Bill Hurley, none of whom appear on his record.

On 2 January 1911, in Pittsburgh, Mansfield faced Jack Dillon, another top-class fighter who went on to hold the world lightweight title between 1912 and 1916. The outcome of this contest was another example of questionable reporting as the *Pittsburgh Post and Pittsburgh Press* both had Dillon winning. The latter stated that Harry did not appear to be in good shape. The

Indianapolis Star made the American a decisive winner, yet the British publication, *Boxing,* subsequently reported that Mansfield won every round and had Dillon on the verge of a knockout defeat in the final round. It added that the Briton had a fourteen-pound weight advantage.

Harry had just five more fights in America before returning home. He drew with Jack Fitzgerald over 12 rounds, lost over six to highly rated Leo Houck, drew with Peck Miller and in the space of three days had two contests in Columbus, Ohio. The last was a 12-round points defeat to Frank Mantell who, eleven months later, would become world middleweight champion.

Harry retuned to London during April accompanied by his American manager, Babe Greenbaum and spar-mate, Willie Beecher. He made no secret of the fact that his return was to force a title fight with Jim Sullivan who had become champion six months earlier by beating Tom Thomas. Speculation grew even stronger when the two were introduced from the ring at The National Sporting Club.

Mansfield had grown considerably since leaving for the United States when he scaled 8st 12lbs. Yet when he squared off with Young Nipper on a testimonial show at the Canterbury Theatre at the end of April, he looked more like 12st 8lbs.

Anxious to get back into action he agreed to face Welshman, Dai Thomas, at Wonderland on 11 May and badly needing to shed some weight, got down to work at Joey Smith's place at Herne Bay. Yet when he stripped off to face Thomas he still looked badly out of condition and was several pounds heavier than his opponent.

Reports from America had described Harry as a tear-in, do-or-die fighter with wonderful assimilative powers, who was able to shake off punishment easily. It was therefore to everyone's surprise that he was outboxed from the opening bell. Furthermore, he didn't box to any rule and frequently placed his left glove behind his opponent's neck and banged away with the right. He hit and held and often went dangerously low.

Thomas frequently appealed to the referee about the foul tactics but was ignored. Amazingly it was later reported that the third man was hard of hearing. After one such rejected appeal, the Welshman was so incensed that he rushed at Mansfield like a wild bull. After grabbing him around the shoulders he attempted a head butt and then appeared to chew at his left cheek.

There was instant pandemonium as the referee attempted to pull them apart. As he did so Thomas stood with his back to the ropes whereupon an angry ringside spectator jumped up and struck him on the shoulder with a chair. Within seconds there was a full-scale riot and the referee hurriedly left the ring. The chair-wielder was knocked to the ground and set upon before Jack Woolf rushed up, grabbed him and hustled him out of the arena but not quick enough to save him from the fury of the mob.

When order was finally restored, Jack climbed into the ring and addressing the audience, apologised for what had occurred. Having spoken to the referee and advised him that the boxers had patched up their differences and were agreeable to continuing the fight, the official declined to re-enter the ring and declared the bout 'no-contest'.

Whatever the reasons were for his poor performance against Thomas, Harry redeemed himself three weeks later at the National Sporting Club against Jack Harrison. The contest was described in the press as being the best bout of the season at the club and despite losing a narrow decision, he boxed brilliantly. Because of his fear of getting disqualified he cut out the rough stuff and complied with the rules. Consequently, there was never an idle moment.

Harry's next two opponents were servicemen. After knocking out Seaman Sykes, billed as from the Royal Navy, Chatham, in the first round, he met Army & Navy champion, Private Jim Harris who was serving with the Coldstream Guards. Despite speculation that, on retuning to England, he would face Jim Sullivan, those hopes were dashed following his poor showing against Dai Thomas. Sullivan, meanwhile, went on to challenge Billy Papke for the world title but was beaten and although no such announcement had been made, the promoters advertised the fact the winner of Mansfield and Harris would face Jim for the Lonsdale middleweight championship belt.

How reliable that claim was became irreverent when, yet again, Mansfield blew his chance. After a rough mauling contest in which he went low on three occasions to shouts of 'foul', he was disqualified in round eight for hitting whilst holding with one hand. Gone, it appeared were his chances of ever fighting for a British title.

Yet after Harry had beaten Arthur Harman by stoppage in eight rounds at The Ring in February 1912, he was matched with Bill Curzon over 15 rounds at the National Sporting Club in a contest billed as an eliminator for the British middleweight title. They had boxed a 10-round draw at Premierland two months earlier but with a formidable reputation stemming from his showings in America in which he displayed considerable ruggedness and stamina, Harry was expected to have too much for his older opponent. It did not, however, work out like that as Bill boxed cagily throughout and even appeared to have Mansfield in difficulty on occasions. The fight was extremely close and although the majority of members thought Harry had sneaked it, the referee's decision of a draw was warmly received.

Two weeks later he travelled to Liverpool for his sixth meeting with the formidable American, Harry Lewis, who was on a European tour as he neared the end of his professional career. It was a gruelling 20-round battle in which it was clear that there was no love lost between them. Rules were often broken but although Mansfield more than held his own, there were occasions when his cast iron jaw saved him. He took a long count in round 18 but was still on his feet at the end. It was extremely close and the referee's decision in favour of Lewis did not please everyone.

When Harry fought Private Jim Harris, fresh from becoming light-heavyweight champion of the Brigade of Guards, Navy & Army, press and public opinion was that he showed a distinct improvement from any performance since returning from America. It was another absorbing contest in which Harris, considered as one of the best boxers in the British Armed Services, pushed Mansfield to the limit. For his part Harry showed more skill and composure than in previous fights and was also careful to observe the rules. The decision of a draw was well received, and general opinion was that both men had earned the right to a title shot.

Dispirited by a sudden lack of fights and nearing the end of his career, Harry agreed to a well-paid contest in Paris against undefeated Jeff Smith from New York. Having been out of action for seven months it was not the most sensible decision to make and the outcome was that the American hammered him unmercifully for six rounds and forced his retirement.

Having given up all hope of ever getting a British championship fight, Mansfield signed a contract to take five fights in Australia under the management of Snowy Baker. He had been approached to go down there some months earlier by trainer Jack Goodwin but declined because he was passionately fond of his parents. He was not prepared to be that far away from them. The lack of opportunity in Britain and the lure of good money, however, changed his way of thinking.

After losing a 10-round decision to Bandsman Dick Rice on 1 March 1913 he set sail along with former British lightweight champion Matt Wells, Sid Stagg and other London boxers. Goodwin had just settled in Sydney and was training Sid Burns for a title fight with Johnny Summers when Mansfield and his colleagues arrived. He was delighted to see them and agreed to handle all their affairs.

Harry's first contest was at Sydney Stadium against Les O'Donnell, a six-foot-tall lightweight, although it was made at the middleweight limit of 11st 6lbs. At the weigh in on the afternoon of the fight, O'Donnell immediately declared that he was overweight and agreed to pay a forfeit of £100. As Mansfield raised no objection, the fight went ahead before a crowd of 15,000 and having a weight advantage of nine pounds, O'Donnell was a strong odds-on favourite to win by a knockout. Jack Goodwin, however, knew Harry's pedigree and contacted two bookmakers and told them to bet heavily on him lasting the distance.

It was a fierce fight from the opening bell in which Mansfield sustained an ugly cut above the left eye in round six. By the tenth, blood poured down his chest but with the referee not inclined to call a halt, he battled on bravely. By round 18 it was extremely close but at this point, however, he started taking a hammering. He was floored heavily in the penultimate round and only saved by the bell.

Goodwin freshened him up the best he could but the pounding continued throughout the final session. Harry's only satisfaction was the fact that he was still on his feet at the final bell only to lose on points. The appreciative audience cheered him loudly for his wonderful game showing. He was not happy, however, when he later discovered that Goodwin and Burns had picked up a tidy sum of cash at the expense of his pain and suffering.

It took a while for him to recover from the O'Donnell beating but once he was fit, he was matched with Jerry Jerome, a talented hard-hitting Aborigine. Mansfield boxed brilliantly for 11 rounds but then sustained two cuts above his right eye forcing him to quit. They met again two months later, and the Londoner was forced to retire after 13 rounds having been floored twice for long counts.

He did have the satisfaction of one success in Australia, outpointing Bill Walsh in Melbourne between the Jerome contests. Overall, however, it was not a successful trip and

Harry was sensible enough to know that he was at the end of his career. Although he got well paid for his pains in Australia he lost quite a lot as he was a compulsive gambler.

On his return to England he quit boxing despite being quite young and in reasonable form. He could have taken small-purse contests, but he was devoted to his parents who pleaded with him to retire. Although he loved fighting, he complied with their wishes and in doing so made a tremendous sacrifice for a man who had great strength and glorified in it.

Harry maintained his interest in boxing and became a referee during the 1920's. A decade later he was recognised as one of the soundest judges and most conscientious of officials. He was a relatively young man when he passed away in 1940 and his commitment and love for the sport should never be forgotten.

Traceable Record;
64 CONTESTS
23 WON
26 LOST
11 DREW
4 NC

—.27.—

HARRY MASON

(Whitechapel)

BRITISH LIGHTWEIGHT CHAMPION 1923-1924 AND
1925-1928 (undefeated)

EUROPEAN LIGHTWEIGHT CHAMPION 1923
(undefeated)

BRITISH WELTERWEIGHT CHAMPION 1925-1926 AND
1934

Harry was one of the smartest and most dapper little men ever to have climbed into a boxing ring. Always immaculately dressed, he was good looking and took great pride in his appearance. He would part his hair down the middle and keep it in place with brilliantine and frequently boasted that he could go through a 20-round contest with the roughest fighter and come out with the parting still intact.

A unique personality in many ways, he became known as 'The Little Fiddler' not just because he was an accomplished violinist, an instrument he sometimes played in his dressing room before a fight, but also for his clever ring tactics and the way he could fiddle his way to victory.

Although he developed into a talented and skilful ring man there were times when his unsportsmanlike antics irritated opponents and spectators alike. He could be unpredictable and had an extraordinary knack of aggravating fans, particularly at Premierland where he had many fights. He was clever, game and provided the East Enders with scores of brilliant performances, yet his perky, saucy mannerisms and temperament got him disliked.

One such occasion was on the afternoon promotion of 21 December 1929 when he entered the ring clad like a mountaineer in cap, muffler, sweater, coat and scarf. Plucking his rather racy cap from his head he tossed it onto a ring post where it remained throughout the preliminaries. During the fight with Charlie McDonald from Sunderland, in which he was giving away a huge amount of weight, Harry was repeatedly cautioned by referee, Jack Hart, for holding. Midway through round six he was disqualified. There was an immediate response from Mason's trainer, Alec Goodman, who told the referee what he thought in very forcible language. The crowd cheered McDonald loudly, but turned against Mason, a professional for nine years, who did not care one bit. He just shouted back telling them in no uncertain terms just who and what they were. He left the ring to a storm of booing.

Born of Jewish heritage in the East End on 27 March 1903, Harry's first experience of fighting occurred during a lunch break in his school playground. A diminutive figure, he stood with his back to a fence as half a dozen bigger boys threatened him. Adopting a stance that would have done credit to an experienced boxer, he parried wild blows aimed at him by his aggressors and prevented them striking his face.

Anxiously looking for a way out, he offered to fight the biggest one but not the lot. The group chose their best fighter whilst the rest formed a ring. Mason was barely half the size of his rival but knew how to jab and move and dancing backwards and sideways, he soon had his opponent bewildered. When blood streamed from his nose, as a result of Harry's accurate left jab, the fight was called off and the group dispersed. He made a lot of friends that day and his natural ability saved him from persecution of bullies in the future.

Before he finished his education, Harry joined the Jewish Lads Brigade solely to get some clothes and join the boxing section. Despite being the smallest member, he perfected his talents and won a 5st 7lbs championship, the lowest weight at which he could box. Even then he gave away weight to his opponents.

When the family home was destroyed during a Zeppelin raid in the First World War, the Mason family moved to Leeds which, due largely to the rag trade, had one of the biggest Jewish communities outside London. Having left school, Harry obtained employment as a trolley boy with London North Eastern Railway but continued to box. He won further boys competitions and then at the age of seventeen turned professional in order to help augment his mother's meagre income. He started by fighting 10-rounders and within two years was a top-liner at venues in the north of England. Always billed as from Leeds, nobody thought anything of him being other than a Yorkshireman.

Like most boxers living in the provinces, Harry yearned for the day when he would be invited to box at The National Sporting Club in London. Amazingly an offer came shortly after his eighteenth birthday after having only seven professional contests. Although he lost a 10-round points decision to Dan Bowling, the defeat did him no harm whatsoever. He fell in love with the London fight scene and quickly realised there were far more chances to make money in the capital than in the north of England.

Fortunately for Harry he met Joe Morris, an established East End boxers' manager who was also connected with promotions at Premierland and Manor Hall, Hackney. Always on the lookout for new talent he had been impressed by the youngster's showing at the National Sporting Club. Joe became particularly interested when Mason explained that he wanted to earn more money in order to support his mother and bring her back to London.

After giving him a six-round try out at Manor Hall, Morris was convinced that he had the ability to have a successful ring career. By the end of 1921 he had won all 11 fights under Morris in the space of eight weeks at Manor Hall, Hoxton Baths, The Ring, Blackfriars and Premierland.

His work rate continued through the following year, taking 33 contests of which 15 were at Premierland. He lost only two. He also travelled back to Leeds where he engaged in four contests and also one each in Manchester and Liverpool. By early January that year, Harry had graduated to 15-round contests and had his first 20-rounder in July at the age of nineteen. By this time he was recognised as one of the leading lightweights in the country.

As the months passed by so the level of opponents got tougher. Thriving on his continued success, Harry outpointed former British featherweight champion, Mike Honeyman, over 20 rounds at Premierland in September 1922. Two weeks later at the same venue, he faced Seaman James Hall who, six weeks earlier had become British and European lightweight champion by outpointing Ernie Rice. After a scintillating battle over 20 rounds, the referee called it a draw much to the disgust of the East End fans. Mason's performances, however, confirmed his entitlement to a championship contest.

Being of an impetuous nature, Harry became irritated when nothing materialised within a few weeks and rather than wait he went ahead and agreed to face Honeyman in a risky return contest over 15 rounds at Mile End three months later. Again, the referee's decision was a draw, but it was nevertheless a good performance by Mason. Recognising his undoubted ability, London promoter Major

Arnold Wilson, put up an enticing purse for Hall to defend his titles against Mason at Olympia on 17 May 1923.

Although only just turned twenty years of age Mason had the experience of almost 60 fights behind him and developed his own unique style in the ring. A brainy, confident boxer, his skill was of the highest order, but he had the cockiness about him which was disliked by some people, both opponents and spectators alike. If he could entice his opponent to lose his temper early in the fight he was happy; he loved it when they were so riled that they wanted to give him a hammering. Remarks he made during a contest only added to their fury, his impudence being designed to cause a rival to abandon a set plan and strive to knock him out.

In some respects, kidology helped him to beat Seaman Hall. He was doing well by the mid-stages of the fight until the champion decided to concentrate his attack on the body. This ruffled Mason and in the ninth, after a flurry of close range exchanges, Hall banged in a right which all of Harry's many fans screamed was foul. He went down acting as if he was in great pain and admonished the champion for what he claimed was a low blow. Referee, Joe Palmer, usually a cool-headed individual, motioned to Hall to step back and signalled to Mason to get up. Harry half rose but was ordered by his corner to stay down which he did for about 20 seconds. The official then called them together and warned Hall and told them to box on.

With an element of needle having developed, there were some fierce exchanges with Mason setting a fast pace and showing no sign that the earlier body punch had caused lasting pain. Not able to score consistently to the challenger's head, Hall chanced the occasional body punch and twice Mason complained of being hit low for which the champion was again cautioned. Then in the middle of the 13th Hall threw a more powerful shot to the body which despite being dangerously low, was not, according to press opinion, a foul. Mason was hurt and went down clutching his stomach and without any hesitation, referee Palmer ordered Hall to his corner. The titles had changed hands on a disqualification. It was not a satisfactory ending for many of the fans who were not impressed by Harry's tactics.

Five months later they met again over 20-rounds at Premierland in a non-title bout. Before his own supporters, Mason boxed brilliantly to secure a well-deserved victory and deprived Hall of any chance of securing a return title shot.

Four weeks later Harry successfully defended his titles against a former champion, Ernie Rice at the Royal Albert Hall. Ernie chased and swiped for 20 rounds, but at the end the sleek-haired champion was still on his feet despite having been floored twice in the 14th round and again midway through the last.

Early the following year, Harry went to America in the hope of securing a world title fight with Benny Leonard. During his seven months stay he had eight fights in New York, Brooklyn, Chicago, Detroit and Columbus, mostly against welterweights. Although he lost only three and earned plenty of money, it was not a very successful transatlantic venture. He found that especially in New York, the referees were less particular about the whereabouts of the bodyline while his opponents were deaf to his tongue-lashing tactics.

On arriving back home Mason was infuriated to find that The National Sporting Club, which never regarded him as a champion, due to his title fights having not been under its jurisdiction, had matched Ernie Izzard with Jack Kirk for the vacant lightweight title which Izzard duly won. Grimly determined to get his title back, Harry was unbeaten in eight contests, mostly at Premierland. In doing so he created such a stir that the club had little option but to match him with Izzard under championship conditions.

The fight was set to take place on the 24 June 1925, but due to the intense rivalry between the two camps, public interest was massive. The huge numbers clamouring for tickets meant that the club premises were hopelessly inadequate to accommodate them, so a decision was therefore made to stage the contest at Holland Park Ice Rink.

In some respects it became a disappointing occasion as a number of fans who had purchased ringside seats were unable to reach them because others from the cheaper areas had already occupied them. The fight commenced amid uproar and the referee, who sat outside the ring, was powerless to exercise proper control. Despite the disruption, Mason boxed brilliantly to become champion again and claim the Lonsdale Belt when Rice failed to come up for the ninth round. In doing so he showed a degree of aggressiveness which nobody believed he possessed but his actions were designed partly to show indignation for being slighted by The National Sporting Club.

To demonstrate his prowess, Mason faced Hamilton Johnny Brown for the vacant British welterweight title at the Royal Albert Hall four months later but was beaten on points. It was extremely close and the pair met in a return at the same venue six weeks later, when Harry outpointed the Scot to become dual champion. Despite his achievement, the fans were still unhappy about the way he had originally won the lightweight titles. Mason, however, was not concerned as being of a strong personality he knew they would still turn up at his fights if only in the hope of seeing him get beaten.

Mason's next fight was a defence of his British and European lightweight titles against Ernie Rice at The Royal Albert Hall in February the following year. It only lasted five rounds due mainly to the elusive tactics adopted by the champion. Out of sheer frustration at failing to land a telling blow, Rice swung widely to the body, went decidedly low and was immediately disqualified.

Reverting back to welterweight, Harry defended that crown against Len Harvey at The Albert Hall two months later. It was a contest which fired the imaginations of the fans and proved an absolute sell-out for astute promoter, Harry Jacobs. Although only nineteen years of age, Harvey was a bright young prospect but faced a severe test. Despite having advantages in height and reach, he lacked the top-class experience of the champion who was already a veteran of over 80 contests, including six with titles at stake, plus his American venture.

Mason trained at Brighton under Alec Goodman and had to work hard having allowed himself to balloon up to 11st 4lbs. He made the weight comfortably and at the weigh in told Harvey: 'You're in for a boxing lesson'. There were times during the 20-round battle that the comment was looking accurate, but the talented challenger was equal to everything Mason threw at him and even floored him twice. It was an absorbing battle between two extremely talented young men and at the end, the referee Mr C H Douglas, seated at ringside, called it a draw. Both were smiling as they touched gloves, but Mason wanted the last word, albeit in jest. 'You were lucky', he said cheekily.

Experiencing weight problems, Harry relinquished his lightweight titles to concentrate on the heavier division. His next two contests were against Jack Hood from Birmingham, the first of which took place at Holland Park on 31 May. After an incredibly close affair, Hood got the decision, but there was so much controversy that they met again six weeks later at The Royal Albert Hall. This time Mason was in a petulant mood and didn't seem to care if he won or lost. Most critics expected him to gain revenge, but he gave Jack far less trouble than in their first contest. Hood got the decision and this time there was no dispute.

The defeats put Harry back among the contenders, yet for the next eight years he continued taking on top class opponents winning far more times than he lost. Fellow East Ender Moe Moss was the only man to knock him out. In 1928 he travelled to Australia winning three of six contests before moving on to South Africa where he won all four contests and made himself extremely popular with the local fans.

After more than a year away, Harry began the long haul back in the hope of regaining championship contention. Boxing exclusively at Premierland, he won six of seven contests in just four months, his only defeat being by disqualification. He the outpointed Jack Hood over 12-rounds at The Royal Albert Hall and shortly after made another trip to America where he had two fights one of which was a points defeat to former world welterweight champion, Joe Dundee.

Then came a third meeting with Ernie Rice on a Sunday afternoon show at The Ring, Blackfriars, in September 1930. A few days beforehand both parties met in the tea lounge of the Savoy Hotel ostensibly for the purpose of finalising the signing of contracts. The press were invited and it was quite a party with things being amicable until Mason suddenly shouted at Rice: 'Make sure where you put your punches this time'.

Ernie countered by calling him a cheap crook for going down from a perfectly legal blow in their previous fight and claiming a foul. Before Harry could say anything more Rice pushed over a table and went to seize his old foe by the scruff of his neck. A real rumpus developed with everyone jostling each other until somebody managed to get between the two boxers.

Things eventually quietened down, and Mason's party left followed shortly afterwards by Rice. The whole thing was of course a put-up affair supposedly staged by The Ring, promoter, Victor Berliner but it worked. With the two boxers being sworn enemies, details of the affair were plastered across the pages of the national newspapers the following day. The Ring was jammed full come fight afternoon, but the fans did not get much for their money. Rice attacked fiercely at the start rushing Mason to the ropes, whereupon Harry slid to the floor. Rice promptly clouted him on the head while he was sitting there and that was that. The last entry on Ernie's record showed him being disqualified in round one.

Harry continued boxing regularly and in November 1931 outpointed talented Bristol man, George Rose in a British welterweight title eliminator. No championship contest was forthcoming and in December two years later he won a Southern Area title eliminator followed by a British title final eliminator at Swansea against local man Danny Evans. Trouble, however, seemed to follow Mason and after he was awarded the decision the referee had to be escorted from the ring by the police to protect him from turbulent Welshman who counted on their man winning.

Mason's long wait for another title shot finally came in June 1934 when he faced Len 'Tiger' Smith at Birmingham for the British championship vacated by Jack Hood. Looking far from the fighter he was a few years earlier, Harry got lucky in a contest he was losing as Smith was ruled out for a low blow.

The poor form continued, and Harry lost his next four contests on points, one of which was to Pat Butler at Leicester. It came about following a chance meeting one Sunday afternoon when Butler's manager, George Biddles and East End personality and Master of Ceremonies, Buster Cohen, went into a café in Commercial Road and bumped into Mason and his manager, Benny Huntman. Harry had just come out of hospital and was broke and quickly made it clear that he needed a fight and in particular, the money it would bring him. Biddles immediately saw the possibility of a fight with his rising star Len Wickwar which would have suited Mason. George also managed Pat Butler, another Leicester youngster, so local promoter James Panter offered to match the two with the winner to face Mason.

After a lot of negotiation, they fought, and Butler came out on top. He was then matched with Mason in a non-title fight in Leicester on 19 November. Harry had agreed that if he lost he would put the title on the line in a return. Butler won a close decision, having Harry on the floor in the final round with only the bell saving him from being knocked out. His form was poor, and it was claimed that he had not fully recovered from the illness for which he was hospitalised.

They met again four weeks later with the title at stake, but there had been difficulties when Huntman and Mason demanded a huge purse. Matters were only resolved when Butler agreed not to be paid unless the show made a profit. After a fast and furious 15 rounds, he got the decision but it was unpopular with the crowd who thought Mason was a clear winner. As the promotion lost money, Pat was probably the only British boxer to win a title and not get paid.

During the 12-month period following that contest, Mason was twice beaten by Wickwar and George Biddles always maintained that the shrewd Huntman would never have allowed this man to risk the title against Len. He always believed Harry would beat Butler, but his plans backfired.

After losing his title Mason carried on with top-of-the-bill contests throughout the next two years. His opponents, however, were generally up-and-coming lads and the arenas at which he performed were often smaller and of a less important variety than those of his earlier career. Whilst he was still a capable performer who the fans liked to watch, he suffered almost as many defeats as he gained victories. It was therefore not surprising that after Jack 'Kid' Berg forced him to retire after three rounds at The Ring early in 1937, Harry sensibly hung up his gloves.

Berg was far too good for his one-time stable-mate and subjected him to considerable rough treatment before Harry decided he had taken enough. He had come in at almost a stone overweight and although he had been due to pay a forfeit, Jack did not press the claim.

Mason contested 11 championship contests and despite twice being champion at both light and welterweight, was never able to make a Lonsdale belt his own property. He was, nevertheless, always a talking point among the fans for a variety of reasons. Whilst his ring craft was a joy to watch, many never forgave him for his questionable tactics. He made himself extremely unpopular in some quarters which lead to his car tyres being slashed on a number of occasions. Furthermore, he often had to leave an arena under police escort.

Boxing journalist, Gilbert Odd, who knew Harry very well once wrote;

> Mason could invite trouble. I've seen him leaning over the shoulder of an opponent winking at the audience while throwing kidney punches. The referee was always on the blind side of course and the more the crowd booed the more Mason liked it.

In and out of the ring Harry was a lively individual, never at a loss for words and with a chirpy zest for repartee. After Johnny Brown beat him at The Royal Albert Hall in 1925, he addressed the audience in such a way as to prompt one dinner-suited ringsider to remark; 'This fellow should be in the House of Commons'.

Throughout his career he continued to play his violin and it was once rumoured that he was offered a large sum to play on stage. He was entirely self-taught, and things came about by accident when he discovered an instrument lying in a training camp. With nothing better to do at the time he picked it up and started strumming the strings as though it was a guitar. Within a very short time he learned to play extremely well.

Towards the end of his career Harry was, on occasions, billed as coming from Leicester having bought a house there towards the end of 1934. After retiring from the ring he went to South Africa where he accepted an offer to manage a hotel. He remained there until killed in a road crash in 1977.

Traceable Record:
208 CONTESTS
140 WON
52 LOST
14 DREW
2 ND

28

DANIEL MENDOZA

(Whitechapel)

Born in Whitechapel on 5 July 1763, Daniel Mendoza became the first Jew to earn fortune and fame in the ring. He was extremely proud of his heritage and was recognised as the greatest prize fighter of the late eighteenth century. Only a middleweight by modern day standards, he had a wonderful scientific and accomplished style of fighting which enabled him to beat much bigger and stronger men.

His first recorded battle took place at Mile End when he was just sixteen. Over the next three years he trained hard, perfecting his skill. He progressed well, winning more than 20 contests before suffering his first setback in 1788 at the hands of 'Gentleman' Richard Humphries. Regarded by many knowledgeable followers as the best man in England, it was Humphries who originally persuaded Daniel to fight for pay after seeing him in a street fight.

The fight took place on 9 January at Odiham, Hampshire, for 400 guineas and lasted 29 minutes. The end came when Mendoza fell with his leg beneath him causing a bad sprain to his foot forcing his immediate retirement. They met twice more with Mendoza winning both thereby proving what a talented fighter he was.

Much was written about him over the years and there are varying accounts regarding his period as champion of England. It is generally believed, however, that he laid claim to the championship after beating Bill Warr in 23 rounds at Croydon in 1792 when it was estimated that more than 10,000, many from the Jewish fraternity, travelled from the East End to see the fight. When they met again two years later Warr was pounded to defeat inside 17 minutes as Mendoza showed more aggression than at any time in his career.

Apart from being an exceptional purist, Daniel was also very popular as a person. His reign as champion brought new prestige and security to Jewish people particularly in the poverty stricken East End.

Mendoza's reign as champion came to an end in 1795 when he accepted a challenge of 200 guineas-a-side from 'Gentleman' John Jackson, a two-fight novice who was five years his junior, much taller and 42lbs heavier. They met in a field at Hornchurch, Essex, and after a short vicious fight, which lasted for just over 10 minutes (nine rounds), a badly cut up Mendoza was knocked out. He was so upset that he immediately announced his retirement from the prize ring.

During the ensuing years his life was one of fluctuating fortunes. He served terms of imprisonment for debts and other misdemeanours, took part in races against horses, which he usually won and toured England, Scotland and Ireland with a circus and boxing academy. While in Scotland he became a recruiting officer in the Fifeshire Regiment of Fencibles and a Sheriffs officer, a post from which he was removed for failing to bring himself to arrest his friends. Upon being released from Carlisle Prison, members of 'The Fancy' took pity on him and set him up as 'Mine Host' of a Whitechapel Tavern. That, however, was a short-lived position as he was soon hounded out by creditors.

Eleven years after retiring from the ring Mendoza was in dire straits and poverty, having again just been released from prison. With no other way to earn money he fought and beat Harry Lee at Grinstead Green, Kent in 53 rounds. Sadly, the dire financial problems persisted, and he was still a regular inmate of H.M. Prisons.

Some 14 years after beating Lee he agreed to meet Tom Owen, the Portsmouth publican, to settle an old grudge. They squared up on Banstead Downs, Surrey, on 4 July 1820. Mendoza, despite putting up a good fight was beaten in 12 rounds. It was his final battle, his reward for which was 50 guineas.

Apart from being a talented prizefighter, Daniel also had a flair for writing. In 1816 he published his autobiography – 'Memoirs of the Life of Daniel Mendoza', a 320-page masterpiece which also contained his observations about pugilism and rules for training. He wrote 'The Art of Boxing (1789), 'The Modern Art of Boxing' (1790) and 'Cautions to the Amateurs of Pugilism' (1823). All became valuable much sought-after collectors' items.

In retirement he eventually became a celebrated instructor of the Noble Art with his own school in the City of London. Among his many clients were members of Royalty and Aristocracy. In and out of the ring he did more to progress the art of scientific boxing than any other man before him and for many years after.

It was therefore extremely sad that he died, aged seventy-three, amid utter poverty at Horseshoe Alley off Petticoat Lane in the Jewish section of the East End that he so loved. He left behind a faithful wife, eleven children and a reputation of a boxer which has been detailed endlessly in British journals and various histories of the ring.

29

HARRY MIZLER

(Stepney)

BRITISH LIGHTWEIGHT CHAMPION 1934

SOUTHERN AREA LIGHTWEIGHT CHAMPION 1935-36
(Undefeated)

Of Polish-Jewish extraction, Harry Mizler quickly developed into another of the huge band of never to be forgotten East End fighters. Born in Stepney on 22 January 1913, he had two older brothers, Judah and Morris, and two sisters. With their father being an invalid, their mother worked tirelessly to support the family. Battling the depression, they knew real poverty but like many of their co-religionists, possessed an abiding family love.

The three lads took to boxing from boyhood. Whilst the eldest, Judah, only boxed locally as an amateur, Morris, known in the sport as Mo, developed into a useful flyweight. Although never reaching championship status he was nevertheless an extremely popular performer, particularly at Premierland.

Harry, named Hymie at birth, started boxing at the age of ten when he joined Berners Street Old Boys Club. When it closed in the late 1920's he went to Oxford and St George's which boasted a magnificent boxing section.

With excellent trainers and facilities, it was a nursery for champions.

At the age of fourteen Harry weighed 7st 7lbs and within a few months won London Federation of Boys Clubs and Stepney Boys Clubs championships. His success was due largely to the tuition given to him by his brothers, particularly Mo, and support from his parents. Despite having extreme difficulty in getting about, his father went to watch every contest.

An extremely close family, they lived in Cable Street and the parents ran a fish stall at nearby Watney Street. The boys all helped out and getting up at five o' clock every morning, pushed the barrow to Billingsgate Market and back in all weathers. Harry regarded his shift as daily roadwork and part of his training.

Mizler developed into a fine amateur, winning National Federation of Boys Clubs titles at bantamweight in 1929 and 1930. By winning the senior ABA title at the same weight in 1930 at the age of seventeen he became the youngest man to achieve that honour. His success was rewarded by being selected to represent England at the Empire Games later the same year. He was the youngest member of the team but justified his selection by returning home with a gold medal.

There were further victories at International level when he represented the ABA against Ireland in Dublin and Belfast, but the following year he was surprisingly beaten in the London featherweight final by Benny Caplan. It was described as being one of the most memorable amateur contests ever seen.

The defeat did Mizler no harm whatsoever and in 1932 he won the ABA featherweight title, after which he was selected to represent Great Britain at the Los Angeles Olympics. Although beaten in the quarter finals, he was still good enough to win the ABA lightweight title in 1933.

Very few men could claim the achievement of Mizler, yet the successes and fame he earned did nothing to help his family in desperate times. With more than 150 trophies to his credit, it was time to join his brother Mo as a professional.

At the time, Harry was good friends with Nat Seller, an established and respected trainer in the East End and following discussions with his brothers they all had a meeting with leading promoter, Jeff Dickson and his matchmaker, Ted Broadribb. Although he was offered engagements as a preliminary boy, the financial side was not acceptable. They then visited Victor Berliner who had left Premierland to become general manager and matchmaker at The Ring, Blackfriars. An infinitely better offer was made and accepted, their contract being in the form of a handshake.

One of the conditions was that Mizler would box fortnightly at The Ring, and be trained by Seller alongside ABA champions, Pat Palmer and Dave McCleave. His first paid contest was on 4 June against Bob Lamb from Sunderland who lasted just two minutes thirteen seconds of the opening round. After another first round success, Harry was matched with Nobby Baker, from Trealaw, who claimed never to have been knocked out in 200 contests. Harry duly destroyed that proud claim in just one minute thirty-two seconds of round one.

By the end of the year the Stepney youngster was undefeated in 13 contests, scoring 10 victories inside the distance. He was then matched with Johnny Cuthbert in a challenge for the British lightweight title at The Royal Albert Hall on 18 January 1934. It was a remarkable situation considering he had only been a professional for six months and was still three days short of his twenty-first birthday. Harry was undaunted by the occasion and outboxed the champion, a veteran of over 150 fights, nine of which were for a British title and who had won a Lonsdale belt outright.

The moment his opponent's hands were raised, Cuthbert rushed across the ring and embraced him. 'That is the way I have always wanted to go out of the game', he remarked. 'Here we have a great young fighter to take my place'. Afterwards, referee Charlie Thomas said that Mizler's left hand was the best he had seen since the days of Jim Driscoll.

It had been an incredible fight, not least because such a young and inexperienced man could take virtually every round from a champion who had fought and beaten some of the best men at his weight. Writing in the *London Evening Standard*, Ben Bennison commented:

> Rarely has a championship been won by such a mountain of points, and absurdly there was never a fight so remarkable for rigid observance of the spirit of the sport. There was no holding, not a single punch that was not fair and above board. It was an epic of fighting cleanliness. and never has a champion struck his flag with such grace. It is but once in a very long time, one is privileged to see such a fight as this was.

Before the fight well known East End bookmaker, Benny Lewis, told Mizler that he would get the finest gold watch in Britain if he could win. Years later he still possessed that, as well as other gifts heaped upon him by admiring fans.

Barely seven hours after being declared champion, Mizler was pushing his barrow through the snow to Billingsgate fish market to collect fish for his parent's stall. From his purse money he paid for his sister Hannah's wedding and gave the rest to his mum to look after. With the welfare of his family uppermost in his mind he was anxious to be a busy champion. Boxing regularly, he beat some of the best British and Continental men at his weight, including Welshman, Billy Quinlan, in a title defence at Swansea. In a run of 10 contests between February and September, Jimmy Walsh was the only man to beat him.

In October that year Harry was called upon to defend his British title against the formidable fellow East Ender, Jack 'Kid' Berg, at The Royal Albert Hall. A former world junior lightweight champion, Jack was a dangerous all-action fighter who had faced the best in America, but never challenged for a British title. Being seven years the elder, he was vastly the more experienced of the two.

During training Mizler suffered serious setbacks in that he sustained damage to both hands. Victor Berliner pleaded with him not to fight but having agreed a purse of £1,750, the largest of his career, he insisted on going ahead. It proved to be a bad mistake because in what turned out to be a fight well below expectations, he was seriously handicapped. Using his tearaway tactics, Berg got on top and by round 10 Harry was almost out on his feet with little choice but to retire at the end of the round.

After a five-month break to get his hands treated he eased back to boxing 10-rounders and remained undefeated throughout 1935. After a run of six victories he faced Gustav Humery, of France in what developed into one of the most incredible fights ever seen in a London ring.

Humery was no pushover, having engaged in three tough battles with Berg, beating him in Paris and The Royal Albert Hall earlier in the year. Every fight fan in the East End desperately wanted Harry to gain revenge but after what Jack had done to him the experts were convinced the Frenchman would be too good.

That quickly looked to be the case once the fight got underway, as although Mizler took the opening round, he was suddenly on the receiving end of a hiding. Humery tore into him and during the third round sent him to the canvas for three long counts. When he was draped across the bottom rope by a vicious body shot, referee Moss Deyong, ruled it was low. It was some time before Harry recovered and before the action could continue the bell came to his rescue.

The pattern of the fight continued and Mizler was sent to the floor again in rounds five and six. During the seventh there were shouts from all parts of the arena for the fight to be stopped, as the East End favourite continued to take fearful punishment. At one point, Humery made a similar gesture to the referee but was ignored. At the bell to end the session, Harry was so exhausted that he sank to his knees and fell through the ropes. Meanwhile, his own fans were laying odds of 10/1 against him.

Moss Deyong did go to Mizler's corner during the interval and asked the boxer if he wanted to quit. He refused, stood up and showing immense courage faced up to Humery for round eight. Although he had been battered from pillar to post for the previous six rounds he caused an absolute sensation by suddenly changing the whole course of the fight. With the Frenchman again on top, Harry suddenly put everything into a classic right cross. It landed flush on the mouth causing blood to spurt like a cascade.

Although Mizler was generally regarded as a stylish boxer who could wear an opponent down, he turned on incredible savage aggression. Seizing his chance, he went for broke raining a salvo of blows on Humery's head and driving him around the ring. His face covered in blood, the Frenchman was defenceless and trapped in a corner, arms dropped at his sides. Harry showed no mercy and when another huge right swing crashed to the jaw, the French seconds threw in the towel. The noise from the 7,000-strong crowd was deafening because it had been one of the greatest fights for a decade and would be written about for many years to come. Mizler was certainly fortunate that the fight had not been stopped some rounds earlier, as it would have been in modern times, yet nothing could detract from his performance and incredible bravery.

Despite the gruelling battle with Humery, Harry was back in the ring two months later when, almost as an anti-climax, he beat Norman Snow on points over 15 rounds to win the Southern Area lightweight title. Five more victories followed, one of which was a defence of his newly won championship, against Alby Day (Old Ford) who he beat on points in one of the most stirring battles ever seen at the Devonshire Club, Hackney.

Meanwhile, Jimmy Walsh had sensationally taken the British lightweight title from Jack Berg leaving the way clear for him to defend it against Mizler. At the same time, he was to seek revenge for his setback two years earlier.

After winning 14 consecutive contests Harry faced the new champion at Empress Hall, Earls Court on 18 October 1936. It was a sparking contest between the two stylish boxers and so cleanly fought that the referee, Mr C. H. Douglas, was able to control it from a ringside seat. Apart from the fourth round Harry was outboxed until the 11th when he suddenly came to life and rocked Walsh. Although he won the later rounds he could not make up the points deficit and the champion retained his title by a close but deserved decision.

Four weeks later Harry was outpointed by Dave Crowley at Harringay but following three consecutive victories early in 1937, one of which was on points over Walsh in a non-title fight, he faced world featherweight champion, Peter Sarron of America on the Tommy Farr – Max Bear bill at Harringay. Despite being outpointed, he put up such an impressive performance that he was invited to have a return in the Union of South Africa two months later. Boxing was still finding its feet there and the bout, staged in Johannesburg, was intended to develop a greater interest amongst sports fans. Unfortunately, from the organisers point of view it was a huge disappointment as Sarron was disqualified in the opening round.

Continuing to box at a high level, Mizler faced Al Roth, an outstanding fighter from New York, who had originally been due to face Jimmy Walsh. In what promoter, John Harding, described as the greatest match he ever made, Harry recorded one of his finest victories. Unlike that with Humery, this was a contest of sheer skill. Roth's walk-in style was made to measure for one of the best exponents of left jabs in the business. He did not make a mistake as he outwitted, outpunched and out boxed the aggressive

American. The victory earned him a *Boxing News* Certificate of Merit.

The win over Roth put Harry back in line for another shot at the British lightweight championship and he was matched with Dave Crowley in a final eliminator at the Royal Albert Hall in March 1938. Sadly, he could not maintain the great form he displayed against the American, partly due to having had weight problems. He lacked fire, thus enabling Crowley to take a clear points decision.

Moving up to welterweight, Mizler continued to delight the crowds with his clever boxing and scrupulously fair tactics. He won most of his contests for a couple of years, but they were generally against lesser quality opponents. He fought less frequently following the outbreak of war and in 1940 joined the RAF as a physical training instructor until discharged on medical grounds with stomach problems.

Not having the necessary training facilities as well as losing the zest for fighting, he never regained his best form and was not the fighter of a few years earlier. The rigors of the ring had taken their toll and consequently there were almost as many defeats as successes during the war years. He was outpointed by Berg, Charlie Parkin, Jim Wellard, Harry Lazar and Arthur Danahar who also stopped him in eight rounds. He did beat a faded Eric Boon in 1943 and ever the sportsman, Eric later told a journalist; 'This was not a fight. I was like a pupil with a master'. Some years earlier they had trained alongside one another at Nat Seller's gym in Whitechapel Road where Harry taught Boon some of the finer points of their sport.

Following his four-round defeat by Jimmy Molloy in December 1943, Mizler retired from the ring at his wife, Betty's insistence. She had seen all his fights since they met and never interfered but when she told him it was all over he knew better that to argue. He once toyed with the idea of a comeback, but Betty stood firm and she was backed by Victor Berliner.

During the later years of his life Harry remained as handsome and unmarked as in the halcyon days of his fame. He was a happily married family man with children and grandchildren. Every Sunday morning, he collected his granddaughter and went shopping for bagels and smoked salmon before returning home for a family breakfast.

Family matters were always at the top of Mizler's agenda and after leaving the RAF he returned to his parent's fish stall. He used his ring earnings wisely and after attending to the needs of his family, left the stall and set him and Betty up in a fashionable gown salon in Golders Green. He soon had the image of a flourishing businessman, smart and bearing no marks to indicate his previously demanding trade.

Throughout his retirement he retained a keen interest in boxing and was a much sought-after celebrity. He was called into the ring with Dave Crowley for the Parade of Champions at the last night of Harringay Arena in 1958. In September 1961, he joined Al Phillips' stable as a trainer and on 14 April 1980 was honoured with a testimonial dinner at the Anglo-American Sporting Club in London.

Harry Mizler was one of the finest amateur boxers of all times and although he had a successful professional career he did not quite live up to expectations. He possessed all the essentials that constituted a great boxer – punches, skill and ability to absorb punishment. He was a classic stylist who used the English straight left as well as anybody. Yet there were two aspects which contributed greatly to the fact that he never became a world champion. Firstly, plagued with hand injuries and secondly his lifestyle, albeit an extremely clean one. Unfortunately, there were many occasions where he would tumble into bed within hours of a gruelling fight only to be up at the crack of dawn to get to the fish market, as his parent's business and welfare were of great importance to him. He frequently reminded journalists of the fight for survival and in one interview said: 'Today people take taxis but back in those days my

Aldgate Bantamweight, Alf Mansfield & trainer (identity not known)

Daniel Mendoza
(Whitechapel)

Tom King
(Stepney)

Samuel Elias (Dutch Sam)
(Whitechapel)

Aldgate Flyweight Sid Nathan who later became
a Board of Control Star Class referee

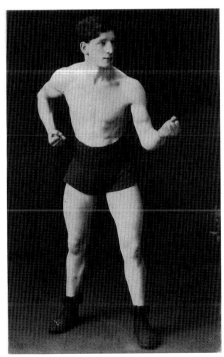

Flyweight, Joe Wilson
(Stepney)

Sam Kellar
(Aldgate)

Former triple British & European
champion Ted 'Kid' Lewis (Aldgate)

Former British Lightweight champion
Harry Mizler (Stepney)

Former undefeated British & European Lightweight champion, and British Welterweight champion, Harry Mason (Whitechapel)

Lew Lazar (left) and Terence Murphy (Canning Town)
weigh-in for their eight rounds contest at Harringay Arena on 7 December 1952,
watched by promoter Jack Solomons

Flyweight, Kid Rich (Aldgate) and Arthur Cunningham square up before their
contest at Victoria Hall, Southend-on-Sea, on 24 September 1926

Former Southern Area
Featherweight champion,
Benny Caplan
(Stepney, St. Georges)

Aldgate Heavyweight
Jewey Smith

Former world, British
and European Flyweight
champion, Charlie Magri
(Stepney)

mother would walk an extra two miles to save a penny on a bus fare'.

Harry was a gentleman in and out of the ring, liked by everyone in boxing and many outside it too. At a meeting back in 1935, he was one of 12 boxers elected to serve on the committee of The National Union of Boxers. He always wore the Star of David on his trunks with honour and distinction and was an absolute credit to his sport and faith.

Tributes poured in following his death in 1990 after battling a long illness. Veteran sports writer, Ben Bennison, who had seen virtually all of his fights described Harry as 'a living text-book on boxing.' He was and still is recognised and talked about as one of the last of the really great Jewish fighters.

Traceable Record
81 CONTSTS
63 WON
2 LOST
16 DREW

30

SID NATHAN

(Aldgate)

To become a successful boxing referee, experience as a competitor inside the ropes is vitally important. Formally a novice flyweight, Sid Nathan rose to the pinnacle as a third man in the ring and when he retired having reached the age of sixty-five, he had refereed a total of 1,246 fights in 30 years.

Sid was born in Aldgate on 1 September 1922. His father boxed as a professional under the name of Jack Arbour, having changed it to avoid his parents knowing what he was involved in. The name he chose related to the area he lived, Arbour Square, where there was also a well-known boxing club Arbour Youth.

As a youngster Jack fought Ted 'Kid' Lewis at the Judean Club on 23 August 1911 and was disqualified for an alleged low blow in the third round. Both featherweights, the two were good mates and the fight was in the early stages of their careers for a purse of sixpence, a cup of tea and a piece of cake each.

Sid was barely 10 years old when he joined the Jewish Lads Brigade and attended boxing classes. Amongst the boys he became friends with was Harry Lazar who was a couple of years his elder. As teenagers they often sparred together at the La Boheme gym in Mile End Road where, one day Harry's manager, former boxer Alf Jacobs, asked Sid if he fancied turning professional. At first, he was apprehensive but the lure of a few shillings during difficult times helped to make his mind up.

Not yet seventeen, his first paid contest was at Kentish Town Baths in March 1939 against Mike Constantino (Soho) who he beat on points over six rounds. Although he suffered the usual first fight nerves, Sid went into the ring quietly confident of victory because Harry Lazar had scored a knockout victory over Mike a few months earlier. Reward for Nathan's debut victory was 25 shillings. 'I was so happy, I thought I had won a world title' he remarked in one interview.

Nathan's ring career was short and sweet having just 16 contests in a little over a year, losing only two. His last was at Holborn Stadium on 3 June 1940 against Idris Pickens (Wales), whom he outpointed over eight rounds. Whilst the effects of the Second World War contributed to the fact that he never boxed again, this was overshadowed by the love and respect he had for Lillian, the young lady who would become his wife. They had met when he was only fourteen and there came a time when she made it clear that she did not like boxing. Without too much debate, Sid agreed to give it up. They were married in 1942 and later that year he was called up for military service but was discharged on medical grounds a short while after.

Still loving the fight game, he couldn't resist the lure of the gyms, and often getting into a sparring routine, contemplated a comeback. His form impressed Jarvis Astaire, an aspiring manager, later to become a top promoter and he even signed a three-year contract with him. Ted 'Kid' Lewis who had remained in the sport as a trainer, manager and promoter also tried to sign him. Following a cartilage operation on his right knee, Sid knew there was no possibility of a return to the ring.

His involvement in refereeing began one night in 1957 when he attended a small hall promotion at Caledonian

Road Baths. At the end of the final contest he vehemently disagreed with the verdict of the referee, Bill Williams. During a conversation that ensued, Bill explained how he arrived at his decision but admired Sid's enthusiasm and suggested that he applied to the Board of Control to become a referee.

After going through the necessary procedures, he was appointed and officiated in his first contest, at Shoreditch Town Hall on May 13 1958, between welterweights Buster Gaffney (Croydon) and Mike Robbins (Camberwell), which he stopped in Robbins favour in round four. The following week *Boxing News* reported; 'Trial referee Sid Nathan, acted correctly when stopping the uneven exchanges in the fourth'.

An alert, sprightly individual, Nathan adapted rapidly to his new role in boxing and in 1971 was appointed to 'A Star Class', the highest grade of official in the United Kingdom. It entitled him to referee and judge fights at every level from world championships downwards. Consequently, he officiated in those roles, not only in Britain, but throughout the world.

After retiring in 1988, he maintained a healthy interest in boxing which, he is always quick to acknowledge, played a huge part in getting him out of the grime and pressures of the East End. Over the years this extremely popular man has given countless interviews and in one with the late Ron Oliver for *Boxing News* he confessed;

> Boxing has been my life. I was just a kid from the East End, but boxing has enabled me to travel the world and meet some wonderful people, experiences money can't buy. I have been fortunate, and I appreciate it very much and everyone along the way.

It was a moving statement from a genuine, honest and hardworking man to whom boxing owes a great deal. He died on 2 April 2016, aged ninety-three.

31

AL PHILLIPS

(Aldgate)

BRITISH EMPIRE FEATHERWEIGHT CHAMPION 1947

EUROPEAN FEATHERWEIGHT CHAMPION 1947

The one great disappointment in Al Phillips life during his 13 years as a professional boxer, was that he never won a British championship. Three times he challenged for the featherweight crown but lost on each occasion. Although he won British Empire and European titles at the weight, he was never presented with a trophy to recognise either success. It was an injustice to a tough and extremely popular fighter.

Al was born at The London Hospital in Whitechapel Road on 25 January 1920. His parents, Harry and Nellie, had come to England from Russia some years earlier. He had six brothers and two sisters. His grandfather was the only member of the family who had ever boxed.

Phillips started boxing at a school play centre in the East End, leaving at the age of fourteen to join the Jewish Lads Brigade Boys Club. As a member he became Stepney Borough Federation champion and went on to win a London Federation of Boys Clubs championship at 6st 6lbs.

At quite a young age, Al gave up boxing and joined the Merchant Navy as a cabin boy for a while. When he returned in 1938 he went to a boxing booth with Freddie Mills and Gypsy Daniels and then at the age of eighteen turned professional with manager Ted Beeber. His trainer was Jimmy Scott who looked after the La Boheme gym at Whitechapel Road which had originally been opened by Nat Seller a few years earlier.

Boxing at venues including Mile End Arena and The Ring, Blackfriars, where most of his early contests ended in the first few rounds, Al quickly became a popular little fighter affectionately referred to as 'The Aldgate Tiger'. In December 1938 he won a Jack Solomons' featherweight competition at The Devonshire Club, Hackney, having two contests on the same evening. Both ended in the second round.

Three weeks later, however, he suffered his first defeat when Red McDonald (Canning Town) knocked him out in the first round of a hurriedly arranged contest. Jack Solomons' bill had collapsed badly on the night and as the two boxers were at the arena they agreed to fight. It would be the only time in Al's career that he failed to beat the count.

Shortly after he had turned professional, Phillips felt he needed more experience, so he joined Sam McKeown's boxing booth travelling around Devon and Cornwall. He joined as a mere novice but on returning to London six months later, felt like a seasoned campaigner with plenty of confidence.

After six further winning contests at the Devonshire Club, war broke out and Al was called for service. With a demand for stokers in the Navy, he served with both The Royal and Merchant branches and in doing so experienced some very difficult times. The ship on which he served was bombed, machine gunned, mined and torpedoed and he was also involved in commando raids. Luckily, he survived the perils to tell the tales.

While on leave between trips to sea, Al squeezed in fights whenever he could. He had several at Liverpool and when he was later posted to Sheerness he was able to box in London. He was fortunate to have a sports minded commander who allowed him time off to fight.

In November 1941 he married his sweetheart, Sonia, known to everyone as 'sis'. They had two children, Joey who was born in November 1942 and Paula in February 1947.

Philips professional career really took off during 1943, during which he had 12 fights, losing only to Jackie Paterson who stopped him in round three at Glasgow in March. It was his only defeat in a run of 36 contests between March 1941 and November 1944 when he was disqualified against Dave Crowley. During that period, he boxed on 14 occasions at Queensbury All-Services Club at the London Casino in Soho but also travelled further afield to Glasgow, where he had four fights, Oxford, Leicester and Bristol.

By 1944, 'The Aldgate Tiger' was a genuine championship contender and boxed three official eliminating contests for the British featherweight title, all of which he won against Jim Brady (points), George Pook (KO.1) and Len Davies (Disq.6). Those successes ultimately led him to being matched with champion, Nel Tarleton, who had held the title since 1940.

They met at Manchester in February 1945 whilst Al was on six weeks leave from the Navy, and hundreds of his fans travelled from London to support him. Being a tough, strong and relentless fighter, he was expected to be too good for the thirty-nine-year-old champion. A crowd of 7,000 witnessed a great boxer versus fighter battle in which Phillips was more than holding his own until he sprained an ankle during round 10. From that moment his mobility was insufficient to cope with the champion's speed and skill and he suffered a points defeat.

Undeterred Al was quickly back in action and had 10 further contests before the end of the year, three of which were against Dave Crowley who outpointed him twice. Al won the other on points.

After a run of six inside the distance victories, one of which was against Canadian star, Danny Webb, he faced Cliff Curvis in a British title eliminator at The Royal Albert Hall in December 1946 winning by a second-round knockout. The success was pivotal to him moving into the most important year of his career because despite only having 10 contests in 1947, four were for major championships.

On 18 March, Phillips outpointed Cliff Anderson, of British Guiana, to win the vacant British Empire title in a fight which was not without controversy. Al was floored three times in round four and although he fought back to take a close decision, many in the crowd believed Anderson was robbed.

Two months later, again at The Royal Albert Hall, Al faced good Frenchman, Ray Famechon, for the vacant European title and again there was a degree of controversy. He took five counts in round seven and despite appearing to have cramp in his right leg, fought back well. In the next round, after appearing to be hurt, Famechon threw a right hook to the body and followed up with a headbutt. Phillips fell to the floor where upon the referee disqualified the Frenchman for a low blow.

In view of the closeness of their first contest it was inevitable that the East Ender would be called upon to defend his Empire title against Cliff Anderson. It was duly staged at Olympia on 1 July and this one also ended in disqualification when Anderson was ruled out for kidney punching.

As a double champion, Phillips was then given the chance to add the British title to his laurels by facing Ronnie Clayton for the vacant featherweight championship and at the same time put his own titles up for grabs. The fight took place on a rain swept evening at Liverpool Football Club's Anfield Stadium on 11 September. Both men set a blistering pace and although there were no knockdowns it was tough going throughout the 15 rounds. At the end Clayton was a worthy winner and took all three titles.

Despite the defeat Al was not out of championship contention and in April the following year faced Johnny Molloy in yet another eliminator. Although he was adjudged to have lost on points, the decision was extremely unpopular. There was considerable uproar, so much so that the Master of Ceremonies could not be heard as he attempted to introduce the next contest.

After an eight-round defeat to old foe Ray Famechon, two months later there were signs that Phillips' best days were behind him. After several months out of the ring due to hand and arm injuries, he had only four contests during 1949, three of which were against Tony Lombard of South Africa. In 1950 he had just three contests but most importantly one was a 10-rounder at catchweight, against Ronnie Clayton. Al won a close decision and left the ring at the Empress Hall to scenes of wild excitement.

After knocking out Ron Cooper of Poplar in four rounds in December the old 'Aldgate Tiger' showed that he had lost none of his punching power. As a result, he secured another shot at Clayton's British and Empire titles. It was staged at Nottingham on 26 February 1951 and several hundred East End fans made the trip to support their man. Although he put up a great fight and finished with his left eye closed and the right badly bruised, he was fortunate enough to survive the full 15 rounds only to lose a wide points decision.

That was enough for the popular Aldgate man and in announcing his retirement told a press gathering 'It seems I was fated never to win a British title. I accept it but I've loved the game'. He paid tribute to his one and only trainer, Jimmy Scott, saying; 'I'm sure he loved me like a son and I will never forget him'. Al also recalled his first manager, Ted Beeber, who he eventually left for Alf Jacobs' 'I don't know if I did the right thing or not, all I know is both looked after me while I was with them'.

The fighting may have been over for Al, but he was never going to be inactive. Just after the war he and his brother-in-law bought a printing business which grew from strength to strength. When they originally opened up, their equipment consisted of a one-foot pedalled press, a few cases of type plus a determination to make a success of their venture. By the early 1950's they employed two men and were equipped with the latest automatic printing machinery. Al handled the sales side of the business as his ring reputation attracted many customers connected to boxing. They included promoters of large and small events who required programmes, leaflets and posters to advertise their shows.

The 'Aldgate Tiger's' involvement in the fight game didn't end the night he was beaten by Ronnie Clayton. It had always been his ambition to have his own gym and hopefully manage a featherweight capable of winning a British title. Never a man to delay things he promptly applied for and was granted British Boxing Board of Control trainer and manager licences after which he set up an office and gym in Essex Road, Islington.

Local man Arthur Howard was the first boxer he handled and with the stable growing rapidly, others soon joined. Over the years Al trained or managed a host of fighters including Jimmy Newman, the Hinson brothers, George Dormer, Joe Bygraves, Brian London and Johnny Prescott, many of whom reached championship level.

Phillips eventually held all Board of Control licences except a promoters. As his business developed he became a matchmaker for the Midlands Sporting Club and eventually an International agent, in association in particular, with the leading Italian promoter, Umberto Branchini. He also did considerable business with South

African promoters and travelled to the Philippines, Ghana and Nigeria.

Away from boxing Al was a devoted family man who often claimed that his wife knew almost as much about the sport as he did. They were a close couple but suffered a horrendous tragedy in 1986 when their son Joey was killed in Marbella when a boat he was on burst into flames.

Al loved golf and was a member of Potters Bar and Stanmore clubs claiming to have played most of the courses in Middlesex. He was also a regular at Champion Golfing Society events together with many other former champions, including Sir Henry Cooper, Dick Richardson and Terry Downes.

A modest, quietly spoken man outside the ring, Al was a rough tough battler who wore the Star of David on his trunks with pride and distinction. When he passed away on 7 February 1999, he was the last of the great Jewish fighters produced in Britain and that is how he will be remembered.

Traceable Record:
89 CONTESTS
72 WON
14 LOST
3 DREW

——.32.——

JOHNNY QUILL

(Stepney)

Shock and horror spread throughout the East End when folk learned of the untimely death of John Patrick, 'Johnnie' Quill on 29 June 1935 at the age of just twenty-four. He was a tremendous young prospect who, having amassed a professional record of 97 contests in a little over nine years, was on the verge of a British title fight.

Born in Stepney in 1911, he lived with his parents at 77 Brook Street, just around the corner to Premierland where he would have his first paid fight at the age of fifteen. Living in this densely populated area, Johnnie quickly learned how to look after himself, but in many respects, became different to the average street urchin and hooligan. He was intelligent and although he soon took to boxing, was also able to turn his hand to other things as he got older. He became singularly well-read and his conversations were not always about boxing and the men he had beaten. With an incredible memory he was always able to quote the exact date of any of his fights.

He was always very astute and looked to the future. After his death he left behind a small library of books including a dictionary with folded pages and manuscript notes. It had been his intention after finishing with boxing to make a career for himself in journalism and was already embarking on the rudiments of the art.

Quill's first contest was another example of the sheer rawness of boxing at the time. Not only was it over 10 rounds but his opponent was only thirteen years of age yet had the experience of 20 professional fights. Nipper Pat Daly, despite being two years Johnnie's junior, was an incredible youngster. He was quicker, sharper and generally much the better boxer and earned the points decision.

The two lads became good mates after the contest and soon took to sparring together at Professor Andrew Newton's famous gym at Marylebone Road. Whilst Daly was by far the more experienced, his skill rubbed off on Quill who was a quick learner. A tall, rangy upright boxer, he took the sport seriously from the start and had a huge appetite for training.

Once he was established as a professional, Quill boxed regularly, mostly in London with Premierland being his favourite venue. He was gradually matched with better quality opponents and within a four-week period during April and May 1929, he outpointed Harry Berry, Lew Pinkus and Mick Hill in 15-rounders at the East End venue.

In 1930, Johnnie entered a lightweight competition at The Ring, Blackfriars, for a belt donated by the trade paper *Boxing*. In the first and second heats, staged during the afternoon of Sunday 10 August, he outpointed Billy Granelly (Wales) and Jim Hunter (Scotland), both over four rounds. In the semi-final the following evening he was awarded a dubious six-rounds decision over Jim Learoyd (Leeds) and left the ring to a storm of booing. The final took place a couple of hours later and for what was probably the only time in his career, Quill was given an unpleasant welcome despite fighting in his hometown against a man from Walsall. Peter Nolan, however, proved to be the better man and although most exchanges were close he won a clear decision which pacified an angry crowd.

Johnnie's first serious setback came in June 1931 when he travelled to Paris and faced good prospect, Gustave Humery who, in 1937, would become European lightweight champion. Although the Londoner put up a game performance he was gradually worn down by ferocious body attacks. When he was sent heavily to the floor in round four, his corner promptly threw in the towel but in accordance with Continental rules, the referee counted him out. It would be the only knockout defeat he would suffer in his whole career.

Although the defeat was damaging only to his ego, Johnnie sensibly took a five month break from boxing. It freshened him up and, putting himself under the management of Ted Broadribb, he eased back with an unbeaten run of six contests. By this time he was considered to be approaching championship contender class, so in order to assess his true capabilities he was matched with established contenders, Fred Webster, Haydn Williams, and Leo Phillips over a three-month period at The Ring, Blackfriars. Although he was outpointed by all three and four months later stopped in four rounds by Arthur Unwin due to a cut eye, the experience gained in those contests was invaluable.

Quill was an exceptionally intelligent young man who used everything to his own benefit. Following the unfortunate loss to Unwin, his only defeat in a run of 28 contests between June 1933 and April 1935, was to Leo Phillips who outpointed him over eight rounds at Holborn Stadium.

Following victories over Fred Webster, Stoker George Reynolds, Pat Butler and Dave McCleave. Johnnie established himself as one of the top welterweights in the country and a genuine championship contender. He also avenged the defeat by Arthur Unwin with a three-round stoppage victory at Mile End. The victory over Butler, who he stopped in 11 rounds, however, was particularly significant because seven months later Pat would become British champion by outpointing Harry Mason.

Another important victory was in December 1934 when he outpointed Billy Bird in a final eliminator for the Southern Area title. It had already been agreed by the British Boxing Board of Control that the winner would meet Charlie Baxter for the vacant title. The winner of that contest would go on to face Harry Mason for the British title.

It was at this point, however, that nature became unkind to Johnnie in that Baxter had to withdraw from the contest through illness. It was agreed that Pat Butler would take his place, but fate intervened. Whilst training at Brighton, Quill fell ill with a heavy cold which worsened within a few days. It became so severe that he returned to London where he was admitted to St Georges hospital and underwent an operation for pleurisy. He failed to recover and died on 29 June 1935 aged just twenty-four.

It could be argued that Quill was one of the finest East End boxers never to have fought for a championship. A model professional, he could box, and he could punch hard and his record alone of 62 victories and 12 draws from 97 contests qualified him for a tilt at major honours.

He was focused and dedicated to his sport but outside the ring he never belittled an opponent. In victory or defeat he was always generous. Talking to a reporter one day he referred to Paul Schaeffer whom he outpointed at Whitechapel Pavilion in November 1934, just five months before his death. 'He's the hardest hitting welter in the country', he remarked. The reporter pointed out that Johnnie was something of a puncher himself, but the response was; 'No, Paul hits harder than I do'.

By the time of his passing, Quill had moved to Manchester Road on the Isle of Dogs, but the people of Cable Street and the surrounding areas had not forgotten him. They followed all his fights and he was very much a local hero. He had an extremely generous nature and was always willing to support any charitable cause and help those less fortunate than himself.

At 2pm on Wednesday 3 July, the funeral cortege left his old address at 77 Brook Street and proceeded to Leytonstone Catholic Cemetery. Hundreds of people lined the streets of the East End to pay their respects. Many were in tears. It was an incredible turnout, and mounted police had to clear a way for the hearse to proceed. More than 100 wreaths were laid out at the cemetery as people gathered to mull over the injustice that had occurred.

Johnnie Quill was given an incredible send off as local people as well as others from the boxing community remembered him for who he was; a talented young boxer in the ring and one of nature's gentlemen outside it.

Traceable Record
97 CONTESTS
62 WON
22 LOST
12 DREW
1 NC

—.33.——

HARRY REEVE

(Stepney)

BRITISH LIGHT-HEAVYWEIGHT CHAMPION 1916-17

Despite being generally billed from Plaistow where he lived. Harry, real name Harry Issacs, was born in the St Georges area of Stepney on 7 January 1893. 'Reevo', as he called himself from an early age, was the eldest of a large family and began boxing professionally in 1910 at the age of seventeen. Showing great promise, he lost just one of his six contests that year and was undefeated in 1911 during which he won 14 and drew one. After having half a dozen fights at The Ring, Blackfriars, he became a regular at Wonderland which was close to his home at Whitechapel Road. When the arena was destroyed by fire in 1911, he automatically continued his career at nearby Premierland.

During the early stages, all contests were of six and 10 round durations. Despite a points defeat to Harry Rudge at Premierland in January 1912, he continued to make good progress and as a consequence the duration of contests increased to 15 and 20 rounds. After stopping Ike Pratt in the 20th round of a fight at Newcastle in early 1914, Reeve was matched with Pat O'Keefe (Mile End) for the vacant British middleweight title and Lonsdale belt at The National Sporting Club on 23 February the same year.

O'Keefe was a crafty old veteran, 10 years older than Harry and vastly more experienced. He had won and lost the middleweight title in 1906 and challenged Bombardier Billy Wells for the heavyweight crown in 1913 only to lose by knockout in round 15. Four weeks before facing Reeve he had been knocked out in five rounds by George Carpentier in a challenge for the European heavyweight title in Nice. He had also campaigned in the United States, Australia and Paris between 1907 and 1910.

Unperturbed by the task he faced, Reeve rose to the occasion. He had O'Keefe on the verge of defeat in the sixth and fourteenth rounds but using every trick in the book to avoid defeat, the former champion fiddled his way through the 20 rounds to take a close decision after a stirring contest.

Disappointed but not downhearted, Harry was soon back in action but was beaten in his next two contests. He was forced to retire against tough American, Joe Borrell and then outpointed by Sergeant Pat McEnroy. Refusing to let the defeats get him down, 'Reevo' proceeded to rack up another winning run of 11 contests during a period of just eight months. Three of these were against a crowd pleasing knockout specialist, black Canadian, Johnny Holland. He had become a real favourite at Premierland by hammering everyone put in front of him.

Badly needing a man who could absorb his destructive power, the promoters made Harry a good offer. Not only did he take the Canadian's big punches but gave him a boxing lesson and took a well-earned decision. Those behind Holland could not believe it when Reeve repeated the treatment in a return three months later, and insisted on a third contest. Harry duly agreed, and this time left no doubts by stopping the tough Canadian in 10 rounds.

Another notable achievement during this period was when he stopped up-and-coming Joe Beckett from Southampton in seven rounds. Having stopped Reeve in the previous year, Joe was a huge odds-on favourite and during the early rounds was by far the better man. He shook Harry badly in round four but the tough East London man recovered, boxed skilfully throughout the next two rounds and then in the seventh put the young prospect down and out with a great head and body combination.

Not prepared to refuse a generous offer, Reeve travelled to Australia where within a few months he agreed to five 20-round contests in Sydney and Melbourne. Although he lost the first two inside the distance, he demonstrated his toughness by winning the next three on points, all over 20 rounds.

Like other men before him, Harry loved the life down under especially the local beer which he downed in generous quantities. Consequently, when he returned home he was more than a stone heavier than when he left. Nevertheless, he kept fit and ran up another string of victories including a 20-round decision over reigning British light-heavyweight champion, Dick Smith. His success earned him the right of a return for the title and with a newly allocated Lonsdale Belt at stake.

Reeve had five months in which to prepare but instead of being thoroughly professional and taking the matter seriously, he spent much of his time drinking heavily at his local pub. Utterly dismayed by the situation, his manager, Dan Sullivan, knew that if his man was to have any chance of being ready for the fight he had to get him away from the East End. He therefore arranged for him to set up camp at The Black Bull at Whetstone in Hertfordshire where fighters had trained from the bare-knuckle era.

Harry eventually got down to serious training but could not shift the surplus weight. When Sullivan paid him a visit a week before the fight he found to his horror that he scaled in the region of 14st meaning that he had seven days to shift 21lbs.

Reeve appeared unconcerned and nonchalantly insisted that he would make the light-heavyweight limit of 12st 7lbs. Sullivan, however, knew that the only way that could happen was in a Turkish Bath but in doing so would leave him extremely weak. Only Harry knew what exactly went on during the days leading up to the fight but come the day he surprised everyone by scaling 12st 4lbs.

Although Smith possessed all the physical advantages, he could not cope with Harry's bustling style. Appearing strong and oozing confidence, the East End fighter proceeded to outbox the champion to take a well-earned decision and claim the British championship at the age of twenty-seven.

Looking forward to earning good money by being champion, things started well for Reeve when he stopped former middleweight champion Jim Sullivan, in 11 rounds at the Holborn Empire. Within a couple of months, however, war was declared and like many other fighters, Harry was called up for Army service early in the summer of 1917 and within two months was sent to France. By the end of the year, however, he was home again having been seriously injured in combat. His right leg was full of shrapnel and half the calf blown away. When he was finally discharged after a long spell in hospital he was told that his army and boxing careers were over. Harry therefore reluctantly notified The National Sporting Club that his injuries would prevent him from defending his title, which accordingly was declared vacant. He also returned the Lonsdale Belt.

When the war ended in 1918, boxing in Britain received a massive boom as many professionals got back into ring action. Money was short in the Reeve household and Harry badly needed much more than his war pension of six shillings and fourpence a week to support his wife and large family. With his injuries healed he trained himself back to reasonable fitness and put the word out that he was looking for action. When the promoters at The Ring, Blackfriars, offered him a return with Joe Beckett he jumped at the chance despite not having boxed for almost two years. Having got himself into reasonable shape, he was confident he still had the beating of the Southampton man.

After a good opening round Harry caused a sensation by flooring Beckett for two long counts but couldn't finish him off. His great effort put immense strain on his injured leg which burst open in the fifth forcing him to retire. The damage was in fact so bad that a photograph showing several shrapnel scars duly appeared on the front page of the next edition of the trade paper *Boxing*.

It was a sign of the times that despite the worrying setback, 'Reevo' refused to quit the ring. Having regained the taste for action plus his urgent need for extra cash, he beat Seaman Powell in nine rounds at The Ring two months later. Harry feared nobody and next faced good heavyweight, Eddie McGoorty, who knocked him out in four rounds at The National Sporting Club.

He continued by fighting mostly heavyweights but with only limited success. After being outpointed by Bandsman Dick Rice in January 1920, he was out of action for exactly a year but returned to face British champion, Bombardier Billy Wells, who knocked him out in four rounds. It was a further 12 months before he fought again and this time he was stopped by Herbert Crossley. Dutch champion, Piet Van der Veer knocked him out in Rotterdam as did Bert Kenny at Lime Grove Baths.

After being outpointed by Tom Berry (Custom House) at Canning Town, Harry fought abroad more often than at home. During the period between January 1921 and August 1922 he took 14 contests in the Netherlands, Germany, Denmark, Belgium and France as opposed to six in England.

The first in this sequence of away fights was in June 1921, against the talented Battling Siki at Rotterdam in which he was outpointed over 10 rounds. They met twice more at Antwerp and Marseilles with Senegalese winning on points and latterly by stoppage in six rounds shortly before he took the world light-heavyweight title from George Carpentier.

In many respects this was a successful period for Reeve because apart from earning good money, he won four, drew four and lost six of his fights abroad. Only Siki beat him inside the distance which demonstrated his toughness and sheer determination to overcome what had been horrific physical handicaps.

Prepared to fight anyone, Reeve again went in against world class opposition in January 1923 when he faced Mike McTigue in Liverpool only to be knocked out in three rounds. In his next contest two months later McTigue beat Siki to take the world title.

Before the end of the year, Harry was on his travels again taking five fights in Germany and Poland in the space of two months but was successful in only one. Despite being in the journeyman class he was very popular in Germany but was forced to return home when his wife became ill.

Despite all the obstacles, Reeve kept issuing challenges to heavy and light-heavyweights and was rarely short of work. Another example of his toughness was when he held heavyweight contender, Phil Scott, to a draw at the Royal Albert Hall in July 1924. The following year he got a similar result in Hamburg against Dutch champion Piet Van der Veer.

The majority of his fights by this time took place in the small halls of East London such as Hoxton Baths, Ilford Skating Rink, Forest Gate and East Ham Baths. With the capacity to fight regularly he also travelled to Plymouth, Manchester, Southampton, Nottingham, Sheffield and Wales. He was particularly busy in 1927, taking 13 contests but Phil Scott was the only man to knock him out. Most of his contests over the last few years of his career were over 15 rounds and he was rarely beaten inside the distance.

Harry decided to retire in 1928 following a 15-round draw with Reggie Meen in Leicester but six years later at the age of forty-one, this remarkable man returned to the ring and took a further four contests. He lost only one on points over eight rounds to Jack Cannons in Ilford after which he retired for good.

Living at Queens Road, Plaistow, he became a stevedore in the London Docks but also maintained an interest in boxing. He was an instructor for many years and ran a school at Plaistow. Many youngsters benefited from his tuition both before and during the years following his final retirement.

Had it not been for war Harry may well have made a bigger name for himself, despite the fact that he was not always the most conscientious of trainers. Physically, at only five feet eight inches tall, he was too short for a light-heavyweight but he more than made up for such a handicap with an abundance of courage. He overcame his obstacles and never complained. With a dry wit he just got on with life and was another man who was a credit to his chosen sport. His death in December 1958 at the age of sixty-five was a shock to all that knew him.

Traceable Record:
154 CONTESTS
83 WON
49 LOST
20 DREW
2 ND

—.34.—

JEWEY SMITH

(Aldgate)

Born in Spitalfields on 7 January 1884 of Jewish parents, Jewey Smith, birth name Joseph, lived in Aldgate most of his life. Very little is known about his early years or his introduction to boxing due largely to the fact that contests during that period often went unrecorded.

He joined the Navy at a relatively young age and in all probability, became involved in boxing (during this time due to it being a must-do-sport within the services). On returning to London, Jewey was managed by Harry Morris who, apart from owning the Lion Club, a billiard hall in Whitechapel Road, also handled a number of professional fighters including Sid Burns and Bandsman Rice.

Morris was a good businessman but needing somebody to train his fighters, approached Jack Goodwin, a former fighter who was making a name for himself in the East End as a trainer. They reached a deal whereby Jack was installed in part of the club where he created an up-to-date gymnasium. Jewey Smith became one of his new batch of pupils.

Being only 5ft 8ins tall but very squat and stocky, Smith boxed at heavyweight. Goodwin had first seen him in action at the Judean Club and despite his lack of height was impressed by his all action style, power and skill. That view

236

was endorsed at Wonderland a few weeks later when he saw Jewey knock out Mike Crawley in three rounds after flooring him several times.

As part of their training routine all of Jack's fighters did their roadwork early in the mornings at Victoria Park. This, however, did not suit Jewey who being very shy, could not be persuaded to run in public. Instead, he would arrive at the club earlier than the others and spend up to half an hour running flat out around the billiard tables. After going half a dozen times in one direction he would stop, shadow box for a few minutes and then run in the opposite direction. It was completely unorthodox but still ensured that he reached the right level of fitness.

Another of the trainer's routines that Smith hated was his method of freshening boxers after training. As there was no bath he used a hosepipe, but with Jewey he threw buckets of water over him instead. Jack insisted that his methods ensured that each boxer went to the ring in a perfect state of fitness.

Smith settled under Goodwin and in April 1908 was matched with world heavyweight champion Tommy Burns in a title fight at Neuilly, Paris. The circumstances under which it was arranged, however, were extremely unethical. The champion was on a tour of England and Europe taking fights against poor quality opposition to earn as much money as possible and delaying an inevitable meeting with genuine challenger Jack Johnson. While in Paris he contacted small hall promoter Leon See, offering to fight for him for half the box office takings. With no suitable opponent in France, See travelled to London and met with Wonderland matchmaker, Harry Jacobs, and offered him £25 plus expenses for two for Jewey to fight in Paris.

Although an agreement was eventually reached, there were strings attached on both sides. At the outset, See declined to name the opponent, whereupon Jacobs insisted that it be written into the contract that Smith would meet anyone provided he was not an Englishman or American. He reasoned that the clause would prevent See from giving him a dangerous opponent for such a small purse. When the French promoter eventually revealed that Jewey would be facing Burns, Harry was furious but with the world champion being French-Canadian he was forced to concede that he was powerless to do anything about it.

During the build up to the fight, Smith was billed as being Champion of Africa and France. There was a strong indication that he had some connection with South Africa and although no conclusive evidence has ever emerged to support it, several boxing historians accept that he at least began his boxing career in Johannesburg. Reporting on the Burns contest, the *Montreal Daily Star* stated categorically that Jewey hailed from South Africa.

The contest was a huge attraction in Paris, and always being a man with an eye for showmanship, promoter See had the large hall decorated with dozens of flags and streamers. Before the fight Burns allegedly agreed to take it easy for a few rounds to give the crowd a show. For his part Jewey charged forward from the opening bell, snorted and swung wildly while the champion ducked and weaved and generally made it look as though the Aldgate man had a chance. In round five, however, he decided it was time to end matters and sent Smith to the floor with a sharp shot to the chin. The large gallery of photographers snapped away enthusiastically, but one magnesium flashgun set fire to a streamer. When somebody shouted 'fire' the crowd made a panic-stricken stampede for the exits.

In the meantime, Jewey struggled to his feet only to be knocked out by the champion's next shot. Suddenly aware of what had occurred outside the ring, Burns jumped over the ropes and ran for safety. He was already fully dressed by the time someone told him that he had won by knockout. Although the fire quickly fizzled out, hardly a person was left in the hall.

Jewey became extremely popular in Paris, returning there to fight on seven further occasions, losing each time but nevertheless earning reasonable money. He recovered quickly from the Burns defeat and nine days later scored a second-round knockout over Charlie Allum at Wonderland. Four weeks later he returned to Paris where he was knocked out in three rounds by the immensely talented black American, Sam McVea, one of the most feared hitters of the era. The punch with which he finished Smith landed on the forehead with such force that it raised a huge lump making it impossible for him to wear a hat for several weeks.

Showing no obvious ill effects, the tough man from Aldgate was back in the ring at Wonderland within three weeks, losing a points decision to Jack Scales who he subsequently faced on four further occasions, winning three. It was the beginning of a good spell for Smith because in the next 12 months the only man to beat him was good American, Willie Lewis, who outpointed him twice in the space of two weeks in Paris.

The level of opponent Jewey faced was generally good, one being former British heavyweight champion, Iron Hague, who he outpointed over 20 rounds at Sheffield in February 1910. Harry Morris had been after the contest for some time and the local crowd warmed to Smith who withstood some tremendous punches throughout the thrilling contest but gave back more in return. Ahead of the start Hague had been a 5/1 on betting favourite to win by knockout.

After five more straight victories Jewey was matched with Petty Officer Matthew 'Nutty' Curran over 20 rounds at Wonderland on 26 September. Jack Woolf went to extreme lengths to hype up the importance of the contest, advertising it as for the heavyweight championship and championship challenge belt of England for a purse of £400. Articles were signed at the offices of *Sporting Life* who were the stake holders.

A near record crowd packed into the historic old arena and raised the roof as Smith and Curran entered the building during a supporting bout. At ten o' clock, the ring was cleared, and the atmosphere was intense as they waited for the main event as if it were for a world title.

Curran went to the ring first surrounded by an entourage larger than one which would accompany a Continental celebrity. Smith was not without a hefty clan, carrying bottles, towels, sponges, smelling salts and other aids to successful seconding. The preliminaries were long and wearisome with Curran making an exhaustive examination of his opponent's hand wraps. Not to be out-psyched, the Londoner put on a similar show.

The belt, a magnificent piece of goldsmith's artwork was then carried to the ring and displayed. When announcing the officials and principal guests, the Master of Ceremonies stated that it would be presented to the winner on condition he agreed to defend it in any part of England for £500.

Curran was at least a head taller than his opponent and with a longer reach. He was heavier by a stone but when stripped revealed surplus flesh around his middle. In contrast, despite his squat appearance, Jewey looked in great shape and as hard as nails. The fight, however, did not live up to expectations, although for his part the Aldgate man probably never fought better, winning the first four rounds.

Using his extra weight, Curran relied on roughhouse tactics to try and wear his opponent down and succeeded in flooring him in rounds five and six. In the meantime, however, he persistently mauled, held and hit on the break.

The fight ended in the seventh when, following a toe-to-toe skirmish, Curran slammed a right hook into Smith's groin. There was a storm of booing as he slumped to the floor, but when it had quietened down, it was announced that the referee, who had issued warnings to both men, had disqualified them for hitting in the clinches and declared the bout 'no contest'.

It was an unfortunate outcome for Jewey because the doctor in attendance subsequently issued a certificate stating; 'Jewey Smith is suffering from contusion of the groin caused by a blow and such an injury would have rendered him incapable of continuing a boxing contest'.

Despite the disappointing ending, a rematch was immediately agreed and took place four weeks later at the Cosmopolitan Gymnasium, Plymouth the venue for most of Curran's fights. It was again billed as being for the English heavyweight title and was again a huge attraction. A crowd of 7,000 crammed into the arena only to witness another poor contest.

Despite its billing, neither man looked championship class and in some respects the ending was similar to that of their first encounter with Curran flooring Smith with a body punch. Again, a foul was claimed but referee, Eugene Corri ruled it legitimate. A doctor called into the ring to examine Smith stated that, in his opinion, there was no evidence of a foul blow having been struck.

Although Jewey continued his ring career for a further three years, it was very much a roller-coaster ride with just eight victories from 21 contests. He returned to Sheffield six weeks after losing to Curran and was outpointed over 20 rounds by Iron Hague. On this occasion he was badly handicapped by twisting a shoulder muscle in round 11. By the 17th the pain was so acute that his left arm was practically useless.

Smith thrilled the Paris crowd in his next fight on New Year's Day 1911 in a gallant battle against George Gunther, only to be knocked out in the seventh. Three weeks later at Wonderland he again showed immense courage before going down in the eleventh to big punching American, Battling Jim Johnson. He was forced to quit on his stool having injured his left arm which twisted under his body when he was knocked to the floor.

Fully recovered, Jewey returned to Wonderland three weeks later and knocked out Harry Croxon and followed that up the following month with a points victory over Ben Taylor. Meanwhile the Sheffield fans wanted to see more of him, so he was matched with black American Alf Langford in early April.

As it was an important fight Jack Goodwin decided they should train in the region and set up a gym at Waleswood, a small colliery district near Sheffield. Although he succeeded in getting Jewey to do his morning road work, the boxer, still feeling self-conscious, wore a woollen cap which he pulled down to his eyes while his sweater covered his chin. It was the first time a boxer had ever trained in the village and when the local women saw him approaching they ran into their houses and slammed the doors. Eventually, once they realised who he was they got excited about the forthcoming fight and crowded into the gym every afternoon to watch him train. Even when a small charge was made in order to keep the numbers down, people still arrived in their dozens. Jewey had become so popular that on the day of the fight the village was decked with bunting and the small streets were lined with well-wishers who gave him a tremendous send off.

Alf Langford was a huge man but Smith still succeeded in flooring him three times during the early rounds. Eventually size and weight were the deciding factors. Jewey faded badly as the contest wore on and the American took the 20-round decision. Remaining in the north of England, Jewey faced another black American, Young Johnson, at Mexborough three weeks later and won on points.

Influenced by other Jewish boxers from the East End he then decided to try his luck in America and between July and December 1911 had eight contests, mostly in New York, of which he won four. The first was against Dan Flynn who four months earlier had lost a 20-round decision to Bombardier Billy Wells at Olympia. Flynn beat Jewey courtesy of a newspaper decision over 10 rounds.

In November Smith scored his best victory in America when he outpointed Tom Overby, another big man who was being touted as a 'black hope'. In the first round Jewey broke his opponents jaw, then floored him twice in the third. Despite his handicap the tough American lasted the distance.

Two weeks later the Aldgate man scored another victory outpointing Jack Fitzgerald, but the following week was out of his depth when pitted against the smart Joe Jeannette who had lost only seven of about 70 contests. Jewey was knocked out in three rounds by a man who had faced world champion in waiting, Jack Johnson, on six occasions.

Smith's final contest in America was on 28 December when he was beaten in five rounds by Jim Stewart who two years earlier had knocked him out in six rounds in Paris. This time the ending came when police intervened.

In March the following year Jewey returned to Paris where he was outpointed by 'Kid' Jackson of America but two weeks later returned to London and faced Fred Storbeck of South Africa at Premierland. The result was a draw which apparently flattered the Londoner. The following month he met another South African, George Rodel, but was outpointed in what was described as a poor contest.

In reality, Jewey had reached the end of the road. Although he made two further trips to America for single fights, he bowed out following a 20-round points defeat to Iron Hague at Sheffield on 5 December 1913.

The popular, ginger-haired Jewish fighter was remembered as an extremely brave and rugged performer, but he took far too much punishment. Facing up to punchers such as Tommy Burns, Sam McVey, Joe Jeannette and Iron Hague to name but a few, was a testimony to his toughness. Sadly, such foolhardiness invariably comes with a price. After retiring from the ring, he fell on hard times, living at Rowton House in Fieldgate Street, Stepney. Unable to work, he was reduced to living off local charity and could barely afford to pay the ninepence a week lodging fee.

Traceable Record:
54 CONTESTS
28 WON
23 LOST
2 DREW
1 NC1

—.35.—

GEORGE WALKER

(Stepney)

The elder brother of heavyweight Billy by 10 years, George was born in Stepney on 14 April 1929. They were the sons of an East End brewery drayman.

He started boxing while in the RAF before joining Thames Refinery ABC and went on to win the ABA light-heavyweight title in 1951 having won all his preliminary rounds inside the distance. In the final he knocked out Ron Crookes (Army) in the first round.

In less than three years as an amateur, George had 50 contests losing only eight. In November the previous year he represented England against Austria twice, winning on points at Graz, but lost on a disqualification four days later at Bregnez.

George signed professional terms the day after winning the ABA title and had his debut at Earls Court on 10 July, on the undercard of the Randolph Turpin - Sugar Ray Robinson world middleweight title fight. He stopped Frank Raven on a cut eye after two rounds.

It was three months before he boxed again, this time on Jack Solomons' big bill at Harringay when the main event was Don Cockell against Albert Finch. Little did the Stepney man know that just a year later he would face Finch in two very important contests.

245

Walker's opponent on this occasion was Dave Williams, a professional since 1948 and ranked at number four in the light-heavyweights. It was an ambitious pairing but, boxing intelligently, George won on points. In November on another big Harringay bill he continued to progress by stopping Tommy Caswell in round three.

George's first fight of the new year was a return with Williams at The Royal Albert Hall. After a terrific contest in which both were covered in blood, Dave got the decision.

Up until this point, all of the Stepney man's contests had been on large promotions at major venues but in February he had his first small-hall fight before a packed house at Leyton Baths. It was also his first eight-rounder. In a very one-sided affair he stopped Alf Hines in the final round, having floored him on eight occasions and cut his left eye. Hines took a real battering and eventually collapsed from exhaustion midway through round eight. After staggering to his feet at the count of 'nine', he was subjected to another vicious attack whereupon the referee stepped in.

The victory for Walker, however, came with a price as he sustained a hand injury which side-lined him for four months. When he returned to action at the White City on the Cockell – Turpin bill, he stopped Ted Morgan in two rounds.

Despite having had only six fights, *Boxing News* rated George at number four in the light-heavyweight division. Apart from being a good prospect he was also a good ticket seller and another full house saw him stop Billy Dean in four rounds at Mile End Arena in July. He returned to the same venue the following month and outpointed Johnny Barton over eight.

Having a fight, a month, his next opponent was Welsh light-heavyweight champion Dennis Powell at Earls Court at the end of September, but he was disqualified during round three. In reality, he had only himself to blame having ignored numerous warnings from referee Frank Wilson, as he struggled to cope with the experienced Welshman's tactics. In addition to blatant holding he was also guilty of misuse of the head and some dubious body punching.

Although the defeat was seen as a setback to his progress, promoter Freddie Mills matched George with Albert Finch (Croydon) over 10 rounds at Earls Court on 28 October. No sooner had terms been agreed the Southern Area of the British Boxing Board of Control recommended that the fight be for the vacant area title. The promoter duly put this to both managers who insisted that their boxer's purses be increased if a title was to be at stake. As no agreement could be reached the contest went ahead as a non-title affair as originally made.

It turned out to be an incredible contest in which Finch was superior in every department, except power of punch. Walker attacked from the start and never stopped pressing forward, raining blows from both hands despite being out-jabbed. The Croydon man stood up to his task magnificently for several rounds, but George would not be denied sending his opponent to the floor in round four from a hard right, which appeared to land on the protector. Referee Mickey Fox counted to 'five' and when Finch rose he spoke to Walker indicating that the blow was dubious.

The Stepney man appeared to stray low again with a hard right in the fifth, but when Finch dropped to one knee, Fox told him to get up. He was clearly hurt and subjected to a rough time until the bell came to his aid. By the start of the sixth most of the resistance had been knocked out of the Croydon man, and when George attacked viciously a right hook sent him down for a count of 'nine'. As he rose Walker went for the kill and another heavy right brought matters to an end with Finch failing to beat the count.

The two met again at Earls Court on 2 December for the Southern Area title as ordered by the Board of Control. Walker was ranked at number three in the division, with Finch immediately behind him. The fight began in similar fashion to their first encounter with the Croydon man attempting to outbox his aggressive opponent, yet again struggling to cope with his rough house tactics.

By round five, Albert was noticeably weak, and his sole aim was survival. The end came in unexpected fashion as in sheer frustration, Finch blatantly head-butted his opponent and was disqualified. *Boxing News* described his action as 'a momentary lapse of bad manners'.

The victory put George in line for a shot at the vacant British title, and promoter Johnny Best matched him with Dennis Powell at Liverpool Stadium during Grand National week. Although the Welsh champion was vastly more experienced, having taken part in 62 fights to the Stepney man's 11, Walker started as the odds-on favourite in what turned out to be an incredible fight. Subsequent media reports described it as one of the most gruelling, gory punch-ups ever seen in a British ring.

At the end of the seventh Powell went to his corner with blood streaming from a jagged gash on his left eyelid. It was so bad that one of his seconds glanced apprehensively at the referee who, fortunately for the Welsh champion, was attending to his scorecard.

George was also hampered by damage to his left eye from the third round onwards. It worsened as the fight progressed and by the 11th it was completely closed at which point his chief second Dave Edgar indicated to the referee that he was retiring his man.

The Stepney fighter was in a bad way when he left the arena, his mouth puffy and swollen in addition to the eye problem. His brother Billy was quoted as saying years later, that he took a week off school and stayed at home to keep him company whilst the injuries healed. George did not want to leave the house.

It was six months before George boxed again and still holding the Southern Area title he had three fights in as many months, all at London venues. In September he was disqualified against Brian Anders (Brighton), outpointed

Fred Jackson and lost on points to Joey Parsons, both over eight rounds.

His final contest was an Area title fight at Harringay on 16 February the following year against Anders. In a fight which kept the crowd absorbed, Walker set the early pace, although he received warnings for low punches and use of the head. Anders for his part kept a cool head, and by the fifth had taken the initiative. Although George never stopped rumbling forward, he was outboxed and outpunched. The end came in round nine when, after taking a short count, he was subjected to accurate methodical punishment which forced the referee to step in.

It was announced afterwards that he would retire from the game, but his efforts were rewarded when the readers of *Boxing News* voted him the gamest loser of 1953 referring presumably to his defeat by Dennis Powell.

In retirement George was a garage proprietor but in 1961 when his brother Billy turned professional he became his manager and trainer. Whilst Billy never succeeded in winning British title, his partnership with George was an extremely lucrative one. With the passing of time George embarked on massive business ventures and it is doubtful whether any former boxer was ever as successful. He once told Ron Olver, writing for *Boxing News,* that they owed a lot to boxing because it gave them the start. 'It's a tough sport', he continued, 'but you won't hear me knocking it!'.

Tracable Record
16 CONTESTS
10 WON
6 LOST

JOE WILSON

(Stepney)

Back in the early 1900's a boxer would rarely have been considered for a championship challenge unless he had been around for several years and endured the discomforts of dozens of battles. Joe Wilson therefore had to be one of the most fortunate men of his era to be able to step into the ring at The National Sporting Club and contest the British flyweight title after only a handful of contests.

Born in Stepney in 1889, Joe was a late starter, having reached the age of twenty-one before he had his first paid contest, a six-round draw at Brighton. After winning a few six-rounders at Wonderland and The Ring, he was matched with Bill Kyne (Poplar) over 20 two-minute rounds at St James Hall, Newcastle, for what was billed as the unofficial English 110-pound championship for a purse and side-stakes of £25. It was Kyne's third contest at the venue in as many months, all having been billed as for the title. As he and Wilson lived in close proximity to each other, there would have been greater interest in their fight in the East End than in the North of England, particularly as it was described by the press as a brilliant contest in which the Poplar man won by a six-round knockout.

Wilson had very few contests over the next six months, yet good fortune suddenly and unexpectedly came his way due to being in the right place at the right time. By late 1911, six Lonsdale belts had been put into circulation with only the fly and light-heavyweight divisions still to be honoured. With the latter not at all popular, The National Sporting Club decided to award one for the eight-stone division and stage a contest for the first official British championship.

Only Sid Smith stood out as an obvious contender but finding the right man to oppose him proved difficult, as there was a number of excellent rivals. The first choice was Bill Kyne but he could not make the weight. Sam Keller was then installed but two weeks before the fight, which was to take place on the 4 December, he was taken ill and admitted to hospital with appendicitis. This gave the chance to Wilson who had the necessary backing and jumped at the chance.

Besides being a championship fight, it was an auspicious occasion at the club, which had been closed for alterations and redecoration. Subsequent delays set the opening night of the season back by about three months. With more seats than before, over 4,000 members assembled for the contest which the critics saw as a good thing for Smith and he entered the ring a heavy odds-on favourite.

Wilson was unfazed by his task and did everything in his power to make the most of his big chance, but by round five Sid was well ahead. Joe, however, oozed determination and suddenly landed a heavy left hook which sent his man crashing to the floor. He took a count of 'nine' and on rising immediately fell into a clinch trying to smother Joe's efforts to follow up. The Stepney lad, however, pulled and pushed, managed to break free and threw a wild right hook to the jaw which sent Smith straight back to the floor. This time he took an 'eight' count and when he rose hung on grimly. A combination of Wilson's inexperience and over-eagerness enabled him to survive.

By round 13 all Joe's advantage had evaporated and he was well behind on points. Believing in his own power, he then set up a big attack and caught his man flush on the mouth sending him briefly to the floor. Smith got up too quickly and another good right sent him down for 'three'. This time he rose, went straight into a clinch and used his know-how to control his over-eager opponent.

Had Wilson steadied himself and picked his punches more carefully he may well have ended it in that round. Instead he allowed himself to be outboxed and by the end of the final round, Smith was a clear winner. Although disappointed, Joe was the first to congratulate him and the pair received a wonderful hand for an excellent contest. There was massive respect between them and they became good friends, frequently meeting at boxing shows in London long after their boxing careers had finished.

It became customary for the Master of Ceremonies to introduce them from the ring prior to the main event, one particular occasion being at The Stadium Club, Holborn, shortly before the start of the Second World War. Sid was short, bespectacled and carrying a bowler hat, whilst Joe was a dapper little fellow, smartly attired in evening dress. Few people knew who they were until the MC made his announcement at which point they received a huge ovation. The knowledgeable patrons at the club knew all about their thrilling contest almost 30 years earlier.

Some 35 years after his fight with Smith, Joe told reporter Charlie Rose that their purse was £100 split £60 to the winner and £40 loser. 'Charlie,' he said, 'By the time I paid my training expenses I hadn't enough left to buy a turkey for my Christmas dinner. Don't I wish I was doing my stuff now!'

Another example of the close friendship which existed between the two arose in December 1947 by which time Smith was in poor health having contracted tuberculosis. On the 36th anniversary of their fight Joe wrote to the Sportsman's Aid Society on his old opponent's behalf with the outcome that Sid subsequently received a cheque for £100 to aid his misfortune. Sadly, he died the following year.

The contest with Smith did much to enhance Joe's career, his performance not only exciting the fans but also the promoters who saw him as a good attraction. Consequently, he received offers to face other leading flyweights. With his confidence high, his next contest was a return with Bill Kyne, at the Poplar Hippodrome in February 1912. Billed as for the English 114lbs championship, it was a huge attraction, in that it was between two well-matched East End lads and on Bill's home turf. After a very close contest, Joe took the decision much to the disgust and unsporting reaction of his opponent and the local crowd.

Five days later, Wilson faced another top contender, Bill Ladbury, from Deptford over 12 rounds at Premierland. Again, the decision this time a draw, was unpopular with the crowd. Reports suggested that everyone except the referee thought Ladbury had earned the nod.

Next up for Joe was a trip to Dublin for a 20-rounder against local favourite Johnny Curran. After what was described as a clean, thoroughly sporting and scientific contest representing boxing at its best, Curran took the decision. The crowd, however, remained impartial and Wilson was given huge applause as he left.

Respect for the Stepney man had grown massively since his fight with Sid Smith and on 3 June he was invited to box a six-round no decision bout with young undefeated Welsh prospect, Jimmy Wilde at The National Sporting Club. Two months later another young prospect, Joe Fox (Leeds), who had beaten most of the top flyweights in the country, faced Wilson at Premierland. The Stepney lad's aggression just about mastered the skills of Fox to take a close 10-round decision.

Joe's form then dipped somewhat and in a fast, clean, scientific bout at Premierland, he lost a wide decision to

Nat Brooks (Aldgate). He then suffered two knockout defeats to Bill Ladbury in 12 rounds at Plumstead in October and 17 at New Cross in February the following year. Four months later the impressive Deptford man took the British lightweight title from Sid Smith by stoppage.

Still facing top quality opponents, Wilson's form remained inconsistent. After knocking out Jack Morris in 18 rounds at Premierland, he faced Sam Keller at The National Sporting Club and was stopped in seven. Although he outpointed Alf Mansfield over 10 rounds at Premierland, he then suffered four consecutive inside-the-distance defeats.

At Plymouth in August 1913, he was involved in a strange, even unsporting, situation in his contest with Joe Symonds, made over 15 rounds for a purse of £40, with the winner to take £25 and side stakes of £10. Wilson looked considerably heavier when they removed their dressing gowns, prompting shouts from the crowds, 'What's their weights?' It was announced that both men were inside the eight-stone limit.

For eight rounds it was a slow and often dull affair, but despite taking two counts, Joe looked to be significantly ahead. Then came an astonishing incident in the ninth. Following an attack by Symonds, Wilson went down on one knee but was up quickly. When forced back into his corner, he held up a hand as if to indicate he had hurt it or that he was surrendering. Symonds immediately dropped his gloves while waiting to see what was happening whereby Wilson suddenly lunged at him. Although caught unawares, the Plymouth man evaded the punches, but as he made to hit back, Wilson fell heavily to the floor from the impetus of his own action. He laid there while the crowd booed loudly for what they considered a mean trick to try and sucker their man. When Joe was unable to continue, the referee awarded the fight to Symonds.

The following month Wilson went in as a late substitute at The Ring against Arthur Ireland (St Pancras). He narrowly avoided being knocked out in round three, after being heavily floored and almost fell out of the ring. He recovered well and took most of the next rounds but in the tenth sustained a leg injury. Despite vigorous massaging by his seconds during the interval, he failed to recover sufficiently, and the referee called a halt at the start of round 11.

Joe then suffered two defeats to unbeaten Percy Jones at Tonypandy. In the first during October, he extended the Welshman to the point where his supporters feared his record would be shattered. Joe hit him hard and often in the early rounds and opened a bad cut over the left eye. Expert corner work, however, limited the damage and Jones regrouped. By round 12 he was well on top, then floored Wilson twice in the next before knocking him out. A return was a natural attraction and at the same venue, three weeks later, Wilson was totally outclassed before retiring after 12 rounds.

With little hope of getting another championship shot, Wilson concentrated on taking fights anywhere in the UK, many at short notice. Although very much a journeyman by this stage he had some success along the way. A six-round draw with Joe Symonds and a 15-round decision over Alf Mansfield, both at The Ring, and a draw with Tommy Harrison at New Cross were the highlights.

In his final contest in 1920, Joe faced Bert Moughton who he had met in his first professional bout in Brighton. They had also met in 1914 in Burton-on-Trent when Joe won by a ninth-round knockout. This time at Bow, Moughton retired after seven rounds.

In a busy career spread over 11 years, Joe faced the best men at his weight, albeit with limited success. Bill Ladbury became flyweight champion in 1913, Percy Jones took the title from him the following year. Joe Symonds was bantamweight champion from 1915-16, Joe Fox held the same title between 1915 and 1917, and was undefeated featherweight champion between 1921 and 1922. Tommy

Harrison held the European bantamweight title from 1921 to 1922 and was British and Empire champion at the same weight from 1922-23.

During his career, Joe was firm friends with fellow professional Sam Russell (Limehouse) and they were frequently in each other's corners on fight nights. He also got to know Jack Solomons who, before he took to promoting, was a regular at East End shows. Years later Jack told a story about a night when Wilson was due to fight but was clearly unwell. Sam wanted him to pull out of the contest, but Joe insisted on going ahead. Believing he was on to a good thing Russell had a hefty bet on the opponent but came unstuck when Joe hammered him to defeat.

After retiring from the ring Wilson trained a number of East End boxers and during the mid-1930's was also instructor to groups of Army Cadets. He also became a masseur to several leading Jockeys.

Having retained close contact with Solomons, he worked for him shortly after Jack began promoting. He acted as a ticket seller and more latterly as a steward at big London promotions. On fight nights Joe always wore a carnation and usually arrived at the venue for work carrying two – one for himself and the other for Jack.

Joe Wilson was a credit to boxing and in particular the East End, where he was massively popular and remained so until he passed away at the Whittington Hospital, Highgate in May 1965 aged seventy-six.

A number of sparse reports over the years claimed that Joe had over 100 contests during his professional career, yet by often fighting as a late substitute, many were never reported in the sporting press of the time. His traceable record below is therefore thought to be far from accurate.

Traceable Record:
45 CONTESTS
25 WON

13 LOST
6 DREW
1 NC

—.37.—

JACK GOODWIN

(Trainer)

There can rarely have been a better coach than Jack Goodwin, real name Goldstein. As a judge of boxers, he had few equals and certainly no superiors as a second. He knew every punch and counterpunch and could demonstrate them perfectly. He taught his pupils how to develop a knockout blow at a young age, maintaining that unless it was ingrained into a boxer in his youth he would never develop it. 'One punch pays for it all', was his favourite motto as he emphasised time and again that even when well behind a fight could be pulled out of the fire if a man had learned how to hit hard enough.

Born in the East End in 1878, fighting came naturally to Goodwin and he was doing it for pay by the time he was fifteen. In the early 1900's he had plenty of fights at Wonderland and was known as 'the man with the right arm' because he had such a tremendous punch in that hand.

Jack lived in Calvert Avenue in Shoreditch and when illness cut short his ring career he turned his hand to training. He first gym was at nearby Kingsland Road before moving to a billiard hall on Whitechapel Road owned by boxer's manager, Harry Morris. Among those he looked after were Sid Burns and Bandsman Rice who Goodwin agreed to train.

Having been brought up the hard way, Jack controlled his gym with rigid discipline and it was strictly business once training commenced. No boxer, manager or promoter had the slightest say in the way he coached his men and he fully justified the trust. He was not just a trainer, but a weight specialist and doctor as well. He never took a man to the scales over weight or with bad hands, nor did he often go wrong in advising a boxer's backer how to place his bets.

Smoking was strictly forbidden in the gym and anyone caught breaking that rule was ordered to stop or get out. Veteran journalist, Charlie Rose, who for some years had been a successful boxing manager, once challenged Goodwin about his stance. He reasoned that as boxers performed in a smokey atmosphere it was as well to accustom them to it in training. Jack, however, wouldn't hear of it. 'Listen here,' he snapped, 'how the devil do you expect to get a fighter into condition if his lungs are being daily clogged up and poisoned by foul tobacco. It don't make sense'.

Jack excelled at establishing the strengths and weaknesses of his boy's opponents, and organised training accordingly. He was meticulous in every aspect of his work but made it clear that he resented liberty takers. Not being one himself, he had his own way of dealing with them and those who dared try it on with him, only did it once.

He never had any difficulty in getting particular sparring partners for his men no matter what the weight. He was known and trusted as a man of his word and those he engaged knew they would be paid well and looked after generously. There was the added bonus of learning a great deal from the man known as 'the master' who more often than not managed to get them to fight on the bill for which he was promoting.

Aside from his strict discipline Goodwin was an expert at repartee. The wit, humour and the kindness that was hidden beneath his rugged features was a rarity. This shone to the fore one Sunday morning, at a time when he was training American middleweight Augie Ratner at Hampton Court. Although it was a day off for everyone, regular sparring partner, Tom Berry from Custom House who had a very large family, took them to the camp for a social visit. When he saw all the children get off the bus, Jack, who loved children, said he thought it was an orphanage come to look over the place. Yet, when he realised what the situation was, he pulled out all the stops to make sure they had a good time.

Jack put his heart and soul into boxing but ultimately paid the price for long hours and exertion. After training Phil Scott for a British Empire heavyweight championship defence against Larry Gains, at Leicester in June 1931 which Gains won, he reluctantly decided to retire having been advised by doctors that he had a weak heart. In order to stay in the sport, he became a matchmaker at the Boulevard Rink, Leicester, later that year and even contemplated taking up promoting. One of the first major contests he made was between Gains and French heavyweight champion Maurice Griselle which was staged on 30 November 1931.

By this time Larry had taken on Harry Levene as his manager and in January the following year drew with South African, Don McCorkindale in defence of his Empire title at The Royal Albert Hall. A return was fixed for 3 March at the same venue and in order for his man to be in prime condition, Levene asked Goodwin to train him. Jack had reservations because, as he told Charlie Rose; 'I took a dying oath when I started training that I'd never train a coloured man. I hoped I'd be struck down if I did'.

Charlie laughed and insisted that Larry was a really good fighter who would be relatively easy to prepare. Against his better judgement, Goodwin swallowed his pride, struck up an agreement with Levene and set up camp for a month at Shoeburyness. They returned to London on the morning of the fight and after the weigh-in Jack went to see his wife and family at Shoreditch, telling Gains that he would pick him up from his hotel in Soho at six o'clock before making their way to The Albert Hall. Gains later recalled that when the trainer returned he looked very pale and admitted having been sick, but by the time they left for the arena he insisted that he felt much better.

The fight was going Gains way by the end of the twelfth round, but as he returned to his corner he saw Jack climbing the ring steps and then suddenly fall backwards. People at ringside caught him and as he sat on his stool Larry asked Harry Levene what had happened only to be told; 'he's fainted'. It was only as his arm was raised at the end of the contest that news filtered through that Goodwin was dead, stuck down by a massive heart attack. Although Gains triumphed, there were no after-fight celebrations that night.

The following week, the trade magazine, *Boxing* paid a fitting tribute to the man it described as a tremendous character, adding that no trainer was more competent and conscientious than Jack;

> To every boy and man, he took under his wing, he gave his all. A born student of character, he knew to a nicety how to handle men. He could, in that humorous manner of his, bring the most obtuse fellow to his way of thinking.
>
> It was woe betide any fighter who did not do his bidding, for when he deemed it proper and helpful he waged a tongue of vitriol. He could wither a man by a single sentence. His fund of stories was inexhaustible, and he was always full of quips and cranks. He never grew up in the sense that, except when he was out to do a spot of work, he refused to be serious.

Many men passed through Jack Goodwin's hands and everyone benefited from his advice and attention. It is no exaggeration to say that that he produced more British champions than any other trainer prior to his passing and probably for many years after. Ted 'Kid' Lewis frequently referred to him as 'the world's greatest trainer'.

Many tears were shed as he was carried away from the ring he loved so well, because there had been rumours about his failing health. Many in the great arena feared the worst.

The following Monday, a glorious Spring day, Jack's body was laid to rest at the Jewish Cemetery at Marlow Road, East Ham in the presence of sad faced mourners from all walks of life. Larry Gains, the last boxer he had trained, laid a wreath in the form of a boxing ring inscribed simply, 'To my pal Jack, from Larry'. He was so moved at the graveside as to be on the point of collapse.

Charlie Rose never forgave himself following Jack's collapse at The Royal Albert Hall ringside, because it was he who convinced him to train Gains despite the fact that he had been told by doctors to quit the work. Charlie's close association with Goodwin began when he became Ted 'Kid' Lewis' manager and asked Jack to train him. In one conversation he told Rose how he would hate to linger on after life reached a stage where he could no longer train boxers.

Prior to his death Jack was probably known to more people in boxing circles than any other man. Consequently, a committee under the chairmanship of Victor Berliner, manager of The Ring, Blackfriars, was set up to organise a special benefit evening for his dependants. It took place at the arena during the afternoon of Sunday 12 June 1932, before a full house and consisted of three 15-round contests and another over 12 rounds.

A surprise item featured Larry Gains in a special three-round exhibition with Lord Douglas Hamilton, the Scottish University Amateur Champion. There followed a 'great parlour scene' in which many of Britain's best boxers, past and present, were introduced. A number had been trained by Jack. A sale, auction and collection by referee, Moss Deyong, raised over £130 for his dependants

*   *   *

Joe Goodwin, Jack's younger brother, was also heavily involved in boxing. From flyweight to feather he had over 100 fights between 1900 and 1911, almost 70 of which were at Wonderland. Billed out of Spitalfields he faced a number of top men and always gave a good account of himself. In October 1904 he was outpointed by Johnny Summers, but 10 days later he drew with the man who just 15 months later would become British featherweight champion.

In June the following year, Joe drew with former world featherweight champion, George Dixon, in Manchester. Five months later, on a booth promotion in the West Midlands, he lost on points to Jim Driscoll, who then six months later would also be crowned British champion.

After retiring he turned his hand to training and between 1925 and 1934 worked at the Webbe Amateur Club at Hair Street, Bethnal Green. Alf 'Kid' Pattenden was a club captain between 1925 and 1927 when Harry Paulding, later to become a top referee, took over.

Joe was a boxing man through and through and in the late 1920's was matchmaker at Premierland. He also acted as the whip at The Ring, Blackfriars, for a number of years, where he had the reputation of being a 'good fixer'. Part of his job was to match novice youngsters starting out on their careers. There was no weigh-in, he just picked lads who to him looked like a good pairing.

Traceable Record
100 CONTESTS
64 WON
24 LOST
12 DREW

——.38.——

NAT SELLAR

(Trainer)

Another of the successful East End trainers from the early 1900's, Nat Sellar, started boxing at the age of eleven at Watney Street school and also for the Jewish Lads Brigade. As a youngster he also learned all about the great East End venues such as The Whitechapel Pavilion, Judean Club, Wonderland and Premierland.

Shortly after he enlisted for National Service, the Provost Sergeant, an Army Chaplain, persuaded him to box. Success came quickly; he won Army bantamweight and featherweight championships and was undefeated for three years before becoming an instructor with the Army Gymnastic staff during the First World War.

Back in civilian life, Nat developed his training skills under Jack Goodwin. He became a recognised authority on physical culture who knew how to make a boxer concentrate on his job. He was highly respected in the East End for his strict discipline and in October 1937, after looking after fighters for 20 years, opened his La Boheme Gym at Mile End Road.

Early the following year, Jack Solomons who was promoting good quality shows at the Devonshire Club, approached Nat and persuaded him to take over the training of Eric Boon. Whilst the Chatteris youngster was an extremely hard hitting young prospect, he had been beaten in seven rounds by Johnny Softley (Poplar) in July the previous year.

At the time Nat was training Harry Mizler for a British title eliminator against Dave Crowley at The Royal Albert Hall on the same bill as a return between Boon and Softley. Although he claimed never to have seen Boon fight, Seller knew he was a great prospect and had no hesitation in agreeing to the promoter's request. It was the beginning of what would be a great partnership, although Nat would experience plenty of day-to-day headaches which only ceased when he stopped training the Chatteris fighter.

Seller really put the youngster through his paces working with Frank Hough, Pat Palmer, Harry 'Kid' Silver and Mizler, all of whom were due to box on The Albert Hall bill. All the hard work was rewarded because Eric won a stirring-eight round contest and went on to become British lightweight champion with Nat in his corner.

Just after the war, Boon had ambitions to set up his own business in London and after a lengthy search found a disused billiard hall at Great Windmill Street on the edge of Soho. He took Jack Solomons along to view it but quickly acknowledged he couldn't afford the rent. Solomons, however, realising the need for a high-quality gym in the West End, quickly agreed the tenancy.

The establishment opened in March 1946 with Nat Seller running the gym and training a number of Jack's fighters. It was there that he met Freddie Mills who was training for his first world title fight with Gus Lesnevich. Their only previous meeting had been in 1938 when Nat took former British welterweight champion, Dave McCleave to Bournemouth when he outpointed Freddie.

Mills lost to Lesnevich but was trained by Seller for the return two years later which he won. Freddie always claimed it was Nat's training routine that got him into peak condition for the fight. He overlooked nothing and even stayed in his room at night to ensure he got proper sleep.

The pair continued to work together until Freddie retired in 1950.

Nat was highly respected throughout his career as a trainer. He knew triumph and defeat for almost 50 years, working with men such as Dai Dower, Vince Hawkins, Ernie Izzard, Benny Caplan, Mizler, McCleave and a host of others.

He lived in the East End for most of his life until passing away in 1975.

39

JOHNNY SHARPE

(Trainer)

Born in Spitalfields in 1894, Johnny Sharpe, like his five brothers (one of whom was Young Jack Cohen), learned the noble art the hard way. He had not reached fifteen when he made his professional debut at The Judean Club in 1909 and beat fellow East Ender, Kid Levine, on points over six rounds.

In his third contest at the same venue a few weeks later he outpointed Ted 'Kid' Lewis who was having his second contest. It took place on Alf Goodwin's benefit night show and afterwards club secretary, Sam Kite took Sharpe aside and pressed 15 shiny coins into his hand. He was thrilled thinking they were half crowns, but on a proper look later found they were new pennies. It was still a pricey sum in those days and in addition he was also given a cup of tea and two cakes. As loser, Ted got six pennies and one cake.

During 1912 Johnny was due to meet an unknown Welshman named Jimmy Wilde at The Ring, Blackfriars. On the day, however, the fights were switched and instead Wilde met Matt Wells' Nipper and knocked him out in the first round. 'I was very grateful to the Nipper', Johnny told a reporter some years later. 'It could have been me on the canvas'.

Sharpe continued boxing on small hall shows with limited success until 1916 when on the advice of his brother, Young Jack, he ventured to America in search of better purse money. He remained there for five years, having about 65 contests with a best purse of $300. In all he had about 80 contests before turning to training and the managerial side of the sport.

His first gymnasium was at Darling Road, Brockley before moving back to the East End and opening premises at the rear of 45 Mile End Road which he eventually advertised as 'The largest gym in England'. He trained fighters of all levels there for 15 years, the first of whom was Laurie Raiteri, an exciting light-heavyweight from Stratford.

In 1933, Johnny was instrumental in arranging the first televising of professional boxing in England when he took Raiteri, Archie Sexton, Bill Lewis and Freddie Baxter to studios at Broadcasting House in London to box exhibitions.

Another boxing man through and through he could turn his hand to all aspects of the sport. He was matchmaker for a series of Jewish National Fund promotions at Holborn Stadium and also dabbled in small hall events at venues in the East End. For more than 40 years he was the British correspondent for the American monthly magazine *The Ring*.

Right from the start the gym at Mile End Road was a hive of activity as Sharpe worked tirelessly with a host of good fighters mostly from the East End. Although the majority never looked like winning titles they were nonetheless all good drawing cards. Raiteri, his brother Sid, Sexton, Wally Dakin, Jimmy Thornton, Harry Jennings, Peter Howard, Harry Brooks, Moe Moss, Dave Keller, Kid Farlo, Harry 'Kid' Silver, Johnny Boom, Jackie Lucraft, Bob Frost and others were all trained and managed by Johnny over the years.

He also spent time with former British feather and lightweight champion, Johnny Cuthbert and acted as British manager for world featherweight champion Freddie Miller when he campaigned in Britain during the 1930's. Yet his biggest success originated in 1942 when Harry Droy, who promoted at Caledonian Road Baths and Prince of Wales Baths in North London, recommended Islington flyweight, Terry Allen to him. They quickly formed a solid working relationship in which Terry progressed to win British, European and world flyweight championships.

On the administration side of the sport, Johnny was a member of the Southern Area Council of The British Boxing Board of Control for 24 years from its inception. Towards the end of his working life he became promoter Jack Solomons right hand man and occupied a room at his Great Windmill Street Gym in the West End of London.

Johnny had very strong views about boxing generally and in an interview in the late 1960's made it clear that he was one of the many who believed that modern day fighters didn't even measure up to those of yesteryear. 'Today's fighters have false records and can't stand up to international competition', he embarked. 'I only wish we had some of the old ones with us now'.

Johnny died suddenly in June 1968, aged seventy-four in Johannesburg where his cruiserweight, Dickie Owens, was due to fight. His funeral was at Bushey Cemetery on 21 June. He left wife Jean and two sons, Lawrence and Bob.

40

HARRY JACOBS

(Promoter)

Loud, arrogant and aggressive are all terms that fittingly described the personality of East End born promoter, Harry Jacobs, real name Harry Cashtein. That said, he was renowned as one of the most astute matchmakers and promoters boxing had ever known. Although disliked in many quarters, even his most bitter enemies could not deny he was top class and to most fans he was considered the leading promoter in the country.

Despite his fiery personality Harry was a real character and some of the greatest boxers in British fight history, especially the London ones, graduated with him at Wonderland. Yet when it was a poor house, he gave fighters a few shillings less than they had been promised. The fact that they wanted future work usually made them agreeable to his terms as there were no contracts as such in those days.

Jacobs had his own way of forming a bill, particularly during his days at Wonderland. He would consider the talent at his disposal, remember those who entertained the crowds and then merely write down on paper particular matches that looked like money spinners. The bill would then be dispatched to the printers after which he may or may not send a messenger to tell the boxers when they were fighting. There were plenty of occasions when he left it to them to see their names on the billposters of which there were many plastered on walls around the East End. If a particular boxer did not turn up, Harry would not be concerned as he knew there would be plenty of ambitious youngsters in the hall willing to step in and have a go in the hope of being offered more work in the future.

He frequently made rules fit the occasions and wouldn't hesitate to bill a particular fight for a so-called championship. It made no difference that the contestants were no more entitled to the honour than were a pair of novices. An attractive pairing would always draw a good crowd to Wonderland and an attractive belt up for grabs to the winner of a competition guaranteed a good entry.

Jacobs was always prepared to take risks but on one occasion caught a cold over a competition at the East End venue. The first prize was a belt previously belonging to Ted Pritchard which he had picked up at a sale. It was a gaudy arrangement of embossed leather, gold buckles and enamelled studs but of dubious value. Harry had it polished up and exhibited on a royal blue velvet cushion making it look all of the advertised value of £250.

The 10-stone competition attracted a large entry including good class American, Jack Clancy, who became the eventual winner. In and out of the ring, Jack was no fool and when he went to claim his prize found nothing but a broad band of stained leather studded with a few gilt medallions.

The American at once set the law in motion and his counsel, producing bill matters and articles of agreement as evidence, got judgement for the advertised value of the belt of £250. It was never established if Jacobs ever paid up.

At Wonderland, Harry presided over a bizarre institution furnished in shabby Victorian music hall style. Although his partnership with Jack Woolf was a stormy one, practically everybody who was anybody in boxing appeared on their shows. Consequently, the game suffered when the two parted company on bad terms. It was an inevitable severance because there had been many bitter rows and hurling of insults between them, which often spilled over into the ring between fights.

Determined not to be outdone Harry soon began promoting at the nearby Paragon Music Hall at Whitechapel Road in direct competition to Wonderland, but the operation was short-lived as he was forced out by the London County Council following complaints from local residents.

Jacobs had an abundance of grit, determination and above all, ambition to maintain his reputation as the top promoter. Totally confident of his own ability, he wasted no time before renting an empty warehouse at Backchurch Lane and, at considerable cost, created Premierland which opened to the public in December 1911. Although successful while it lasted he brought about his own downfall when he was declared bankrupt early in 1914.

Harry disappeared from the boxing scene for a while only to reappear after the war more flamboyant and extravagant than ever. With his wide sense of the ring he created a sensation by acquiring a lease at The Royal Albert Hall for a series of promotions each year. He was in his element and revelled at pairing boxers in fights of tremendous public appeal and on an even more prestigious stage. In doing so he gave his patrons the best possible value for money, often providing several championship bouts on one programme. With up to 100 rounds of boxing in a single evening his shows frequently went on past midnight.

Although the Board of Control of the time which preceded the current regulatory body claimed the right to make the title fights, that power held no terrors for Jacobs. He calmly went about making his own such contests and was able to do so with total disregard and, simply because he paid so well, most of the top boxers clamoured to appear on his shows.

Despite his sharpness and success in business, Harry made one costly error during his time as a promoter. It was entirely due to ignorance because he thought that Boxing Day had something to do with the Noble Art. Consequently, he came up with the idea of staging a big all-star bill at The Royal Albert Hall on that Bank Holiday in 1919 with Ted 'Kid' Lewis facing Matt Wells in the top-liner. There were five fights, all of which would fill an arena in modern times, but only a few hundred tickets were sold. With all the boxers on good purses, he lost a fortune.

Harry always maintained a healthy relationship with Ted 'Kid' Lewis. It began towards the end of 1911 when he was preparing to open Premierland and was on the lookout for new young talent. Ted fitted the bill perfectly, having had about 80 contests mostly at The Judean Club. He was a potential ticket seller which prompted Jacobs to offer him a deal of 16 fights at the rate of two a month, for which he would be paid £4 a fight. Ted jumped at the chance and between January and December the following year had 34 contests at the new arena, losing just three.

Lewis went to America in 1914 and remained there until the end of 1919. Having lost the world welterweight title, the relationship with Harry was revived with The Albert Hall contest with Matt Wells. Apart from that contest the promoter paid him £3,500 to top a bill at The Royal Albert Hall in January 1925 against Francis Charles. Ted won, and the promoter put him on again two months later against Tommy Milligan. Both contests were sell-outs.

Although forced to leave Premierland for financial reasons, Harry could never quit boxing. He had his usual ups and downs whilst promoting at subsequent venues (Queens Hall, The Opera House, Olympia and The Royal Albert Hall), but was never discouraged. There were times when rival antagonists thought they had him beaten only for him to rise up again. Doggedly determined he carried on and on the whole, was a winner more often than a loser right to the end.

It was a fitting that Jacobs wound up his last performance in a blaze of glory with another full house at The Royal Albert Hall in early January 1929. He was a very sick man when he put together the bill topped by heavyweights, Phil Scott and Ted Sandwina (USA) backed by East End favourites Jack 'Kid' Berg, Archie Sexton, Kid Brookes and Peter Howard. Although he insisted on being there his medical advisors would not permit him to be at ringside. Harry died a few weeks later.

Despite his faults and enemies, he was missed in more quarters than generally accepted. As a mark of respect, the crowd at the first Premierland show after his death stood in silence for two minutes.

—.41.—

HONOURABLE MENTIONS

Throughout preceding chapters attention has focused generally on the achievements of champions, title contenders and a selection of other fighters who showed exceptional talent and commitment throughout their careers. Yet, no matter how many form the backbone of this book, countless others warrant inclusion, even if only briefly. Outside the ring trainers, seconds, promoters and referees also had a massive input.

It was not unusual, particularly during the early part of the 20th century, for boxers to engage in over 100 contests provided they were dedicated, kept fit and avoided serious injury. One of the busiest during that period was Moe Moss (born Maurice Waterman) from Aldgate. Starting at welterweight before moving up to middle, he amassed a total of 176 contests of which he won 96, drew 29, lost 49 with 2 no contests in a career extending from 1928 to 1943. It was a sign of the times that on 28 September 1928, he fought twice, firstly at The Ring, Blackfriars, in the afternoon and then travelling across London for another contest at Hackney during the evening. He won both on points.

Moe was particularly active between 1929 and 1931 when he partook in no less than 89 fights. He was incredibly tough and skilful and lost inside the distance only once in his first 127 recorded contests. At the age of sixteen he became a sparring partner to his idol, Jack 'Kid' Berg, despite not long having turned professional. His sheer ambition impressed Jack and he became a fixture in the training camps and did well.

Moss faced plenty of good men during his career beating the likes of Harry Corbett, Harry Mason and Glen Moody amongst others. He drew with Mason, Mick Hill and Leo Phillips twice. He had three good fights with South African, George 'Panther' Purchase, losing a 15-round decision at The Ring in 1932, getting a draw over 12 at the same venue two years later but losing in five rounds six months later at Mile End. On that occasion Moe was in poor condition and as he stripped off he looked fat. He was also suffering from an attack of boils which had no doubt made it difficult for him to train, in which case he should have pulled out of the fight. Furthermore, an appointed doctor should have refused to allow him to compete. Instead, the fight went ahead but after a promising start Moe weakened and retired after taking a count in round five.

In August 1938, he faced a young Freddie Mills at Boscombe Football Ground. He gave it everything including standing toe-to-toe in a vicious punch-up during round four. Then suddenly, Moe was floored heavily for a long count in the next round before being knocked out.

Suffering no ill effects, he beat Seaman Tommy Long at Plymouth and Tommy Ireland at the Stadium Club, both inside the distance before joining the armed services at the outbreak of the Second World War. After being discharged in 1942, he went to live in Manchester where he became a docker. He retired from the ring the following year, his last three contests being in Glasgow where he had fought on four occasions in the past, scoring three knockouts.

Moe, who had a younger brother who boxed as Young Moss, eventually became a second and trainer with Johnny Sharpe's huge stable at Mile End Road. Moe Moss typified fighters of his era and had a long life after retirement before passing away in 1974.

Aldgate flyweight Young Joseph's Nipper was another prime example of what many young fighters put themselves through during the early part of the 20th century packing in over 130 contests into an eight-year period commencing in September in 1909. The fact that he avoided serious injury and was rarely stopped or knocked out enabled him to cram almost 100 of those into just four years between 1910 and 1913. He rarely ventured outside London with many of his early fights being at The Judean Club. After appearing on the opening bill at Premierland he quickly became a firm favourite there taking 38 bouts in less than three years.

Stepney lightweight Dave Finn was another exceptionally active fighter. He started boxing at the age of fifteen changing his name from Fineri. Within two years he had won 32 of 40 contests losing four and drawing four. The losses were reversed in return bouts. During the early days he rarely ventured outside the East End where he became very popular. Being a nephew of Jack Solomons, who was also born and bred in the region, he often featured at the Devonshire Club after it opened in 1934 and also at Mile End Arena.

In 1936 he went to America where, boxing as Dave Fine, he had seven fights in five months facing generally good opposition. In his penultimate contest he was out-pointed by Benny Bass who had held the world feather and junior lightweight titles between 1927 and 1931 and amassed a record of over 200 contests. Five weeks later he faced former world featherweight champion, Freddie Miller but was stopped in six rounds. It was one of the only occasions he was ever beaten inside the distance.

On returning to Britain, Dave became one of the busiest men in the country, yet the nearest he came to a title was when he won the Southern Area championship in 1945. At best he was a crowd-pleasing journeyman who ducked nobody and in fact usually excelled against better fighters. Those he beat included Dave Crowley, Dick Corbett, Tommy Hyams, Ronnie James, Johnny Softley, Alby Day, Boyo Rees and Jack Carrick.

When he lost to British champion, Billy Thompson in 1946, Dave hung up his gloves with a credible record of 91 victories and 17 draws from 172 contests. Had it not been for a shortage of promotions during the second World War, he would almost certainly have notched up 100 victories. Following his retirement Boxing News referred to him as:

'An industrious and clever lightweight who fought the best at his weight without getting a title'.

Determined to remain in boxing Dave took out a promoter's licence and staged his first show at Hove on 2 April the following year

Another busy Aldgate fighter was featherweight Young Joe Brooks who in a professional career between May 1909 and December 1924 had over 160 contests. A typical journeyman, he fought in many parts of the UK as well as in France, USA, Canada, Australia and New Zealand.

Afraid of nobody he faced Ted 'Kid' Lewis twice, Mike Honeyman and Charlie Hardcastle (both on four occasions), Tancy Lee and Digger Stanley, all of who were, would be, or had been at least British champions. He also met French champion Paul Til twice. Tough hard punching Aldgate man Freddie Jacks failed to stop him in any of their three meetings. Joe's most frequent opponent was gritty Hoxton man, Seaman Arthur Hayes who he faced on 11 occasions, winning seven.

A huge East End favourite particularly at Premierland was Aldgate bantamweight, Phil Lolosky. Active during the 1920's and 30's he was a fine performer with a great left hand and beat plenty of good fighters including Frankie Ash, Dod Oldfield, Harry Hill and Mark Lesnick. Although he was beaten by Alf Pattenden and Young Johnny Brown, his greatest performance was against Teddy Baldock.

Phil had repeatedly issued challenges to Baldock and when a match was made at Forest Gate in February 1928, the venue was packed. Although Teddy got the decision after an absolute thriller, Lolosky's performance was such that many in the crowd thought he deserved at least a draw. Press reports described it as one of the best non-title fights seen in the East End for years. They met again eight months later but Phil was not the same man and was knocked out in the third round.

It was Lolosky's last fight for three years and when he came back he was outpointed by Alf Pattenden. He had a few more contests before another lengthy break, but when he gave it another try the old flare was gone and he quit for good.

Born in Stepney, St George's in 1909, flyweight Moe Mizler never had the success of his younger brother Harry. Unlike his brother, Moe loved a tear-up and after winning Schoolboy and Federation of Boys Clubs championships he turned professional at the age of sixteen. His first 11 fights were at Premierland where he became another young East End favourite. In a six-year period he had 32 of his 51 contests there, his best achievement being when he stopped Nipper Pat Daly on a cut eye.

Another flyweight from Aldgate, although often billed from Bethnal Green, was Kid Rich whose Jewish-Ukrainian parents had fled to Britain to avoid persecution. Like many immigrants they escaped the massacres only to end up living a poor life in the slums of London's East End. Rich was a squat little man built on the lines of a pocket Hercules with a bulging muscular physique and an all action style. He took fights when and wherever he could as a means of survival and thought nothing of giving away half a stone or more.

Many of his fights were over 15 rounds, the first being in 1925, his first year as a professional in which he engaged in 21 battles in just nine months. A total of 17 others that year were made over 10 rounds duration and another, Young Johnny Brown, over 12

In a career lasting 11 years, Rich took part in at least 170 traceable contests of which he won only 40 with 21 draws and 108 defeats. A total of 65 took place at Premierland where he became another established favourite. His set-to with Mark Lesnich in November 1928 was not quickly forgotten as the two stood toe-to-toe throughout the 15 rounds, each stubbornly refusing to take a backward step. A draw was a popular decision, but when they met again three weeks later Mark got the verdict.

The fact that he lost so many fights was not surprising considering the quality of opponents he faced. His best performances were probably those against Nipper Pat Daly who outpointed him three times during 1928, twice over 12 rounds and the other over 15. It was a very busy year for Rich in which he engaged in at least 26 fights and only once failed to last the distance. Defeats to future world champion, Emile Pladner in Paris during 1927, Cuthbert Taylor, Jack Hyams, Dick Corbett (four times) and Moe Mizler were certainly no disgrace either.

After retiring he became a trainer, but when eventually suffering ill-health he found it difficult to secure regular employment.

Lightweight, Phil Richards from Stepney, St Georges was another extremely busy fighter, amassing more than 150 contests during the 1920's and 30's. The elder brother of Benny Caplan, he had two tours of the United States, losing nine of the 21 contests. A man with great political beliefs, he died fighting for the republicans in the Spanish Civil War.

'The Aldgate Assassin' was how promising middleweight, Joe Root became known after building a string of quick knockout victories shortly after turning professional in 1946, at the age of eighteen. He had started boxing at the Eton Manor Club, but after winning a divisional championship in 1945, eventually decided to turn professional.

Apart from being an exciting big-hitting fighter, he was also a busy one, taking 13 contests in the first 10 months of 1947, winning eight by knockout and losing just one. He established himself as a top-of-the-bill fighter when out-pointing Johnny McGowan (Wakefield) at Caledonian Road Baths, in which both men were down several times.

Joe saw army service in 1947 and 48 as a physical training instructor, but despite keeping in good shape his form began to fade. In the four years between 1949 and 1953 he had only 10 contests winning just three. Although he had beaten some good men earlier, he found former British Empire champion, Bos Murphy, Alex Buxton, Ron Groghan and Alby Hollister just a shade too clever so he hung up his gloves at the end of 1953.

Stepney bantamweight, Nipper Fred Morris had a 16-year career starting in 1930. He showed great promise losing only one of his first eight contests but then developed into a journeyman taking fights all over the United Kingdom but was a particular favourite at Mile End Arena. A tough little fighter, he went the distance with a number of vastly experienced men including Dick Corbett, Tommy Hyams, Jim 'Spider' Kelly, Ronnie James, Len Benyon and Phineas John who he beat twice. He did win the vacant South-Eastern Area bantamweight title in October 1932 by outpointing Fred Baxter but vacated it without making a defence. He retired in 1946 having won 26 and drawing 4 out of a record of 64 contests.

Stoker Ramsden, a featherweight of some merit was born in 1883 and featured regularly at Wonderland between 1900 and 1911. He was always value for money to the hard-boiled fans who patronised the arena. His faith in his boxing ability and toughness together with his readiness to lay money to back himself, was expertly revealed in the columns of *Sporting Life*. After retiring from boxing, he worked at the Thames Gas Works for 30 years. He later suffered serious chest problem after being caught between the buffers of two trains. It spoke volumes for his toughness that he survived.

Billed from Whitechapel, but latterly Mile End, exciting lightweight cum-welter, Harry 'Kid' Farlo had over 120 contests in under 10 years during the late 1920's and 30's. An exceptionally busy fighter he averaged at least a dozen fights a year with 21 in 1931 alone. Many of his bouts were at The Ring, Blackfriars, where he beat Alf Pattenden and Lew Pinkus amongst others. Although he never quite reached championship class Harry had a good record, winning more than 80 and drawing many others.

He loved a 'tear-up' and against Len Wickwar at Mile End in September 1933 had Len down three times in the opening round yet still lost on points. Guaranteed to thrill the crowds, he boxed in a number of supporting contests on major London promotions, including that between Larry Gains and Primo Carnera at The White City in May 1932 before a crowd of 80,000. He was often accompanied by his friend and stablemate Moe Moss from Aldgate, another busy fighter.

Born in Leeds on 14 August 1882, Cockney Cohen was billed as from Whitechapel for most of his career, hence the nickname Cockney. Like the East End, Leeds had a huge Jewish population many of whom were involved in the rag trade. It was there that the youngster, real name Morris Cohen, started boxing. Details of his early career are sparse, and it was not until mid-1901 that details began to appear in the press. By this time he was winning 15 and 20 round contests mostly at Leeds County Athletic Club.

The following year Cohen moved to Whitechapel and quickly became a favourite at Wonderland where over six years he met such formidable opponents as Digger Stanley and Johnny Summers. Against the latter he scored a victory and a draw only to lose a third. He also had four enthralling contests with Pedlar Palmer with one victory, one draw and two points defeats.

Cohen often returned to the North of England for fights and in the space of three months between December 1903 and March the following year he had three great encounters with former world featherweight champion, George Dixon, a professional since 1886. He lost the first two in Newcastle but was victorious in a third with a 15-round victory in Leeds.

In the last bout of his career he faced Johnny Condon at Premierland and committed virtually every foul in the book before being thrown out in round five.

An extremely capable man, he won more fights than he lost before retiring in 1912, but with several other Cohens boxing in the East End at the time, there was often confusion over their true identity thus causing inaccuracy in records. He died at his London home in October 1976 aged seventy-four.

Harry Lazar, real name Lazarus, was the elder brother of Southern Area middleweight champion Lew who challenged for British and European Honours in 1954. He was born into a crowded Jewish household in Aldgate on 6 September 1922, his father being a street bookmaker and his grandfather a bare-knuckle fighter.

In a 12-year career firstly at lightweight and then welter, Harry had almost 120 contests of which he won 84. Boxing almost exclusively at Mile End Arena and The Devonshire Club, he looked like a champion in the making after winning his first 26 contests. Unfortunately, he lost his dedication to training with the consequence that he failed to reach the heights expected. He did, nevertheless beat a number of top men at his weight including Dave Crowley (twice), Johnny McGrory, Dave Finn, Henry Hall, Tommy Armour, Tommy Hyams and Harry Mizler. One of his most exciting battles was an all-Jewish, East End affair with Harry 'Kid' Silver who he beat on points in 1940.

The nearest Harry got to a championship fight was in 1948 when he outpointed Jim Wellard in an eliminator for the Southern Area welterweight title but as he was in the twilight of his career nothing further materialised. After winning two of eight further contests over the next 16 months he hung up his gloves. Harry suffered considerable ill health during later life having a lung removed in 1984. He died the following year age sixty-three.

Stepney St Georges lightweight Fred Halsband was a good quality fighter and very unfortunate not to get a championship fight. In a career lasting from September 1909 until July 1921, he lost only 30 of 106 traceable contests. Starting out as Young Halsband of the Judean Club, many of his early fights were at that venue where he was highly regarded. A gifted, upright boxer, he was undefeated in his first 27 contests packed into an eight-month period. He was willing to face anyone and amongst his opponents was an up and coming Ted 'Kid' Lewis who he faced on three occasions. They drew over six rounds at the Judean Club in September 1911, Halsband won on points over ten rounds at Premierland the following year, before losing to the future world champion at The National Sporting Club two months later. Ted had a high regard for Fred and in his memoirs, years later described him as a top-class fighter.

After Premierland opened in December 1911, Fred became as popular there as he was at The Judean Club but in 1913 the prospect of big money lured him to America. There he quickly endeared himself to the fans, particularly in New York and Philadelphia, during a successful spell of 15 months in which he lost only six of 17 contests. Such was his popularity that the boys of the Young Solly Association in New York staged a dinner in his honour at Kraft Hall, 5th Street. There were 75 boys, wives and sweethearts present, most of the boys having migrated from London and Leeds. During the event, Halsband was presented with a silver cup.

On returning to London, Fred was past his best and took only the occasional fight. He won just five of 15 in seven years before retiring in 1921 but remained in the sport as a trainer and worked as a house second at Premierland for several years.

After Fred passed away in early 1940, a grand all-star boxing tournament headed by Jack 'Kid' Berg against Harry Watson (Bethnal Green) was staged at the Devonshire Club on 4 April in aid of his dependants.

Another East End youngster attracted by the big paydays in America was Little Joe Shears, a useful featherweight from Aldgate. Born during the early 1890's he learned his trade in the small halls of the East End and despite being very small, progressed well. In September 1909, he was matched with Young Joey Smith of Mile End over 20 two-minute rounds in a contest billed for the English 7st to 7st 2lbs championship. Although he lost on points he could have claimed the title by default because Smith scaled 7st 8lbs.

Joe had two more contests which were billed as title events. On 13 November he faced Llew Probert over 15 rounds at Merthyr which was billed as being for the English 7st 4lbs title. The result was a draw. Three weeks later in Glasgow he outpointed James Easton over 20 rounds for the English 6st 12lbs – 7st title.

Moving to the United States in early 1911, Shears based himself in New York where he joined forces with fellow East Ender, Sam Keller, who had been there for six months on what was his second tour. He was put under the guidance of world featherweight champion, Abe Attell, who touted him as a boy of class and great promise. The big build up, however, did Joe no favours as for his first fight in an American ring was matched with promising youngster, Johnny Dundee. Despite putting up an impressive showing for three rounds, Joe suffered a heavy knockout in the fourth but nevertheless greatly impressed local critics. In one article he was described as 'a pocket edition of Stanley Ketchell'. Another reporter wrote;

> Shears is about the size of a cider keg and is as full of fight as a battleship. He is so short that he can barely look over the highest rope of the ring.

The defeat did not deter Joe and he got regular work at arenas in and around New York, including two further contests with Dundee. Just two months after their first meeting, he lost a close six-round decision to the American but in July that year was awarded a 10-round points victory. Dundee was a big name to appear on Joe's record as 10 years later he would become world junior lightweight champion, the highlight of a 20-year career in which he had over 300 fights.

Shears remained in the States until March 1913 during which time he had at least 30 contests of which he lost 14. Reports which filtered back to Britain described him as a brave, aggressive and entertaining little battler. Nothing much was heard of him following his return home other than the fact that he boxed a 10-round draw with Freddie Jacks in May 1915.

Alf Goodwin from Stepney was another of the many capable Jewish fighters during the early 1900's with a number of his contests taking place at Wonderland. In 1909 he acted as a second for Ted 'Kid' Lewis in his professional debut at the Judean Club but the following year went to Australia. During a period of three years he boxed all over the country. Billed as Al 'Lightning' Goodwin he had over 20 contests with varying success, including one for the vacant Australian lightweight title in which he was beaten in 12 rounds. Four months later he boxed for the West Australia State lightweight title but was disqualified in round six.

Affectionally referred to in the press as 'The Shapely Jewish Boxer', Alf returned home during the summer of 1913 having been knocked out in nine rounds before a crowd of over 5,000 by Johnny Summers who held the British and Empire welterweight titles.

Trained by Dai Dollins and described in the media as one of the best welters in England, he forced Jack Goldswain to retire after 14 rounds at The Ring. Three weeks later he faced Tom McCormack at Plymouth for a purse of £250 with side stakes of £50 before a huge crowd in what was seen as a title eliminator. After being stopped in six rounds he returned to Australia where he had further contests. His career ended in 1922 following consecutive defeats in Melbourne, America and Paris.

Lightweight Sammy Bonnici was born in Malta in 1930 but came to Britain with his family as a child and settled in Stepney. Called up for National Service in the late 1940's he joined the Army Catering Corps where he took up boxing. He reached the final of the Army championships and although he lost on points boxed in the Imperial Services final following the withdrawal of his conqueror. Again, he lost narrowly on points.

After being demobbed, he worked in his father's restaurant near Aldgate Pump but still had the desire for boxing. He turned professional in 1951 having his debut at Mile End Arena in July. He quickly developed into a capable and popular performer and within four years had engaged in 35 contests, losing only seven. Although he beat some good men along the way, Sammy lacked a big punch and consequently fell short of championship class.

He boxed mainly at East End venues but also ventured abroad to Italy, France and Spain on occasions before emigrating to Australia in 1956. There he had 16 contests all over 12 rounds, of which he won nine. He retired in 1958 with a credible record of 35 victories and six draws from 58 contests in which he was stopped only once.

St George's featherweight Jackie Hurst was one of the toughest little men of his time. In over 60 contests between 1935 and 1940 he was stopped only once, that being in February 1939 by former British bantamweight champion, Johnny King, a veteran of over 200 bouts. A number of other centurions featured on Jackie's record, yet King was the only one of eight to beat him inside the distance.

Jackie was a real favourite at the Devonshire Club where he had 34 contests. Only Alby Day (38) and Eric

Boon (37) had more. Hurst passed away in May 1997 aged eighty.

There were countless other boxers, particularly in the lower weights, who were an important part of East End boxing but for a majority of reasons failed to make the most of their talent. Stepney based Tosh Humphries and Peter Howard in the late 1920's and 30's and Alf Drew during the mid to late 1950's all showed promise but failed to graduate to championship status. Humphries, a welterweight, amassed 90 contests, winning 53. He was particularly busy between 1928 and '30 when he engaged in 57 bouts, the majority of which went the full distance, often of 15 rounds. He was another Premierland regular.

Howard, also a Premierland welter stalwart, had 19 of his 29 fights at the venue between 1925 and 1930, 18 of which went the 15-round duration. His most notable achievements were decisions over Jackie Brown and Johnny Quill and draws with Alf Pattenden and Neil Tarleton both of whom also outpointed him. He was one of about 40 East End boxers trained by Johnny Sharpe.

Drew was on the scene some years later but rarely boxed in the East End due mainly to the absence of arenas as compared to decades earlier. Although unbeaten in his first 11 contests, he then lost form, winning just three of 14 before retiring in 1958. His situation was an indication of how promotion of the sport had declined in the East End by that time.

Heavyweights rarely featured in the East End but a man who warrants mention is Stepney born Joe Crickmar, who was active during the 1950's. He didn't become interested in boxing until he was seventeen and then only by accident. Having gone to the Stepney Institute for carpentry lessons, he met up with several old school friends who were there for boxing training with club coach Johnny Gudge.

Joe took to the sport quickly and had about 10 amateur contests before being called up for National Service. He joined the Royal Engineers and was posted to Singapore where he won an Inter-services championship, was beaten in the Far East championships, but won an amateur championship of Singapore.

After being demobbed he resumed his career with Stepney Institute and won the 1951 London ABA title, progressed to the National final but was beaten on points. Turning professional the following year, Joe won his first three fights in style but then lost more than he won. He did, however, have some notable successes twice stopping Joe Bygraves, later to become Empire champion, and also lost to him on points. He became the first man to defeat good prospect, Peter Bates from Doncaster but towards the end of his career lost to future British champions, Joe Erskine (points) and Henry Cooper (stopped in five rounds).

At just under 14 stone, Joe was small for a heavyweight, but his main problem was susceptibility to cuts around the eyes. One sustained against Cooper required eight stitches and ultimately led to him calling it a day.

Big-hitting, 6'5" tall, Damien Caeser from Stepney, boxed as an amateur with the Repton Club. After turning professional in April 1991, he looked an exciting prospect, winning all of his first eight fights inside the distance. In February 1995, however, he was stopped in eight rounds by Julius Francis for the vacant Southern Area heavyweight title. In a return the following year, he was knocked out in the opening round and quit boxing.

Neville Cole, one of two fighting brothers from Stepney, was a top-class amateur. Boxing for Fitzroy Lodge ABC he won a Schoolboy Junior B Class championship in 1966 and a National Federation of Boys Club (Class A) title in 1968. After moving up to senior level he won ABA lightweight titles in 1970 and 1972 and the light welterweight crown in 1973, his elder brother Eamonn having also won it in 1968.

At international level, Neville first represented the ABA in December 1970 and was only one of two winners in an 8-2 defeat to Poland at The Royal Albert Hall. In October the following year he was a member of an ABA team for a three-match tour of Zambia. During 1972, he gained points victories against USA and France but was outpointed in a match against Ireland. He also boxed in the Munich Olympics the same year.

Cole's ring career came to an abrupt halt in October 1973 when he was beaten in the European championships at Belgrade by eventual lightweight champion Marijan Benes in controversial circumstances. Benes landed a series of heavy punches to the head, the last of which was after the bell. Neville sustained serious facial injuries which necessitated hospital treatment. He never fought again and eventually passed away in March 2009 at the age of fifty-six.

Trained by Alec Goodman, welterweight Fred Archer (St Georges) was another extremely popular man in the East End. A game, big hearted warrior, he faced some of the best men at his weight but in doing so invariably took terrible punishment. Following a fight at Premierland on 2 October 1924 in which he was stopped in eight rounds, *Boxing* commented:

> Never in our long experience of boxing have we seen a man take such gruelling punishment and still keep going as we did when Fred Archer went down to defeat in sensational fashion against Leo Darton of Belgium.

There were so many other brave and skilful fighters in the region who are worthy of mention. There were Dave Sharkey and Jack Fox from Aldgate, Bobby Ramsey, Billy Ambrose and Dennis Booty all from Stepney, crowd pleasers of their time. The list is endless.

The latter showed particular promise after turning professional in November 1956 winning his first 12 contests. When he faced Lew Lazar 12 months later he was outpointed and after four consecutive stoppage defeats, he retired.

Apart from the fighters, trainers, seconds, promoters and referees who, despite working on safer side of the ropes, were all an integral part of a sport in huge demand and therefore warrant mention.

Alec Zalig Goodman was one of the top trainers during the early 1900's, second only to Jack Goodwin. A much sought-after man who had been a good boxer and runner, he made his name as guide and supervisor to Ted 'Kid' Lewis, taking him to the United States when he beat Jack Britton to become world welterweight champion in 1915. He later handled Jack 'Kid' Berg and in the view of some journalists, taught Jack all he knew. Alec handled many other good men, taking Harry Mason to a British title and working with Sid Burns and Harry Mansfield in Australia.

Dave 'Tatt' Phillips, a respected trainer with a gym off the Commercial Road, was often in Berg's corner although he exercised no control over his training routine or social life. He also trained Jack Hyams, Phil Lolosky, Young Johnny Brown and others.

Of all the East End Referees, Moss Deyong was probably the most prominent. Born in 1877 in the Petticoat Lane area of Aldgate, where he spent the early years of his life, he was the second eldest son of a family of 12. He first became involved in boxing at the old Netherlands Club in Bell Lane. Although he won schoolboy championship at the Jewish Free school, he suddenly gave up the sport after causing serious injury to another lad in a sparring exhibition.

As a boy Moss regularly attended shows at Wonderland where he became particularly interested in Young Joseph who had not long turned professional. He lived in Cutler Street opposite Deyong's warehouse and the two of them often engaged in sparring sessions together. Joseph was an extremely promising youngster, but Moss became incensed when he discovered that Harry Jacobs had paid him only £90 for a series of 10 contests all over 10 rounds. Deyong knew the promoter from his days at the Netherlands Club where Harry, boxing at flyweight, became the club's first champion. The situation caused a series of rows between the two because Moss was convinced Joseph had been ripped off.

With the passing of time Deyong transferred his interest to other aspects of boxing including training, seconding and in the late 1920's and early 30's, promoting at Ilford Skating Rink with Ted 'Kid' Lewis as his matchmaker. It was in refereeing, however, that he made his name. Starting with small shows at the Judean Club, where he became chairman for four years, he eventually became a licenced Board of Control official. A regular at arenas including the Stadium club, Holborn, The Royal Albert Hall and Wembley, he was regarded as truly conscientious and one of the best in the country. He was also widely respected in Europe, officiating in the world heavyweight title fight between Primo Carnera and Paolino Uzkudun in October 1933 in Rome. He also acted as auctioneer at many charity shows and in 1934 one national journalist estimated that he had collected at least £175,000 for respective causes.

Harry Grossmith affectionately known as 'Harry the Hat' because he had been in the hat-making business all of his life, was a popular small hall promoter. He made his name at Shoreditch Town Hall where he promoted good value shows for almost two decades between October 1956 and January 1975. One of his greatest matches was the set-to between Terry Downes and Dick Tiger long before either won a world title. Apart from Shoreditch, Harry staged shows at Mile End Arena and Wandsworth as well as further afield in Manchester and Blackburn. He was also a member of the British Boxing Board of Control Benevolent Fund Grants Committee for many years before moving to Miami in the early 1970's. He lived to the ripe old age of eighty-five.

Jack Solomons who was born in December 1900 in a basement flat at Flying Pan Alley, Aldgate developed into Britain's top promoter in the 1950's and 60's. Having had just three professional contests under the pseudonyms of Harry Grossman and Kid Mears, Jack decided promoting was a safer option. Having been a regular visitor to Premierland and Manor Hall, Hackney, he began his new career by staging shows at the Devonshire Club in 1934. It became an East End favourite until 1940 when it was destroyed by German bombs. After the war was over he moved into the big time and remained at the top for many years.

REFLECTIONS

Back in the early decades of the 20th century boxing was a way of life in the East End where most locals knew somebody who was a fighter. The list of young men who embarked on a ring career during that period either through need, desire or both is endless.

Reflecting back even further, history shows that the Jewish fan was the mainstay of London ring promotions since the days of Mendoza and Dutch Sam. In the words of respected writer A.J.Liebling, 'They did more to establish the Jew on the English scene than any other two historical figures.'

Between the early 1880's and the commencement of the First World War it was estimated that approximately 120,000 Jews emigrated to England. Although some settled in Leeds and Liverpool, the majority flocked to the wretched poverty-stricken district of Whitechapel which, like neighbouring Aldgate, was already heavily populated by Jewish folk.

Relations quickly became strained and it was common place for young Jewish lads to be picked upon by hardened born and bred London bullies. In school playgrounds and back alleys, they were frequently subjected to fearful beatings. It was racial hatred pure and simple.

Such happenings, however, led to many Jewish youngsters taking steps to learn how to look after themselves by attending establishments in the area set up for that very purpose. Success in subsequent confrontations during a time of widespread unemployment encouraged many to try their luck in the boxing ring and get paid. For many it proved to be a wise move and they reaped the rewards for their courage.

On a lesser scale the situation became very similar to that in America as featured in the excellent publication '*When Boxing was a Jewish Sport*,' by Alan Bodner & Budd Schulberg. First published in 1937, it highlighted the success of many Jewish fighters in the States during the early decades of the 20th century.

Despite the popularity of the Judean Club, Wonderland and Premierland, there were many other venues in the East End which staged professional Boxing shows on a regular basis, often more than once a week. They were essential work places for not only the many seasoned fighters, but also novice youngsters seeking to ply their trade. In the Whitechapel and Stepney areas alone during the early 1900's it was not uncommon for at least half a dozen promotions to take place on Sundays.

The Stepney Social Club at Bancroft Road was particularly popular with shows on Friday evenings and Sunday mornings. Run by former local flyweight Mark Lesnick, it provided good opportunities for novice boxers to get work on a regular basis.

In Mile End Road, The Whitechapel Pavilion first opened its doors to boxing on 11 October 1931 and featured a battle-royal top-of-the-bill between locals, Harry Brooks and Phil Richards. Moe Mizler featured in the chief supporting bout. Promoter for this and some subsequent shows was Young Joseph backed by a syndicate. He was followed by Victor Berliner who staged weekly events. In 1935, the venue changed its name to the Whitechapel Arena.

Luna Park, later to re-open as the Luna Park Sports Club, was situated at 94 Whitechapel High Street and operated during the 1930's. Former boxer, Alf Stewart, promoted shows on Sunday afternoons and evenings until 1932 when he moved to the Eastern counties. When the club opened under new management, shows were staged weekly on Wednesday and Friday evenings and Sunday afternoons.

Another venue to stage Sunday shows in the early 1930's was Beaumont Hall, Stepney, whilst the nearby Osbourne Social Club promoted on Friday evenings and Sunday afternoons during the same period. The Yiddish Theatre at Whitechapel and the Shadwell Amphitheatre were also popular small arenas, albeit not promoting as frequently as those previously mentioned.

That, however, is a situation long gone as technology created the need for serious modernisation and redevelopment of the area. Consequently, residential areas, particularly those adjacent to the huge London docks, also now confined to history, were razed to the ground to be replaced by huge banking, financial services and other corporate outlets.

Meanwhile, the professional boxing scene, already in decline in the East End, changed considerably. Whilst there remains a huge fan base for the sport in the area, the numbers of top class fighters and venues have diminished rapidly over the past 50 years or so.

Jewish boxers are now a rarity yet many of their brethren have, over the decades, become successful officials such as promoters and referees. Others have held responsible positions with the Board of Control. Yet boxing in the East End bears no resemblance to that of yesteryear. All is confined to history.

BIBLIOGRAPHY

BOOKS

BLADY, Ken   JEWISH BOXERS
HALL OF FAME
SHAPOLSKY.NY.1988

BUTLER, James   KINGS OF THE RING
STANLEY PAUL 1936

CORRI, Eugene   GLOVES AND THE MAN
HUTCHINSON 1928

DEYONG, Moss   EVERYBODY BOO
STANLEY PAUL 1951

FLEISCHER, Nat   THE RING BOXING ENCYCLOPEDIA
RING BOOKSHOP 1969

GOODWIN, Jack   MYSELF AND MY FIGHTERS
HUTCHINSON 1924

GREYVESTEIN, Chris   THE FIGHTERS
DON NELSON 1981

GUTTERIDGE, Reg   THE BIG PUNCHERS
STANLEY PAUL
1983

HALDANE, R.A   CHAMPIONS AND CHALLENGERS
STANLEY PAUL 1967

HARDING, John   WHITECHAPEL WINDMILL
ROBSON 1987

HUGMAN, Barry   BRITISH BOXING YEARBOOK
NEWNES 1986

LEIGH-LYE, Terry	PERSONALITIES OF BOXING SCION 1952
LEWIS, Morton	TED KID LEWIS – HIS LIFE AND TIMES ROBSON 1990
McINNES, Peter	CLOUTING FOR CASH PRIM 1962
MILES, Henry Downes	PUGALISTICA VOLs 1,2 & 3 EDINBURGH 1906
ODD, Gilbert	DEBATABLE DECISIONS NICHOLSON AND WATSON 1953
ODD, Gilbert	LEN HARVEY-PRINCE OF BOXERS PELHAM 1978
ODD, Gilbert	RING BATTLES OF THE CENTURY NICHOLSON AND WATSON 1948
PALMER, Joe	RECOLLECTIONS OF A BOXING REFEREE BODLEM HEAD 1927
RIBALOW, Harold	FIGHTER FROM WHITECHAPEL FARRA, STRAUSS & CUDAHY INC USA 1962
ROSE, Charlie	LIFE'S A KNOCKOUT HUTCHINSON 1953
SOLOMONS, Jack	JACK SOLOMONS TELLS ALL RICH AND COWAN 1951
	HAMBLYN ENCYCLOPDIA OF BOXING HAMBLYN 1983

NEWSPAPERS

BOXING / BOXING NEWS

BOXING, RACING AND FOOTBALL

SOUTHERN EX BOXER

SPORTING LIFE